# GLORIOUS TRUTHS ABOUT
# Women of the Restoration

OTHER BOOKS AND AUDIOBOOKS
BY SUSAN EASTON BLACK

*400 Questions and Answers about the Book of Mormon*

*400 Questions and Answers about the Old Testament*

*400 Questions and Answers about the Life and Times of Jesus Christ*

*400 Questions and Answers about the Doctrine and Covenants*

*Women of Character*

*Men of Character*

*Glorious Truths about Mother Eve*

*Glorious Truths about Mary, Mother of Jesus*

*Glorious Truths about Emma Smith*

*The Other Martyr: Insights from the Life of Hyrum Smith*

# GLORIOUS TRUTHS ABOUT
## *Women of the Restoration*

SUSAN EASTON BLACK

Covenant Communications, Inc.

Leaving Nauvoo © Annie Henrie Nader, for more information go to www.anniehenrie.com

Cover design copyright © 2021 by Covenant Communications, Inc.

Published by Covenant Communications, Inc.
American Fork, Utah

Copyright © 2021 by Susan Easton Black
All rights reserved. No part of this book may be reproduced in any format or in any medium without the written permission of the publisher, Covenant Communications, Inc., P.O. Box 416, American Fork, UT 84003. This work is not an official publication of The Church of Jesus Christ of Latter-day Saints. The views expressed within this work are the sole responsibility of the author and do not necessarily reflect the position of The Church of Jesus Christ of Latter-day Saints, Covenant Communications, Inc., or any other entity.

Printed in the United States of America
First Printing: March 2021

26 25 24 23 22 21    10 9 8 7 6 5 4 3 2 1

978-1-52441-822-9

To Ever,
my beautiful granddaughter

# Contents

Preface ................................................................. ix
Elizabeth Haven Barlow ........................................... 1
Jane Johnston Black ................................................. 7
Caroline Farozine Skeen Butler ............................... 13
Margaret Gay Judd Clawson ................................... 19
Polly Matilda Merrill Coltrin ................................... 25
Martha Jane Coray .................................................. 31
Elizabeth Walmsley Corbridge ................................. 37
Caroline Barnes Crosby ........................................... 41
Mary Dunn Ensign .................................................. 47
Mary Field Garner ................................................... 53
Rachel Ridgeway Ivins Grant .................................. 57
Drusilla Dorris Hendricks ....................................... 61
Mary Isabella Hales Horne ...................................... 67
Vienna Jacques ........................................................ 73
Jane Elizabeth Manning James ................................ 79
Sarah Granger Kimball ............................................ 85
Vilate Murray Kimball ............................................. 91
Lydia Goldthwaite Knight ....................................... 97
Mary Alice Cannon Lambert ................................. 101
Sarah Studevant Leavitt ......................................... 105
Mary Elizabeth Rollins Lightner ............................ 109
Mary Elizabeth Lott Losee ..................................... 113

Permelia Darrow Lott ............................................................. 117
Sophronia Smith Stoddard McCleary ............................ 121
Lucy Smith Millikin................................................................ 127
Mary Adeline Beman Noble.............................................. 131
Louisa Barnes Pratt ............................................................... 135
Elizabeth Hancock Redd..................................................... 141
Sarah De Armon Pea Rich.................................................. 147
Jane Snyder Richards............................................................ 153
Katharine Smith Salisbury.................................................. 159
Patty Bartlett Sessions ......................................................... 165
Amanda Barnes Smith......................................................... 171
Bathsheba W. Smith.............................................................. 175
Emma Hale Smith ................................................................. 181
Julia Murdock Smith............................................................. 189
Lucy Mack Smith................................................................... 193
Lucy Meserve Smith.............................................................. 199
Mary Fielding Smith............................................................. 203
Eliza Roxcy Snow .................................................................. 209
Eunice Billings Snow............................................................ 215
Priscilla Mogridge Staines................................................... 221
Leonora Cannon Taylor ...................................................... 227
Mercy Rachel Fielding Thompson................................... 233
Nancy Naomi Alexander Tracy......................................... 239
Emmeline B. Wells................................................................. 247
Mary Musselman Whitmer ................................................ 253
Elizabeth Ann Whitney....................................................... 257
Mary Ann Stearns Winters................................................. 263
Zina Diantha Huntington Young..................................... 269
Epilogue..................................................................................... 273

# Preface

THE STORY OF CHURCH HISTORY has in large part been "his" story. Names like Brigham Young, Heber C. Kimball, and Hyrum Smith are well-known in Latter-day Saint households. Their faithful deeds of yesteryear are legendary, as are their stories of willingness to stand in support of the Prophet Joseph Smith.

While I have written and spoken about "his" story for decades, there has been a constant nudge within me to tell "her" story—a story of women who also knew the Prophet Joseph Smith but whose faith and deeds have been obscured by the limelight of "his" story. Since few women in the Prophet Joseph's era wrote memoirs or kept diaries or journals, I rationalized for too long that "her" story would unfortunately remain unknown. But not anymore! There is a great need for the rising generation of talented young women to have faithful exemplars—women who faced persecution, danger, heartache, and disappointments but never lost sight of the prophetic calling of Joseph Smith or the covenant path that leads to life eternal. To have female exemplars to mirror who stood firm when faced with temptation and prayed for Joseph Smith in his extremities is to reach into the past for blessings today.

I wasn't sure what could be found in archives about "her" story. To my surprise, by combing through archival material, I found "her" story, and it is exceptional. It is as exceptional as stories of Brigham Young, Heber C. Kimball, and Hyrum Smith. Within this book are brief biographical sketches of fifty women who knew the Prophet Joseph Smith. They wrote of him and of their faith. Not being able to resist some advice, I included a section about how each woman impacts our lives for good. I am a better person from what I have discovered of their lives. What I have learned is that faith is not just a choice—it is *the* choice. No matter the circumstance, faith will have its reward.

I am grateful to my two research assistants—McKenna Swindle and Eliza Allen. They, like the women in this book, are exceptionally talented and have chosen the covenant path. Both have served missions and returned from their mission fields retaining the sacred ground captured as representatives of the Lord Jesus Christ. I am appreciative of Ashley Gebert for her willingness to share with me her editing talents and ideas for improving the book. I am grateful to Samantha Millburn for her confidence in me. And, of course, there is my husband, George. What joy he has brought to my life.

# Elizabeth Haven Barlow

(1811–1892)

---

On February 24, 1839, Elizabeth wrote to her cousin about the incarceration of Joseph Smith in Liberty Jail. Yet she also wrote optimistically of Church growth—"Our Prophet is still in jail, and many others whom we love. To look at our situation at this present time it would seem that Zion is all destroyed, but it is not so; the work of the Lord is on the march. Never has there been a time since the Church was first organized that the work spread so fast as it has within the past six months."[1]

---

Elizabeth greatly admired her father. She wrote, "He was a man of excellent morals and strove diligently by example and precept to instill into the minds of his children the principals [sic] of virtue, integrity and honor. He taught us to venerate our Father in Heaven and Jesus Christ our Savior, which caused me to be a great lover of the Scriptures." As for her mother, she died when Elizabeth was nine years old. Upon her death, Elizabeth "wept and refused to be comforted."[2]

Difficult days followed for Elizabeth. She often read for hours at a time, hoping to find comfort and peace. Developing the characteristic of optimism did

---

1  Pamela Emeline Smith Grant (as told by Pamela E. Barlow Thompson), "Biography of Elizabeth Haven Barlow," FamilySearch.
2  Pamela Grant, FamilySearch.

not come easy to her. It was not until she was twenty years old that she discovered optimism was found in trying "to live a godly life, but I hardly knew what to do or how to get the spirit I wished for." She joined the local Congregational Church, but "there seemed to be something lacking . . . which troubled my mind."[3]

While attending classes at the Amherst and Bradford Colleges in Massachusetts, she attended a "sort of Sunday School meeting at regular intervals" with other young women. Elizabeth recalled, "We would sing and pray and read the scriptures, and have lengthy discussions regarding our various religious beliefs and the churches we belonged to. . . . I was appointed the lady minister."[4] Still, she knew that something in their discussions was missing. She wanted hope and did not know where to find it.

In 1837, her cousins Brigham Young and Willard Richards gave Elizabeth a Book of Mormon. "I read very attentively," wrote Elizabeth. "The Spirit of God rested on me and I felt convinced to say in my heart 'This is the way I long have sought and mourned because I found it not.' I resolved that I would be baptized the first opportunity."[5] Elizabeth was baptized a member of The Church of Jesus Christ of Latter-day Saints by Elder Parley P. Pratt, an Apostle of the Lord Jesus Christ.

Following her baptism, she bid farewell to family and friends in Massachusetts and journeyed with her brother Jesse Haven to Missouri to be with the Saints of God. Elizabeth was teaching school in Gallatin, Missouri, when word reached her of the Battle of Crooked River. "The next word to reach our ears was that the Governor had raised an army of three thousand men to drive us out of the country," wrote Elizabeth.[6] Ellen Whitney recalled,

> I well remember the morning the mobbers came into Far West to take the Prophet Joseph and other brethren. I was at the school taught by Jesse Haven and his sister, Elizabeth. She was a very sweet woman, beloved by all her scholars and all who became acquainted with her. As the mobbers passed the school house they sounded their bugle causing excitement so great that the teachers allowed us children

---

[3] Pamela Grant, FamilySearch.
[4] Pamela Grant, FamilySearch.
[5] Pamela Grant, FamilySearch.
[6] Pamela Grant, FamilySearch.

to go to the windows and look out. Some of the Prophet's children were there.[7]

In a letter to her cousin dated February 24, 1839, Elizabeth wrote of the Latter-day Saint plight in Missouri as they fled the state under an extermination order: "Between five and seven thousand men, women and children driven from the places of gathering, out of the state from houses and lands, in poverty to seek for habitations."[8] As for Elizabeth, she made it out of Missouri to safety in Quincy, Illinois, and thanked the Lord for her blessings.

In Quincy at age twenty-seven, Elizabeth confessed that "[she] never had really fallen in love and seemingly, as yet she had not met the right one but believed firmly that he would come."[9] When younger friends were marrying, Elizabeth was optimistic that her turn was coming. In Quincy at age twenty-nine, Elizabeth met and fell in love with thirty-three-year-old Israel Barlow. They were married on February 23, 1840, by Isaac Morley. Theirs was a marriage of love. To their union were born eight children: six sons and two daughters.

Soon after their marriage, Elizabeth and Israel made their home in Nauvoo, Illinois. Elizabeth taught school to supplement their income. Attending her classes were children of Joseph Smith, Hyrum Smith, and Brigham Young. Her teaching career ended when she gave birth to her first child. Elizabeth had little time for socializing, but she managed to attend the Female Relief Society of Nauvoo and Church functions. She sorrowed over the deaths of Joseph and Hyrum Smith and attended the August 8, 1844, meeting in which Brigham Young addressed the Saints. Elizabeth later told her family, "When Brigham Young, the President of the Twelve, began speaking I saw a change come over him, saw him take on the form of Joseph Smith, and heard his voice change to that of the Prophet's."[10]

During the winter of 1846, Elizabeth described Nauvoo as "a huge work shop. Hundreds of wagons were built. The blacksmith anvils rang out night and day. Everyone made ready to go as soon as possible."[11]

Elizabeth and Israel joined other Latter-day Saints in fleeing from religious persecution in Illinois. They crossed the Mississippi River and journeyed across

---

7   Pamela Grant, FamilySearch.
8   Pamela Grant, FamilySearch.
9   Pamela Grant, FamilySearch.
10  Pamela Grant, FamilySearch.
11  Pamela Grant, FamilySearch.

the hilly countryside of Iowa to reach the Missouri River in 1846. It was not until 1848 that they journeyed on to the Rockies. Of their journey, Elizabeth recalled, "Many a time when we baked bread, since no wood was to be had, we made our fire of buffalo chips. . . . Once we had a stampede. Several hundred of our frightened oxen, cows, and steers raced away at full gallop bellowing into the darkness with the men on horses after them."[12] Elizabeth and her family arrived in the Salt Lake Valley on September 23, 1848, and thanked the Lord that they had reached their westward Zion.

They spent the first winter in the Salt Lake Fort. By spring, they had moved into the Salt Lake Eighth Ward. Frequent visitors to their home were Brigham Young, Heber C. Kimball, and Willard Richards. Israel supported his family as a farmer. When the family moved to Bountiful, Elizabeth was called to be president of the local Relief Society. She held the position for thirty-one years. During those years, she encouraged the sisters to see the bright side of life and to help those in distress find relief and happiness.

Elizabeth learned the "millinery trade and became an expert in the fads of those days, that of braiding and making various shaped bonnets and hats of straw." She also became an excellent seamstress, "becoming a dressmaker and making beautiful pin laces and other delicate trimmings which she handled in her trade."[13]

On Christmas Day in 1892, Elizabeth died at age 81. Her daughter wrote of her,

> To mother, the gospel had meant everything. No sacrifice was too great in order to send her husband or kindred into the mission field. She dug sego roots and thistles and went to the canyon for wood while her husband was on his mission and she would have done it again had it been necessary. Nothing stirred her soul more than repeating the events she had passed through in Missouri and Nauvoo. The Gospel, coupled with seeing her family live righteously, was the joy of her life.[14]

## A Bridge to the Past

The old adage "heartaches strike when the skies are clear" applies to Elizabeth Barlow. Yet through it all, Elizabeth remained optimistic. As she aged, her

---

12   Pamela Grant, FamilySearch.
13   Pamela Grant, FamilySearch.
14   Pamela Grant, FamilySearch.

optimism did not dim. Optimism is never a bad choice. An optimistic person expresses gratitude, is interested in others, easily forgives and often smiles. The optimist donates time and talents to a cause and finds joy in her own company.

# Jane Johnston Black

(1801–1890)

On September 17, 1846, Jane waited at the ferry to cross the Mississippi River. She related what happened next: "The mob rode up and surrounded our wagon and made a demand that I should give up what arms we had. I then had a pistol in my bosom, which I drew out and told them it was there, and that I would use it before I gave it up. They did not take it from me, but threatened to throw me in the river that night."[1]

At age sixteen, Jane was a preacher in the Wesleyan Methodist movement and had a regular circuit, visiting congregations and households in Ireland to spread the good news of Jesus Christ. She wrote, "I remained in that [preaching] position until I was over twenty years of age, and made William Black [II's] house my home, as he was my guardian."[2] When William's son and namesake, William, returned to his parental home at 10 Castle Street in Lisburn after

---

1 Henry Jay Black, "Biographical Sketch of William 'Young' Black and Jane Johnston Black, Wife," 17-page booklet (Salt Lake City: n.p., 1958), as cited in Wendel K. Walton, Guy L. Black, and Harvey B. Black, *Ireland to Utah: Odyssey of the William Black and Jane Johnston Family* (Provo, UT: Brigham Young University Press, 2012), 93.
2 Jane J. Black Autobiographical Sketch, circa 1883 typescript of history dictated to Joshua Bennett at Deseret Utah Territory, May 12, 1883, as quoted in Walton, Black, and Black, *Ireland to Utah*, 15.

years of serving in the British military, Jane made his acquaintance. Within a month, they were married, on July 31, 1822.

Jane and William made their home in Lisburn. Jane became the mother of one daughter and three sons. William supported his family on a military pension and by working in the hosiery business. The family uprooted in 1835, moving to Manchester, England, where the burgeoning fabric mills bolstered the economy. By so doing, the Blacks broke two hundred years of family residency in Ireland to embrace a new destiny.

In Manchester, the Blacks listened to Latter-day Saint missionaries William Clayton and Joseph Fielding preach the gospel of Jesus Christ. Of their preaching, Jane penned in her journal the phrase "Tidings of Great Joy."[3] In January 1839, she and her husband cast aside their Methodist beliefs and were baptized by William Clayton, the famed lyricist of "Come, Come, Ye Saints." William and Jane not only embraced the Restoration message, they also opened their home to any missionaries who came to the area. Wilford Woodruff wrote, "We [he and Brigham Young] stayed a good deal with them in Manchester, England."[4]

On July 7, 1840, William was called to labor as a missionary in Ireland. He wrote, "Brother [John] Taylor did not stop long with me [in Ireland] as the people of that country did not receive the Gospel. . . . Some 4 or 5 were baptized before I left. . . . I came home on account of my family, as I had to draw my pension in Manchester."[5] William served a second mission in the British Isles, this time in Oldham and Rochdale, England.

Wanting to gather with the Saints of God in Nauvoo, Illinois, Jane didn't wait for William to finish his mission and return to her. With courage, which always seemed to attend her actions, she departed on November 8, 1841, with three sons—George, William Valentine, and Joseph—from Liverpool aboard the seafaring vessel *Chaos* bound for America. Their voyage was not without peril. When a blustery storm threatened their safety, Jane and her sons retreated to a secluded berth aboard ship to pray. After praying for protection, William Valentine spoke in tongues. Jane interpreted his words predicting a safe voyage and landing in America.

---

3  Jane Johnston Black, "Journal Entry," FamilySearch.
4  Scott G. Kenney, *Wilford Woodruff's Journal, 1838–1898* (Midvale, UT: Signature Books, 1984), 5:467, as quoted in Walton, Black, and Black, *Ireland to Utah*, 52.
5  Diary of Joseph Smith Black, 1836–1910, as cited in Walton, Black, and Black, *Ireland to Utah*, 55.

The family arrived safely in New Orleans. They then traveled up the Mississippi River to Nauvoo. In that Latter-day Saint community, they pitched a tent on the north side of Mulholland Street and set up housekeeping. By July 1842, they had moved across the Mississippi to Augusta, Iowa Territory. Through industry and economy and her knowledge of medicine, Jane sustained her family until her husband, William, arrived, which was nearly a year later.

Although William was a familiar figure to the brethren, it was Jane and her medical talents that came to the attention of Church leaders. When Elder Taylor was wounded at Carthage Jail on June 27, 1844, Jane was called to attend him. When she asked Elder Taylor why he had sent for her, family tradition purports that he said, "Because I knew there was none better and wanted you to stand at the Morning of the Resurrection and testify to the Lord against the assassins who murdered the Prophet Joseph and Hyrum."[6] There is some speculation about the validity of this account since nothing in the writings of John Taylor suggests this was the case.

It was a call from Brigham Young to move to Nauvoo that brought William and Jane and their children across the Mississippi River to settle in the city of the Saints. In the bustling city, Jane received her patriarchal blessing on July 16, 1845, from William Smith, the brother of the Prophet Joseph. She was told in her blessing,

> It has been thy faith in the God of heaven that has borne thee up in the midst of deep afflictions, and brought thee through the Storm and through the dangers of the deep. . . . Thou shalt be rewarded for all the sacrifices thou hast made even fourfold and thy drooping Spirits shall be comforted, and as a daughter of Abraham and a Mother in Israel thy name shall be handed down to posterity. . . . Thou shalt be called blessed by thousands, and by tens of thousands . . . thy kindred Spirits shall gather round thee and with thee be saved to the satisfaction and joy of thy heart.[7]

When the Saints began leaving Nauvoo in the winter of 1846, Jane and her children remained behind, waiting for William, who had gone to Canada to draw a military pension. Unbeknownst to William, the journey to Canada put

---

6 "Jane Johnston Black," in Kate B. Carter, comp., *Our Pioneer Heritage*. 20 vols. (Salt Lake City: Daughters of the Utah Pioneers, 1958–1977), 6:428.

7 H. Michael Marquardt, *Early Patriarchal Blessings of The Church of Jesus Christ of Latter-day Saints* (Salt Lake City: The Smith-Pettit Foundation, 2007), 326–27.

his family in harm's way. In September 1846, the Battle of Nauvoo was fought on his property. Jane was in the middle of the fray, ministering to the injured. When it became too dangerous to wait any longer for William to return, Jane and her children courageously crossed the Mississippi to Potter's Slough in Iowa. "There were many of the Saints sick and there was nothing to comfort and nourish them but a little cornmeal until the Lord sent the quails amongst us," wrote Jane. "[The quails] supplied our wants." She concluded her words with, "Blessed be the name of the Lord."[8]

After William joined his family at Potter's Slough, they left the camp to journey to Winter Quarters. By 1850, they had joined the Captain James Pace Company and trekked 1,100 miles across the plains to the Salt Lake Valley. The family resided in small settlements in southern Utah—Spring City, Summit Creek, Springdale, Deseret, and Rockville. In these fledgling communities, Jane delivered more than three thousand babies and, on one occasion, amputated a man's leg using a butcher knife and a carpenter's saw. Although she had never witnessed such an operation, she was confident that she could do the deed. Jane also took an active role in Relief Society, being a class instructor. At a Relief Society meeting held on March 4, 1876, in Rockville, she quoted an Eliza R. Snow poem:

> I love the land of Dixie—
> Our mountain Dixie land;
> Where peace is in the atmosphere,
> And wealth, amid the sand.[9]

On July 6, 1874, Jane wrote to Brigham Young, "My health is poor. . . . I wish to have your counsel what I shall do."[10] While waiting for an answer, she remained in Rockville years after her husband died and her children had moved away. During those years, she gave medical assistance to those in need. In 1878, she moved to Deseret to be with her children.

In her eighty-seventh year, Jane wrote a brief history of her life. She confessed, "My memory has failed me in many things, so that I have not been able to give a complete account."[11] Jane died at age eighty-nine. Her grandson Parley Pratt Black was present at her death and wrote of Grandma Jane wanting

---

8  Jane Johnston Black, "Autobiographical Sketch," FamilySearch.
9  Jill Mulvay Derr and Karen Lynn Davidson, eds., *Eliza R. Snow: The Complete Poetry* (Provo, UT: Brigham Young University Press, 2009), 676–78.
10  Letter of Jane Black (Rockville, Utah) to Brigham Young, July 6, 1874, as quoted in Walton, Black, and Black, *Ireland to Utah*, 205.
11  Jane Johnston Black, "Autobiographical Sketch," FamilySearch.

his mother to open the back door. "Grandma said, 'Joseph and Hyrum is out there.' . . . Mother walked over and opened the door to satisfy Grandma." When his mother walked back into the kitchen, "Grandma [Jane] just slumped down in her chair and was gone."[12] Jane was buried next to her husband, William Black, in the Rockville Cemetery.

**A Bridge to the Past**
Jane had courage. She moved forward with courage to face her future. Courage is a choice. Courage is best seen when making a decision to move out of the past and into the future, and the best thing about the future is it comes only one day at a time.

---

12  Letter of Rita Black (Logan, Utah) to Cheryl (Black) Roper, April 28, 1969, as quoted in Walton, Black, and Black, *Ireland to Utah*, 229–30.

## Caroline Farozine Skeen Butler

(1812–1875)

---

WHEN A COMMITTEE FROM THE Female Relief Society of Nauvoo called upon Caroline Butler asking for a donation to the Nauvoo Temple fund, she had nothing to give. Disappointed with herself, she asked the Lord for means to contribute to the temple. A few days later, as she and her children were riding in a wagon across the prairies, Caroline spotted two dead buffalo. She asked her son to stop the wagon and pull hair from the buffalos' manes. She took the hair home and washed, corded, and spun it into yarn, then made eight pairs of gloves for the stonecutters working on the Nauvoo Temple.[1]

---

Caroline knew much of Southern privilege as a child, being the daughter of a well-to-do plantation and slave owner in Sumner County, Tennessee. She knew little of work or chores or what it meant to go hungry or without means to buy the best dress in a store. She never combed her own hair before her marriage, a "mammy" combing it for her.[2] With slaves in her father's fields and in their palatial home, Caroline imagined a long life for herself of wealth and luxury. But if that were the case, she wouldn't have much of a story to tell.

---

1 Caroline Farozine Skeen Butler, "Pioneer to Spanish Fork and Panguitch, from Women of Deseret," FamilySearch.
2 "Caroline Farozine Skeen Butler," *Pioneer Women of Faith and Fortitude*. 4 vols. (Salt Lake City: International Society Daughters of the Utah Pioneers, 1998), 1:454–55.

In Sumner County, Caroline became acquainted with neighbor John Lowe Butler, four years her senior. John stood six feet two inches tall. He was stout and ready to tackle almost any problem. His suffering from inflammatory rheumatics was well hidden. But there was more to John than physical prowess. He had "serious reflections on futurity."[3] Listening to his parents' talk of religious matters and their Methodist faith left impressions on his mind that led to deep reflections. John studied the scriptures and attended religious revivals, but his questions about Jesus Christ and life in general went unanswered.

John courted Caroline and made quite an impression on her. At age nineteen, Caroline married John in a garden-party setting at her home. For a wedding gift, she received an expensive sidesaddle and two slaves from her father. Rather than raise her family, which eventually included five sons and seven daughters, in the lifestyle Caroline had become accustomed to, Caroline and John gave the slaves their freedom. John provided for his family by working as a schoolteacher, farmer, cooper, and blacksmith. Caroline adjusted with few complaints.

In 1835, Latter-day Saint missionaries taught Caroline and John the gospel of Jesus Christ. For the first time, John claimed to see religious truths clearly. They were both baptized on March 9, 1835, in the Drake's Creek area of Simpson County, Tennessee, by James Emmett. Their baptisms greatly upset Caroline's father. After being disinherited, Caroline moved with her husband and children from Tennessee to Clay County, Missouri, to be with others of their faith. By autumn of 1836, they were residing in Far West, Missouri, in a small log house. When Joseph Smith saw how the Butlers were situated, he proposed that John and Caroline move into a large tavern he had recently purchased. They accepted his kind offer and lived in the tavern before moving on to Adam-ondi-Ahman in Daviess County, Missouri.

August 1, 1838, was Election Day in Daviess County. Men like John Butler went to Gallatin, the county seat of Daviess, to cast their vote. Lucy Mack Smith wrote, "At this election the Mormon Brethren went to the polls as usual for the purpose of voting but a party of men were collected there who were determined to prevent them from exercising the privilege of franchise and strictly forbid them from putting in a vote."[4] Ignoring their threats, John stepped up to the

---

3  John L. Butler autobiography, circa 1859 (transcript, undated), Church History Library.
4  Lucy Mack Smith, "Lucy Mack Smith, History, 1844–1845," book 15, page 6, josephsmithpapers .org.

polls to vote. A man struck him a severe blow. John returned the blow, bringing his assailant to the ground. Four others entered the fray. They were also knocked to the ground by John.

Exaggerated reports of the incident and others that followed led to the Battle of Crooked River, a massacre at Hawn's Mill, and an extermination order against Latter-day Saints issued by Governor Lilburn W. Boggs. In 1839, John fled from the state of Missouri, leaving Caroline and the children. Caroline wanted to follow him. She had a team and wagon but no driver. Abraham O. Smoot, who later became president of Brigham Young University, agreed to drive her wagon if his wife could come along. The Butlers and the Smoots started their journey in the bitter winter of 1839 in a light wagon pulled by two horses. On the journey, Caroline had "sore eyes" and could not see for several days. She walked for five days being guided by Sister Smoot. When Caroline, her children, and the Smoots reached Quincy, Illinois, John was waiting for them.

In 1840, the Butlers moved upriver to Commerce (later known as Nauvoo). They resided in the Nauvoo Second Ward. John supported his family as a fireman, a policeman, and an aide-de-camp in the Nauvoo Legion. As for Caroline, she was a member of the Female Relief Society of Nauvoo. As such, she helped raise money for the construction of the Nauvoo Temple by selling her homemade decorated tablecloths. When Caroline became ill with swamp fever and could not continue with her Relief Society projects nor assist her family, she requested that the Prophet Joseph Smith come to her home and administer to her. He was unable to fulfill her request but did not leave her comfortless. He blessed the broadcloth cape (cloak) worn by her husband. Caroline recovered by wrapping the cloak around herself. Whenever a family member was afflicted with illness, the cloak was wrapped around them. As the years passed, the cloak became shabby and was cut into ten pieces and given to the children of John L. Butler II.[5]

Caroline received a patriarchal blessing from John Smith, an uncle of the Prophet Joseph. In the blessing, she was promised "power and benefits of the Holy Priesthood in common with thy companion" and the "ministering of Angels to comfort thee." She was also promised to live "until thou art satisfied with life and every good thing."[6]

Caroline and her children accompanied her husband on a mission to the Sioux Indians. On the mission, Caroline was robbed. In spite of the experience,

---

5 "Caroline Farozine Skeen Butler," *Pioneer Women of Faith and Fortitude*, 1:455.
6 "Caroline Butler," Patriarchal Blessing, in "History of Caroline Farozine Skeen Butler," FamilySearch.

in the fall of 1844, she accompanied her husband on a second mission to the Sioux Indians. It was not the missions or her interactions with the Indians that troubled her. She was angry when her husband received his endowment in the Nauvoo Temple and "took his second wife Aunt Sarah who never had any children with him" to the temple. It was not until 1855 that Caroline went to the Endowment House in Salt Lake City.[7]

In the winter of 1846, Caroline and her family fled from religious persecution in Nauvoo to the Territory of Iowa. They crossed the hilly countryside of Iowa to reach the Missouri River. For six years, they toiled near the river to survive before heading west with the Eli B. Kelsey Company. After arriving in the Salt Lake Valley on October 16, 1852, the family settled in Palmyra near Spanish Fork. The first winter, they lived in a three-sided shanty. Caroline and her family experienced much privation. When her baby became ill and cried for meat, Caroline traded handwork for meat. Many times she walked five miles to milk a cow to have milk for her family. When flour became scarce, she parched corn, ground it, and put milk over it to feed her family.[8]

When the Palmyra settlement was abandoned, the Butler family moved to Spanish Fork. John served as the second bishop of Spanish Fork from 1856 to 1860. During those years, Caroline discovered she had a gift for healing. When a neighbor nearly cut off his thumb shearing sheep, she put a buckskin needle through each side of his thumb, clipped the thread, and tied it. She plastered the thumb with sticky gum, wrapped it up, and put it in a sling. "He'll never use that hand again," a neighbor said. But miraculously, "when [the thumb] healed it was as good as new."[9]

After the death of her husband in April 1860, Caroline moved from Spanish Fork to Gunnison to be with her son John Butler II. There she did farm work, including shearing sheep. She carded, dyed, spun, and wove wool to make clothing. From Gunnison, she moved on to Panguitch. On August 4, 1875, after being ill for three months, Caroline died of typhoid pneumonia. Her remains were taken to the Spanish Fork Cemetery and buried next to her husband. It was said of Caroline, "In all the trials, privations and persecutions through which she passed, she exhibited remarkable fortitude and patience and an undeviating faith in the Gospel."[10]

---

7   Caroline Farozine Skeen Butler, "Pioneer to Spanish Fork and Panguitch, from Women of Deseret," FamilySearch.
8   Caroline Butler, FamilySearch.
9   Luella Adams Dalton, *History of Iron County Mission, Parowan, Utah* (n.p., n.d.), 71.
10  "Died," *Deseret News*, September 29, 1875.

**A Bridge to the Past**

Caroline's early years of ease and comfort were not repeated in her later years. The pivotal turning point from wealth to privation was her decision to be baptized and embrace the gospel of Jesus Christ. Did she regret her decision? No! With unwavering faith in the Restoration, she faced her privations head-on, knowing her decision to enter baptismal waters was right. Likewise, when we make a right choice, we don't need to rethink the choice. Instead, we can move along the covenant path and discover the blessings awaiting us.

(1831–1912)

ONE DAY AS MARGARET WAS walking past the Mansion House, she saw the Prophet Joseph Smith conversing with several gentlemen. She looked at him. "She knew him, but he did not know her. All at once he reached his arm over the fence, grasped her by the hand, and gave her [hand] a hearty shake. He did not hesitate in his conversation with the gentlemen but kept right on talking."[1]

Before Margaret and her family became residents of Nauvoo in 1842, they went to Kirtland and camped not far from the temple. "We were given permission to go through [the temple]," Margaret said. "I well remember with what awe we entered it. My parents looked very serious and spoke quite low and cautioned us children not to speak at all."[2]

When the Judd family arrived in Nauvoo, Margaret's brother William Riley Judd complained about a swelling on his knee. Margaret wrote,

> Poor boy! How he suffered! Mother used to be up with him night after night, working so hard to relieve his suffering, but nothing seemed to do him any good, so she decided to have him baptized in the [temple] font. . . . When they got

---

1 "Mothers of Our Leaders: Rambling Reminiscences of Margaret Gay Judd Clawson," *Relief Society Magazine* 6 no. 6 (June 1919), 317.
2 "Margaret Gay Judd's Journeys," FamilySearch.

there mother lifted him out of the wagon and carried him to the font where an elder took him in his arms and carried him down into the water. [William] could not step or put his foot to the ground without the most excruciating pain, but after he had been baptized and was carried to the steps where Mother was waiting to take him in her arms, he called out, "O, Mother, I can walk!" And sure enough he walked right up the steps. From that time he had no more pain in his knee.[3]

This miracle left quite an impression on youthful Margaret, whose testimony needed strengthening.

As often as she shared the story of the miraculous healing of her brother, she also shared the story of the herculean efforts of her father to build a home for the family in Nauvoo:

[Father] used to go to an island in the Mississippi River to get lumber. He would go Monday morning and stay until Saturday evening, getting out what he called "shakes." . . . This was an all-summer job, to get enough to build a little two-room house. . . . When our house was furnished and we moved in, my parents were delighted. It was their own home, built in the City of the Saints, and this is where they expected to live the rest of their days.[4]

Mob violence thwarted the Judds' future plans. Church leaders advised the brethren "to always be ready to meet the mob and to protect their homes and families."[5] As mobs turned violent and religious persecution raged, the Judd family abandoned their home and moved to Springfield, Illinois. For Margaret, it meant more than leaving her home; it meant leaving Henry Ridgley:

The night before we left my true lover, Henry Ridgley came to bid me farewell and under our trysting-tree (a big tree close by) we each vowed eternal constancy, for 4 years at least. At the end of that time he would be of age, and then he would come to claim me for his own, even if I was at the end of the earth. Well he did come to see me but it was 40 years after instead of 4 years. He had a wife and three children. I had a husband and was the mother of 13 children.[6]

---

3  "Mothers of Our Leaders," 317.
4  "Mothers of Our Leaders."
5  "Mothers of Our Leaders."
6  "Margaret Gay Judd's Journeys," FamilySearch.

From Springfield, the Judd family moved to Council Bluffs, Iowa. For a month, they waited for a pioneer company to be formed and Margaret's father to overcome the challenges of working with oxen. Margaret said, "How well I remember what a hard time Father had breaking in the animals to draw the wagon. . . . Father would get help to yoke them up and then would start to drive them. All at once they would run off in an opposite direction from where he wanted them to go or would run around to the back of the wagon and get all tangled up."[7]

On May 9, 1849, the Judd family left Council Bluffs for the West. On the journey, eighteen-year-old Margaret had more adventures than her parents. She said,

> There were several nice young men in our company. Especially one. He used to say such lovely things to me; told me that I was beautiful and intelligent and even went so far as to say that I was amiable, something I had never been accused of before. He told me that I was the only woman he ever loved and that we were just suited to each other. I began to believe him, and when he proposed what could I say but "yes." Well the course of true love did run smooth at least until we got into the Valley. Then we had the usual lover's quarrel but not the usual making up.[8]

The pioneer company arrived at the mouth of Emigration Canyon the evening of October 15, 1849. The next evening, the Judds dined with the Stringhams, friends they had known in Springfield. "Never was an invitation more gladly accepted," Margaret said. "That dinner, can I ever forget it? Never before nor since have I tasted anything like it. There was a nice juicy fat beef pot roast, baked squash, boiled potatoes, mashed turnips and boiled cabbage. . . . It was a feast fit for the gods."[9]

For a season in Salt Lake City, Margaret and her sister slept in the wagon box. "Many nights we waded knee deep in snow to our little bedroom,' Margaret said.[10] By spring of 1850, the family had acquired a city lot, and by fall, they had a home of their own. Margaret and her sister Phebe liked going to Warm Springs north of Salt Lake City. Margaret said,

---

7   "Margaret Gay Judd's Journeys."
8   "Margaret Gay Judd's Journeys."
9   "Margaret Gay Judd's Journeys."
10  "Mothers of Our Leaders," 317.

> In those days, we could have two free baths a week by taking a walk of two miles out to the Warm Springs. It was a large pool of natural warm water flowing constantly out of the mountain. President Young made the rule that Tuesdays and Fridays should be "Women's Days" and no "Peeping Toms" were allowed near the place. The rest of the days were for the men. The bathing was delightful, and great fun for a lot of us girls to go out there together to play and splash in the water for hours. The banks of the pool were our dressing rooms, without any kind of shelter.[11]

In 1852, Margaret became the second wife of Hiram Bradley Clawson under the law of plural marriage. Of their marriage, a daughter wrote, "My mother and her sister Phebe were old-time belles of Great Salt Lake City; and when my mother turned aside from other distinguished suitors, refusing young and gallant lovers to marry my father, she proved both her own good judgment and her implicit faith in the teachings of the Prophet Joseph Smith."[12]

She was respectful of her husband, Hiram, and taught her children to honor him and obey his counsel.

Margaret was well known in Salt Lake City for her leading roles in plays presented in the Salt Lake Theater. She was a charming actress and often called the "Mother of Drama in Utah." Of taking the role of titular character Clementina, Margaret recalled,

> I well remember my feelings when asked to take the little part of Clementina in that play[.] I felt the great responsibility and feared I could not do it justice. There were seven or eight lines to be spoken[.] In one scene she had to faint[.] Well that did take practice. I started that at home, and fainted four or five times a day, sister Phebe catching me each time. Well after a week she got pretty tired (I was much heavier than she) and would catch me only once a day[.] Well after repeating my lines thousands of times and fainting hundreds of times I went on the stage with fear and trembling. After the play was over I was congratulated on doing so well. Just because they wanted me to take other parts and keep on playing. Well, I did and played off and on for twenty five years taking all sorts of parts, from sentimental to high and low comedy.[13]

---

11  "Mothers of Our Leaders."
12  Rudger Clawson, "The Month for Mothers," *Relief Society Magazine*, May 1919.
13  "Margaret G. Clawson Reminiscences," FamilySearch.

During her later years, Margaret expressed the fear that she was losing her old-time vigor and dreaded the possibility of dying out of the harness. To keep herself busy and avoid idleness, she turned her attention and time to performing vicarious work for her kindred dead in the Salt Lake Temple. In this sacred work, she found relevance and great joy.

Margaret died of general debility on February 10, 1912, at age eighty. Her children reported, "She had not only provided an ample sum for her funeral expenses and the up-keep of her grave, but there was also a little property left to each one of her children."[14]

## A Bridge to the Past

As President Theodore Roosevelt said, "It is not the critic who counts; not the man who points out how the strong man stumbles, or where the doer of deeds could have done them better. The credit belongs to the man who is actually in the arena, whose face is marred by dust and sweat and blood; who strives valiantly; who errs, who comes short again and again, because there is no effort without error and shortcoming."[15] Margaret never sat on the sidelines. Those around her always knew she was in the room. She wasn't afraid to express her thoughts or interject an idea, no matter who was present. Life is too short to sit back and let others participate when we have something to say. Being an observer has its merits, but when it comes to making a difference for good, we must speak up. We must let our voices be heard on the stage, in the political arena, in Church councils, in our neighborhoods, and at home.

---

14   Clawson, "The Month for Mothers."
15   Theodore Roosevelt Speeches, "The Man in the Arena," April 25, 1910.

# Polly Matilda Merrill Coltrin

(1817–1891)

---

On September 2, 1845, Polly received a patriarchal blessing from William Smith. In the blessing, she was promised, "All thy former troubles and the days of thine afflictions shall not be brought into remembrance for thy God shall be thy support yea he shall deliver thee from all thy deep distresses, neither shalt thou mourn for thy Spirit shall be comforted . . . Spirits . . . in heaven will prove unto thee a guardian angel to direct thy footsteps."[1]

---

Philander Coltrin liked to tell the story of his romance with Polly Merrill. "It was common talk among the boys of the village near Utica[, New York,] that no boy could kiss Polly Merrill." He accepted the challenge. One evening at a party, when the young women were seated on benches under the shade trees, Philander slipped up from the back, grabbed Polly by the shoulders, and planted a fervent kiss on her cheek. Polly slapped him in the face. Philander said, "I told the fellows I would, and I shall do it many other times in the future."[2] Their courtship led to marriage on July 3, 1833, in Shelby, Michigan. Philander was age nineteen and Polly age sixteen.

---

1 H. Michael Marquardt, *Early Patriarchal Blessings of The Church of Jesus Christ of Latter-day Saints* (Salt Lake City: The Smith-Pettit Foundation, 2007), 421.

2 Charles Henry Coltrin, "History of Philander and Polly Matilda Merrill Coltrin," read at a Philander Coltrin Reunion in 1953 or 1955, FamilySearch.

Five years later, Parley P. Pratt, an Apostle of the Lord Jesus Christ, was sent on a mission to Michigan. As Philander and Polly listened to Elder Pratt, they were skeptical of the Joseph Smith story. But as they prayed about the Restoration of the gospel, they received a witness that Joseph Smith was indeed a prophet of God. Polly and Philander were baptized in March 1838 by Elder Joel H. Johnson, the lyricist of the hymn "High on a Mountain Top."

Wanting to be with the Saints of God, the Coltrins sold their property in Michigan, bid farewell to loved ones, and moved to Nauvoo, Illinois. They resided in the Nauvoo Third Ward. To support his family, Philander worked as a brick maker, mason, and plasterer, doing much work on the Nauvoo Temple. On July 2, 1840, he received a patriarchal blessing from Hyrum Smith. In the blessing, he was promised, "Thy power and the authority of thy Priesthood shall not fail in thy lifetime and in the new heavens and upon the new earth shalt thou consider it more fully, for a celestial crown is thine, with all thy kindred and father[']s house to sit down in the kingdom of heaven to go no more out."[3]

The faithfulness of the Coltrins in Nauvoo was legendary, filled with stories of service to family, friends, and strangers. Their crowning experience occurred on December 31, 1845, as Polly and Philander received their endowments in the Nauvoo Temple. But their lives were not without sorrow—they buried a son in Nauvoo.

When religious persecution raged in Illinois, rather than deny their faith, in the dreary winter of 1846, they fled from Nauvoo seeking safety in the Territory of Iowa. They traversed the hills of Iowa to reach Council Bluffs near the Missouri River. Just when Polly had seen herself once again enjoying life with her family, in July 1846, Brigham Young called for men ages eighteen to forty-five to enlist in the Mormon Battalion. Philander answered the call. His enlistment meant that Polly had to provide for their five children, ages two to twelve. Adding to it, she was pregnant. Nevertheless, with heartfelt emotion, Philander left her and the children in Council Bluffs and marched with the battalion to Los Angeles.

On June 29, 1847, he and Rufus Stoddard built the first kiln and fired the first bricks in Southern California. During the same month, he was thrown from a horse in San Diego, seriously injuring his right hip. Philander was discharged on July 16, 1847. Following his discharge, he journeyed to the Salt Lake Valley. In August 1847, he left the valley with Brigham Young to journey to Iowa to unite with his family once again. Philander found in his absence that

---

3   Marquardt, 420–21.

Polly had cared for their children and sustained the family, but not without many struggles.

In 1849, Philander brought Polly, now age thirty-one, and their children to the Salt Lake Valley in the Silas Richards Company.[4] Polly told her grandchildren that she walked most of the way from Nebraska to the Salt Lake Valley carrying her one-year-old son, Byron Colton.

Polly, Philander, and their children settled near Cottonwood Creek in Salt Lake. Philander built a home in the wilderness for Polly. When word of Johnston's Army coming to Utah reached Brigham Young, he asked Philander to move his family to Provo. In Provo, Philander opened a brickyard and built a family home—a five-room adobe structure. The house had a large porch but few windows and doors. It had a cupboard but no floor except hard-packed soil.

The most remembered incident occurred on the large front porch of that home. An Indian brave asked Polly's daughter Emily to marry him. Thinking it in jest, Emily agreed to his proposal. A few days later, the Indian brave returned with other braves to claim his bride. He learned that Emily did not intend to keep her promise. In anger, he put a tomahawk to Polly's throat and demanded that she force her daughter to marry him. Philander saw the incident from the fields and rushed to help Polly and Emily. "Now, you get out of here," he said to the Indian braves. They left when Philander brandished a gun.[5]

In her home, Polly was a product of her time. Her granddaughter Rose Moore Searle wrote, "I can see her now pouring the melted tallow into the candle molds; making her own dye for the carpet rags she sewed; spinning the yarn for the stockings she later knitted; making sausage, etc." Yet in spare moments, Polly liked to read: "Grandmother was a great reader, and I can remember as a little girl, when the New York Ledger arrived, listening spellbound while she read about romance and tragedy."[6]

In autumn of 1887, Polly and her husband, Philander, sold their family home in Provo and journeyed to Ashley Valley, where four of their sons lived. A granddaughter wrote, "Grandfather and Grandmother were cheerful on the hard journey taken by team and wagon [to Ashley]. One night while standing around the campfire Philander slipped and sat down in a prickly pear bed.

---

4  "Philander Coltrin" and "Polly Coltrin," in Utah Mormon Pioneer Overland Database, 1847–1868, Church History Library.
5  Coltrin, "History of Philander and Polly Matilda Merrill Coltrin."
6  Coltrin.

With the nettles clinging to his flesh he joined heartily in the laugh that went around the fireside."[7]

As for life in Ashley Valley, a granddaughter wrote,

> As a child my Mother used to send me occasionally over to Grandmother's house to borrow a bar of soap or some other article. (Of course, these goods were purchased by my father and the other sons.) Invariably, I expected to get a good lecture from Grandmother on the extravagance of Nancy's family. Dear soul Polly! She had practiced the most rigid economy all of her life and she couldn't stand to see anything wasted. I remember that she was also very honest. She wouldn't even take a straight pin if it didn't belong to her rightfully.[8]

Philander suffered from rheumatics and, for a number of years, could only walk with the aid of crutches. For six years, he and Polly were invalids. Their last illness was the grippe, an old-fashioned term for influenza. When Polly became bedfast, her bed was craped in mosquito netting to keep out the flies.

On August 13, 1891, Philander was told Polly was dying. "No, Mother won't die yet. We promised when we were married that we would live and die together, and she will wait for me."[9] Polly died on Thursday, August 13, 1891, at 4:20 p.m. Thirty-six hours later, at 4:30 a.m. on Saturday, August 15, 1891, Philander breathed his last.

The funeral service for the Coltrins was held at the ward meetinghouse in Ashley Valley. The meetinghouse was crowded with over three hundred mourners who came to pay their respects to the noble couple who had endured the vicissitudes of life and remained faithful to their covenants. The coffins rested side by side during the funeral service. At the close of the service, the remains of Philander and Polly were placed in one grave in the Maeser Fairview Cemetery southwest of Vernal, Utah.[10]

## A Bridge to the Past

When we wipe away the tears, remove the boxing gloves, and stop to think about what matters most, the relationship between husband and wife is

---

[7] Coltrin.
[8] Coltrin.
[9] "Philander Coltrin," in Find A Grave.
[10] "Philander Coltrin."

paramount. Polly loved her husband, and Philander loved her. They both loved the Lord. It doesn't get much better than that. Cherish the marriage that has an eternal bond. Life is happier for any family when husband and wife love and respect each other.

## Martha Jane Coray

(1822–1881)

---

Before Joseph Smith "was pointed out to her as the man, [Martha Jane] could discern something in him of such a peculiar character that she knew who he was, and from her unbounded confidence in him as the man of God, she took in common hand every discourse that she heard him preach, and has carefully preserved them. [Brother George] A. Smith said that [Martha] had taken more pains to preserve the sayings of the great Prophet, and had accomplished more in that direction than any other woman in the Church."[1] Her husband, Howard Coray, added, "Martha Jane greatly venerated the Prophet counted him as the greatest miracle known to her, saying even on occasion 'that she valued her acquaintance with him above everything else.'"[2]

---

At age ten, Martha was teaching Sunday school in a Protestant church in Ohio. By age twelve, she had applied for admission to the Campbellite Church. Although strong in her religious beliefs, when she heard Elder George A. Smith in January 1840 set forth gospel principles in "such a plain and unmistakable manner, [it] completely upset all her Campbellism."[3] Martha was the first

---

1 "Obituaries—Mrs. Martha J Coray," Newspaper clipping, FamilySearch.
2 Howard Coray Journal as quoted in Noel Reynolds, "Martha J. Knowlton Coray History Forum Assembly Address," Brigham Young University, October 13, 1997, FamilySearch.
3 "Obituaries—Mrs. Martha J Coray."

in her family to be baptized in the icy Mississippi River as a member of The Church of Jesus Christ of Latter-day Saints.

Near the time of Martha's baptism, Howard Coray was serving as a clerk to the Prophet Joseph Smith. One day, Joseph said to Howard, "Brother Coray, I wish you were a little larger, I would like to have some fun with you." Not realizing that Joseph was speaking of wrestling, Howard replied, "Perhaps you can." A wrestling match ensued. Joseph easily won but not before breaking Howard's leg. The next day, Howard said to him, "Brother Joseph, when Jacob wrestled with the angel and was lamed by him, the angel blessed him; now I think I am also entitled to a blessing." In the priesthood blessing that followed, Howard was promised that he would "soon find a companion, one that will be suited to your condition and whom you will be satisfied with. She will cling to you, like to cords of death, and you will have a good many children."[4]

At a Church gathering held some three or four weeks later, Howard scanned the congregation to see if "possibly the fair one promised might be present." He wrote, "My eyes settled upon a young lady sitting in a one-horse buggy. She was an entire stranger to me and a resident of some other place. I concluded to approach near enough to her to scan her features well and thus be able to decide in my own mind whether her looks would satisfy my taste." He described Martha as having

> dark brown eyes, very bright and penetrating, at least they penetrated me, and I said to myself, she will do. The fact is, I was decidedly struck. . . . I discovered at once that she was ready, off hand, and inclined to be witty; also, that her mind took a wider range than was common for young ladies of her age. This interview, though short, was indeed very enjoyable, and closed with the hope that she might be the one whom the Lord had picked for me; and thus it proved to be.[5]

Martha and Howard were married on February 6, 1841, in Nauvoo by Robert B. Thompson, a clerk of Joseph Smith. They were sealed for eternity on July 22, 1843. Howard wrote of their being sealed for eternity: "Hyrum [Smith] asked my wife if she was willing to be sealed to me. After a moment's thought, she answered yes. He then asked me if I wished to be sealed. I replied in the affirmative. . . . He performed the ceremony [in a buggy,] then and

---

4 "Autobiography of Howard Coray," FamilySearch.
5 "Autobiography of Howard Coray."

there."⁶ Howard and Martha became the parents of thirteen children—eight sons and five daughters.

In addition to family life, Martha and Howard shared a profound interest in preserving records of important speeches given in Nauvoo. For example, when Martha attended a Church meeting and saw that a clerk was not present, she wrote down the words of such leaders as Joseph Smith, John Taylor, Brigham Young, and George A Smith. It was said that she was "'a rabid and lucid writer' who often carried a notepad and pencil into meetings and took notes even when it wasn't her official duty to do so."⁷

Martha also taught school with her husband in Nauvoo. She taught law, philosophy, history, poetry, chemistry, and geology. Instruction given to students by Martha and Howard was so well received that in fall 1844, Howard rented the music hall for their classes. The hall could accommodate 150 students.

Their joint teaching efforts ended in the winter of 1844. The reason had everything to do with Lucy Mack Smith. "People are often enquiring of me the particulars of Joseph's getting the plates, seeing the angels at first and many other things," Mother Smith wrote to her son William on January 23, 1845. "I have told over many things pertaining to these matters to different persons to gratify their curiosity. Indeed [I] have almost destroyed my lungs."⁸ She then announced that she was ready to write down every particular of Joseph's life as far as possible. Howard Coray wrote, "Mother Smith came to see my wife about getting her to help write the history of Joseph, to act in the matter only as her, Mother Smith's, amanuensis. This my wife was persuaded to do and so dropped the school."⁹

Sixty-nine-year-old Lucy Mack Smith told her life story to twenty-three-year-old Martha Coray. At the time, Lucy was suffering from rheumatism and lung infection. Lucy dictated from memory vignettes of her childhood through the martyrdom of her sons Joseph and Hyrum in Carthage, Illinois. Where possible, she referred to historical memoranda of events within her reach.

Howard was asked to help Martha revise the manuscript, correct grammar, and clarify chronological statements. "After consulting President Young, who

---

6   "Autobiography of Howard Coray."
7   "100 years at BYU: A Woman's Touch Valuable to BYA," Newspaper clipping, FamilySearch.
8   Letter of Lucy Mack Smith to William Smith, January 23, 1845, as cited in Kyle R. Walker, "Katharine Smith Salisbury's Recollections of Joseph's Meetings with Moroni," *BYU Studies* 41, no. 3 (2002), 5.
9   "Autobiography of Howard Coray."

advised me to do so, I consented," Howard wrote, "and immediately set to with my might. We labored together until the work was accomplished, which took us until nearly the close of 1845."[10] At the close of 1845, the Corays were satisfied with the manuscript and concluded that their work was finished.

In May 1846, Martha and Howard left Nauvoo to join thousands of Latter-day Saint exiles in Iowa. They journeyed as far as the Nishambotany River, where Martha operated a ferry and Howard tilled the ground until they had the necessary means to continue their journey to the Salt Lake Valley. It was not until 1850 that the Corays arrived in the valley.

Howard was employed as a clerk in the tithing office. Once he acquired additional funds, he took his family to Tooele and then to Mona, Utah, where he raised livestock and Martha sold liniments and medicines made from herbs grown on their land. Although the herbs brought medicinal relief to many, Martha was unable to solve her own health issues. The Corays left Mona and moved to Provo in 1857, hoping to find solutions for her persistent cough.

In 1875, Martha was appointed the first dean of students and member of the board of trustees of the Brigham Young Academy in Provo. In accepting these appointments, she wrote to Brigham Young, "My principle of education has been—God's laws of religion first—Man's laws of honor and mortality second—Science of every attainable kind [third]." Knowing that her views may not match the educational thoughts of President Young, she concluded her letter with, "I am mainly desirous to know your will and that shall be my pleasure in everything touching this establishment."[11]

Her tenure as dean and as a member of the board ended all too soon, but not before she voted to fix "tuition at $4.00 per pupil."[12] With her husband nearby and with all that "medicine could do she left us," wrote Howard. Martha died on December 14, 1881, at age fifty-nine. Her funeral was held in the Provo Tabernacle. Hundreds of mourners attended, including Church leaders Wilford Woodruff and Joseph F. Smith. At the funeral, Howard said of her, "A more intelligent, self-sacrificing, and devoted wife, and mother, few men have been blessed with. . . . She lived a consistent Latter-day Saint life up to the time of her demise."[13]

---

10   "Autobiography of Howard Coray."
11   Martha Jane Knowltown Coray, "Life Sketch," FamilySearch; Martha Jane Coray to Brigham Young, April 10, 1876, Brigham Young Papers, Church History Library, as cited in Amy Reynolds Billings, "Faith, Femininity, and the Frontier: The life of Martha Jane Knowlton Coray," MA thesis, Brigham Young University, 2002, 148.
12   "Diary of Martha Knowlton Coray," FamilySearch.
13   "Autobiography of Howard Coray."

## A Bridge to the Past

Joseph Smith blessed Howard Coray that he "should find a companion, one that will be suited to your condition and whom you will be satisfied with." Was Howard satisfied with his wife, Martha? From the first day Howard saw Martha, he was smitten. It doesn't appear she ever gave him a reason to change his mind. Martha was respectful and kind to him and tried to brighten his day. Like Martha, there are good Samaritans everywhere looking for opportunities to brighten another's day. For some, that effort comes through being a conscientious woman—on a crowded bus, she stands so the elderly woman can sit down. Being courteous and kind just comes naturally to her. For others, volunteering at a soup kitchen or donating to charity is more to their liking. Whatever random acts of kindness we choose, our days will be happier if we do something kind for the loved ones in our lives.

# Elizabeth Walmsley Corbridge

(1816–1896)

---

As a young widow with children to attend to, there was little chance of finding meaningful employment in Nauvoo. What Elizabeth found instead was a whirlwind romance with a Mr. Rogers (given name unknown). Unfortunately, the excitement and affection in their marriage was soon replaced with marital problems. Seeking counsel on what she should do, the Prophet Joseph Smith advised Elizabeth Corbridge to leave Mr. Rogers. With resoluteness, Elizabeth followed the prophetic advice. Joseph then hired her to work in the Mansion House so she would have the necessary means to support her children.[1]

---

Elizabeth was raised to maturity in the picturesque settings of Bowland and Chipping, England. Among the barren gritstone fells, deep valleys, and peat moorland in Bowland and Chipping, she passed her days in peace. On February 16, 1835, at age eighteen, Elizabeth married twenty-four-year-old James Corbridge in Chipping. To their union were born four children, two living to adulthood. Elizabeth and James resided in the village of Thornley in county Durham, a distance of 120 miles from their moorings.

Two years after their marriage, missionaries from America came to Thornley, preaching the Restoration and the gospel of Jesus Christ. Elizabeth and her

---

1   Howard K. Bangerter, "James and Elizabeth Walmsley Corbridge," FamilySearch.

husband, James, had both been christened in the Church of England but had not known much about doctrine and ordinances. In 1838, the Corbridges were baptized members of The Church of Jesus Christ of Latter-day Saints by Elder Heber C. Kimball, an Apostle of the Lord Jesus Christ. On the day of her baptism, Elizabeth received a priesthood blessing promising she would be healed of consumption. She was healed immediately.

Learning that the Saints of God were gathering in Nauvoo, Illinois, the Corbridges—James and Elizabeth and their three children, ages four to a baby in arms—bid farewell to extended family members and boarded the ship *North America* in Liverpool. The ship carried over two hundred passengers, most of them English converts. Elders Brigham Young and Willard Richards sailed aboard the ship for a day before disembarking. William Clayton stayed aboard ship during the entire voyage. He wrote of stormy seas and of a gale-force wind. He also wrote of deaths at sea, one being the baby of James and Elizabeth Corbridge. The baby was buried in the stormy seas before the *North America* docked at the New York Harbor.

James and Elizabeth and their two children continued their journey to Nauvoo. In Nauvoo, James and his son William contracted cholera due to drinking contaminated water. The Prophet Joseph Smith was called upon to minister to the father and son. In the blessing Joseph administered to young William Corbridge, William was promised a long life. His father, James, was not. James died in 1843 in Nauvoo at age thirty-three. It is assumed that he was buried in the Old Pioneer Cemetery on Parley Street.

Difficult days followed for Elizabeth. She had an unfortunate brief marriage to Mr. Rogers. Joseph advised her to end the marriage. She would go on to marry John Walker, a widower with nine children. Elizabeth and John blended their families before fleeing from religious persecution in Nauvoo to safety in the Territory of Iowa. They journeyed across the muddy hills of Iowa in dreary winter weather to reach the last encampment of the Latter-day Saints—Winter Quarters. In that cold encampment, Elizabeth gave birth to Joseph Walker, who died two months later.

Her husband, John Walker, left Elizabeth in Winter Quarters and traveled on to the Salt Lake Valley, promising he would make arrangements for her to come later. Time passed, and there was no word from John. When Elizabeth heard that he had entered plural marriage in the valley, she determined to end her marriage. In 1852, Elizabeth and her children, ranging in age from fourteen to two years old, traveled with an unknown company to the Salt Lake Valley.

It is said that when they arrived at the Pioneer Park meeting place in Salt Lake City, John Walker was there waiting to meet them. As the story goes, John greeted Elizabeth with, "Hi there Elizabeth, I'm ready for you!" and she retorted, "You can go to H--- I've made it this far alone, I'll go it the rest!"[2]

Elizabeth and her sons moved in with her daughter Mary Ann Hamblin and her husband, Oscar Hamblin, in Tooele, Utah. On November 26, 1853, Elizabeth married George Marshall, with whom she had three more children. Rather than stay with George in an unhappy marriage, Elizabeth left him and joined her daughter Mary Ann and family on their mission to the Indians in Santa Clara. When flooding destroyed their homes and crops, Elizabeth bid a sad farewell to family and friends and moved to Minersville, Utah. She remained in Minersville the rest of her life, giving much service to others. In that small community, she was known as "Elizabeth Corbridge."[3] On December 19, 1878, Elizabeth and her children were sealed to James Corbridge in the St. George Temple. Of the men in Elizabeth's life, none was more beloved than James. Elizabeth died on April 13, 1896, in Minersville. She was buried in the Minersville Cemetery.[4]

**A Bridge to the Past**
Elizabeth was not a wilting violet when faced with difficult times in her life. She cultivated a stubborn resoluteness that kept her moving forward. Through years of marital strife, she never lost a sense of who she was or the eternal perspective of what awaited her in the future. Find a resoluteness about yourself. Move forward—take piano lessons, run a marathon, climb that mountain, then another—

> Climb every mountain
> Ford every stream
> Follow every rainbow
> Till you find your dream.[5]

Be among the extraordinary people in life who have true resilience.

---

2  "James and Elizabeth Walmsley Corbridge."
3  US Federal Census, 1870.
4  "Elizabeth Walmsley Corbridge," Find A Grave.
5  "Climb Ev'ry Mountain," from *The Sound of Music*, Rodgers and Hammerstein, 1959.

## Caroline Barnes Crosby

(1807–1884)

---

OF THE PROPHET JOSEPH SMITH, Caroline wrote, "How often while [listening] to the voice of the prophet have I wished, Oh that my friends, parents, brothers, and sisters, could hear the things that I have heard, and their hearts be made to rejoice in them, as mine did."[1]

---

Caroline resided with her parents in Massachusetts before moving to Eastern Canada. Her father had a difficult time making a living as a farmer. Yet "he was naturally a cheerful man, caring little for appearance," Caroline wrote. "His memory was of the most perfect kind; his conversation interested everybody."[2] When the War of 1812 broke out, her father fought on the side of the British. He was taken prisoner and carried to Burlington, Vermont, where old friends helped him gain his freedom. As for her mother, Caroline viewed her as a proud and high-spirited woman and fond of entertaining friends. She had such a love of order that her home was a marvel of neatness, yet too often she was sad and despondent.

Most of Caroline's schooling was in her home under her father's instruction. By summer of 1826, she had qualified to be a schoolteacher. From 1826 to 1834, Caroline taught school.

---

1 Caroline Crosby Journal (1807–1882), Holograph, Utah State Historical Society, as cited in Kenneth W. Godfrey, Audrey M. Godfrey, Jill Mulvay Derr, *Women's Voices: An Untold History of the Latter-day Saints, 1830–1900* (Salt Lake City: Deseret Book, 1982), 46–57.
2 "Caroline Barnes Crosby excerpts from journal," FamilySearch.

In October 1832, Jonathan Crosby spent a month in Canada visiting his relatives in Caroline's neighborhood. "We formed our intimacy while he was there, which finally resulted in our marriage," Caroline wrote. "I was happy in many respects, knowing that I had married a man who loved me, and would do all that he could to promote my happiness."[3]

Yet problems arose. "His religion was strange and new to us," Caroline penned, "and some of our friends seemed to feel very sorry that I had fallen in with such a society of people. Some said they would rather bury me if I were their daughter. . . . I could find no fault with the doctrines he taught knowing they were purely scriptural, yet I felt sorry that he should take so decided a stand against other sects of Christians." In January 1835, Caroline entered baptismal waters. Of her baptism she wrote, "The ground was frozen and partly covered with ice and the ice was very plenty in the creek where I was baptised. But my heart rejoiced in the Lord, and I went forward with good courage."[4]

Following her baptism, Caroline and Jonathan moved to Kirtland, Ohio. Caroline wrote,

> The first person that we saw [in Kirtland] was Evan M. Green, one of the young men who first brought the gospel to Massachusetts at the time my husband was baptized. He assisted us in getting our wagon up the hill near the temple, which we found very difficult in ascending consequence of the ground being clayey. We went directly to Parley P. Pratt['] s, [where] they had engaged to board us awhile; and were soon introduced to a score of brethren and sisters, who made us welcome among them. I ever felt myself quite at home in their society.[5]

Jonathan purchased a lot west of the Kirtland Temple and began building a home for Caroline. Before the home was built, he worked on temple construction while Caroline braided palm-leaf hats, braiding near a hundred in one season. Jonathan served in the Second Quorum of the Seventies. Caroline was supportive of his calling and wrote, "I realized in some degree the immense responsibility of the office, and besought the Lord for grace and wisdom to be given him that he might be able to magnify his high and holy calling."[6]

---

3   Edward Leo Lyman, Susan Ward Payne, and S. George Ellsworth, eds. *No Place to Call Home: The 1807–1857 Life Writings of Caroline Barnes Crosby, Chronicler of Outlying Mormon Communities* (Logan: Utah State University Press, 2005), 28–30.
4   Lyman, Payne, and Ellsworth, 31–33.
5   Journal (1807–1882), as cited in Godfrey, Godfrey, Derr, *Women's Voices*, 46–57.
6   *Women's Voices*, 46–57.

Caroline received a patriarchal blessing from Joseph Smith Sr. In her blessing, she was told, "Sister Crosby, let thy heart rejoice. Thy name is written in the Lamb[']s book of life. Thy heart is pure, and thou shalt be blest. Thou shalt never want for blessings if thou wilt keep the commandments. . . . When thou prayest in faith the Lord shall answer thy prayers. Angels shall minister unto thee."7

Caroline and Jonathan attended the Kirtland Temple dedication. Afterwards, Caroline noted that the Spirit of the Lord was present in Kirtland for many days. During those days, there was "healing the sick, casting out devils, speaking in tongues, interpretation," which "animated our hearts. . . It was a general time of rejoicing for several months among the Saints. They frequently met from house, to house, to break bread, and drink wine and administer to the poor and afflicted."8

But all too soon—

> Times became very hard in Kirtland. It seemed that our enemies were determined to drive us away if they could possibly, by starving us. None of the business men would employ a mormon scarcely, on any conditions. And our prophet was continually harassed with vexatious lawsuits. Besides the great apostacy in the church, added a [double] portion of distress and suffering to those who wished to abide in the faith, and keep the commandments. We became very short of provisions, several times ate the last we had and knew not where the next meal was coming from.9

The most poignant of Caroline's remembrances occurred when Jonathan was working on the Joseph Smith home:

> Sister Emma observing that he was laboring there alone, came in one day, and inquired of him whether or where he got his provision. He told her he was entirely without, and knew not where to look, as he had no money. . . . She then went into her chamber, and brought him a nice ham [weighing] 20 lbs. Telling him that it was a present for his faithfulness, and that he should bring a sack, and get as much flour as he could to take home. Accordingly he came home rejoicing, considering

---

7   H. Michael Marquardt, *Early Patriarchal Blessings of The Church of Jesus Christ of Latter-day Saints* (Salt Lake City: Smith-Pettit Foundation, 2007), 64–65.
8   Journal (1807–1882), as cited in Godfrey, Godfrey, Derr, *Women's Voices*, 46–57.
9   *Women's Voices*, 46–57

it a perfect Godsend. It was a beautiful white flour, and the ham was very sweet. I thought nothing ever tasted half as good.[10]

About this time, the Kirtland bank failed. Caroline recalled that the failure "caused a great deal of distress among the brethren" and to themselves.[11]

> As to poverty we could endure that patiently, but trials among false brethren, who can endure with patience? Many of our most intimate associates were among the apostates. . . . We had taken sweet counsel together, and walked to the house of God as friends. . . . I felt very sorrowful, and gloomy, but never had the first idea of leaving the church or forsaking the prophet.[12]

Then began a series of moves for Caroline and Jonathan. It was not until 1842 that they settled in Nauvoo. Caroline wrote,

> My husband bought a house. . . . It was a small frame [house] on Maine and Cutler [Streets]. I was well pleased with the place . . . [as] it was situated in a pleasant neighborhood, where we could see the great Mississippi, with its numerous steamboats passing and repassing. Besides we had fine prospects of the temple[,] could distinctly see the men at work, and hear the sound of their hammers, while cutting the stones.[13]

In 1843, Jonathan accepted a mission call to the Eastern States. He was gone thirteen months. Caroline wrote, "He had very little means to leave with us, but trusted us in the hands of the Lord. . . . Shortly after [he left,] I opened a school, as the only means of raising a little fund to support myself and son."[14]

Caroline was in Nauvoo when news spread through the city that Joseph and Hyrum Smith had gone to Carthage. She wrote,

> June 27th 1844 we arose with heavy hearts, full of doubts and fears respecting the safety of our beloved Prophet and Patriarch who were then incarcerated in Carthage

10  *Women's Voices*, 46–57
11  *Women's Voices*, 46–57
12  *Women's Voices*, 46–57
13  Lyman, Payne, and Ellsworth, *No Place to Call Home*, 59.
14  Lyman, Payne, and Ellsworth, 60.

jail. The city was full of rumors concerning the mob who were assembling at Warsaw and Carthage. . . . That Pm the governor with a large posse came to Nauvoo, and requested the legion to deliver up their arms, which they did. He then made a lengthy address to the saints, exhorting them to keep quiet &C. which they obeyed to the very letter, but felt greatly insulted by him, knowing that there was no occasion for his remarks, or counsel. The next morning at an early hour, the news of Joseph and Hiram's [massacre] was spread throughout the length and breadth of the city. We would not believe the first report, but finally it was confirmed to us beyond a doubt. And Oh the sorrow and sadness of that day! many were made sick by the intelligence, others deranged. Many walked the streets mourning and wringing their hands. I lost my strength and appetite, could not attend to any business for several days. . . . Their bodies were brought home; and arrangements made for their burial. Everybody was invited, or rather had the privilege of seeing them by walking through the house, we went in at one door, passed by their coffins, gave them a short look, and then went out on the opposite side. They were much disfigured. I thought they did not look natural, in the least, could scarcely tell them apart.[15]

More difficult days followed. By February 1846, Latter-day Saints were leaving Nauvoo in great numbers. Among them were Jonathan and Caroline and their family. They fled from Nauvoo to the Territory of Iowa and then to Winter Quarters. They joined the Amasa Lyman Company to journey across the plains to the Rockies, arriving on October 12, 1848, in the Salt Lake Valley.

In the valley, Caroline and her family lived in a small house on South Temple. Jonathan supported his family by building tables and bedsteads until the April 1850 general conference. At that conference, Jonathan was called to take his family to the South Sea Islands. "It took but few moments reflection to reconcile my mind to another sacrifice of house[,] home[,] and friends for the sake of the gospel," Caroline wrote.[16] It took twenty-one days for the Crosbys to reach San Francisco and another thirty-five days to reach the island of Tubuai.

---

15   Lyman, Payne, and Ellsworth, 62–63.
16   Lyman, Payne, and Ellsworth, 90.

Of her days on the island, Caroline wrote, "Tahiti is most assuredly the most delightful place for fruit, flowers, and shadetrees, that I ever beheld.... We found everything to more than meet our expectations."[17] In 1854, the Crosbys left the island. When they reached San Francisco, Jonathan was hired to do carpentry work on the building that housed the Latter-day Saint newspaper *Western Standard*. When the job was completed, the Crosbys moved on to San Bernardino and then to Utah. This was the seventh time in Caroline's life that she'd had to break up her home and was uncertain as to where her next home would be.

The Crosbys settled in Beaver, Utah, where they remained the rest of their lives. Caroline died on February 16, 1884, at age seventy-seven.

## A Bridge to the Past

From the day Caroline entered baptismal waters, she was willing to leave family, friends, and home for the gospel's sake. Her sacrifice was often the reason for her joy. There is a difference between happiness and joy. Pleasure and happiness are often found in the moment. Joy, the greatest of the three, has an element of sacrifice. Joy coupled with sacrifice is never fleeting.

---

17  Lyman, Payne, and Ellsworth, 152.

(1833–1920)

"I VERY WELL REMEMBER THE first time I saw the Prophet Joseph Smith," Mary wrote. "It was in July 1841. We had just arrived in Nauvoo when we met him just below the Temple hill. He stopped and shook hands with all the family, even the baby, and had words of comfort and encouragement for us all. I thought what a good man he must be to notice us little children. After that I saw him often as we located not far from his home."[1]

Mary and her family moved from Van Buren, Michigan, to Nauvoo, Illinois, in 1841. They built a two-story home—the first two-story house in Nauvoo—at the corner of Hyde and Parley Street not far from the home of the Prophet Joseph. Mary recalled, "On one occasion my father, Simeon A. Dunn[,] was sick and the Prophet came to our house to administer to him. He commenced to joke [with] him about our house. He said, 'I don't know as I would have had faith to administer to you if you hadn't built your house two stories high. It can be seen from all over town.'"[2]

Mary wrote of seeing the Prophet Joseph Smith in a variety of settings. One was as the leader of a Nauvoo Legion military parade: "It was one fourth of July and there were ladies in the parade with him. A sham battle was fought.

---

1  "Mary Dunn Ensign Autobiography and Testimony," dated 1908 and 1914, FamilySearch.
2  "Mary Ensign Testimony."

I thought he was the finest looking man I ever saw, riding his black horse and dressed in his military suit. He certainly looked grand."[3] She wrote of him being kidnapped by Missourians: "How dreadful everybody felt! In three hours['] time there were five hundred men ready to go to his rescue. Father was one of the number. How glad everyone was when he arrived home five days later! Then our sorrow was turned into joy. How earnestly we did pray for him day and night, until he was returned and our prayers had been answered!"[4]

Mary concluded that for the Prophet Joseph,

> it was one continual persecution for him until he felt he could stand it no longer, so he concluded to go west and find a place for his people. I remember when the people found he had gone, there were certain ones among us who raised a hue and cry, "The shepherd has deserted his flock." It seemed as though they could give him no rest so he came back and faced his enemies until they took his life, together with his brother Hyrum, at Carthage jail. When he made his farewell speech we could hear him from our home. Gov. Ford had promised protection to him and his people but you all understand how that pledge was kept. They were on horseback when they passed our house the next day.[5]

News of the Prophet's assassination and that of his brother Hyrum reached Mary. She reported:

> It was a sad day long to be remembered. . . . It was after sundown. We heard a man coming on a horse, shouting. We stopped to see what he wanted. It was Stephen Markham, he had just arrived from Carthage, they had driven him out. He told us what he expected had happened, as he had heard shooting in that direction. That night the gloom that was cast over the city no pen can describe. Cows lowed, dogs howled. The whole atmosphere was impregnated with calamity. The next morning news was received of the massacre of our Prophet and Patriarch. The feeling that we had cannot be described. The people expected that the mob would come in body and massacre the entire colony of Saints. We all felt as

---

3 "Mary Ensign Testimony."
4 "Mary Ensign Testimony."
5 "Mary Ensign Testimony."

though we did not care, now that our Prophet was gone. But in contrast to the composure of the Saints, fear seemed to seize the hearts of our enemies, and they did not have power to go any farther. So we had a little peace for a while so far as the mobs were concerned.⁶

"I remember when the bodies of Joseph and Hyrum were brought home and placed in the Mansion House," wrote Mary. "Thousands went to view the remains. I did not go to see them. I felt as though I could not endure it. It seemed more than I could stand to see those poor souls cold in death. When they were taken to the cemetery they passed our house. It was a sad sight."⁷

As Latter-day Saints mourned the deaths of Joseph and Hyrum Smith, a question arose in Nauvoo—"Who will lead the Church?" The question was resolved on August 8, 1844. Mary wrote,

> Sidney Rigdon was one candidate. I was at the meeting when he stood in his carriage and harangued the people nearly three hours. He thought it his place to lead the people. The Saints did not know what to do. It seemed as though everything was at a standstill. . . . Brigham Young stepped to the stand. It seemed as though the Prophet was before us, and had been resurrected. People craned their necks to get a better view of him, he so resembled the Prophet in looks and speech. Surely the mantle of the Prophet had fallen on Brigham. I remember so well, what father said on our way home after [the] meeting. In speaking to a friend about the circumstances he said, "They need not hunt any farther, Brigham Young is the man." And so it turned out to be. Sidney Rigdon went the way of all those who raised their voices against this people.⁸

Mary and her family left Nauvoo in 1846 due to mounting religious persecution. They joined other Latter-day Saints crossing the Mississippi River seeking safety in the Territory of Iowa. After traversing the hills of Iowa, the family crossed the Missouri River and settled in Winter Quarters. In 1848, they journeyed across the plains to the Rocky Mountains in the Brigham Young Company. Mary, not yet fifteen years old, recalled, "I started without

---

6  "Mary Ensign Testimony."
7  "Mary Ensign Testimony."
8  "Mary Ensign Testimony."

shoes, and drove a yoke of oxen. . . . How I suffered with my feet, especially when we went through the cactus!"[9]

After arriving in the Salt Lake Valley, Mary and her family settled in the Salt Lake Eighth Ward. Mary remembered that Brigham Young "called the people together and told them to take out their seed grain and weigh what was left to see how much there would be per day for each person. From then on we lived on three-quarters of a pound of corn meal a day for five persons, until greens came, also thistle roots etc."[10]

In 1852, at age nineteen, Mary wed Martin Luther Ensign. To their union were born nine children. Mary and Martin resided in Centerville, Utah, before moving to Brigham City. In 1856, just three years after their marriage, Martin was called to be a missionary in Great Britain. Mary wrote, "I was left with three children. My step-mother died and left five. We were compelled to move south on account of Johnston's Army. I then had those eight children to care for, and I drove a team and went as far as Payson. Our teams consisted of oxen and cows. I have gone through some very trying times."[11]

After the "trying times," there were better days for Mary. She and her family resided in a commodious two-story frame house in northeast Brigham City. According to her granddaughter Eunice Ensign Nelson,

> the home was always a source of wonder to us, as grandchildren. The attic was a veritable fairyland, filled with magazines, pictures, mottoes, etc., and the cellar always seemed full of smoked hams, delicious apples and Grandmother's appetizing pickles and fruit. If it were summer time, there were fresh fruits and vegetables of all kinds, and Grandmother was an A-1 cook. Her chicken pies will always be a shining light in my memory as a child. She had big feather beds and linsey-woolsey sheets or blankets, and to have windows open in the winter was not known. Before we began a meal the dish water was put on the stove to heat, and after the last one was through eating it wasn't many minutes until the dishes were washed and put away. The rule never varied. No dirty dishes ever sat around in Grandmother's kitchen. Her dishes were interesting: a set with gold bands and brown leaves as

---

9   "Mary Ensign Testimony."
10  "Mary Ensign Testimony."
11  "Mary Ensign Testimony."

a border. Another interesting thing to me was to watch her chop vegetables in a wooden bowl with a two bladed chopping knife. She could sit squatting on her feet while she prepared the vegetables for a meal or picked strawberries for dinner.[12]

Mary and Martin celebrated their golden wedding anniversary in 1902 at the meetinghouse in Brigham City. Martin died on May 18, 1911. Mary died nine years later on November 8, 1920, of acute gastroenteritis and jaundice at age eighty-seven. Mary wrote her testimony just prior to her death:

> I want to bear my testimony to the divinity of the mission of the Prophet Joseph Smith. I knew him to be a prophet then and my testimony has grown with the years, and today I am firm in the knowledge that this work is of God. It is my desire that I and my posterity may ever prove true to the covenants that I have made.[13]

## A Bridge to the Past

Mary had a testimony that Joseph Smith was a prophet of God. From youth to maturity, Mary never wavered in her belief in his prophetic calling. She has blessed generations of her posterity because she wrote her testimony in her autobiography. If you haven't written your autobiography, what are you waiting for? When you write it, include your testimony, knowledge of the plan of salvation, and your desire to keep on the covenant path. In so doing, you will leave a priceless heritage of faith for your descendants.

---

12  Eunice Ensign Nelson, "Remembrance of Grandmother Mary," FamilySearch.
13  "Mary Ensign Testimony."

# Mary Field Garner

(1836–1943)

---

"I WAS A CHILD, BUT I couldn't help but mourn and grieve and cry with those who cried because the Prophet of the living God had been taken from our midst," wrote Mary. "[I tried to] be as calm as possible, although we felt so badly over the terrible tragedy [the Martyrdom]. The bodies of Joseph and Hyrum were placed in rude lumber boxes and put in a wagon and each covered with brush to protect them from the hot sun [and returned to Nauvoo]. I was with the Saints who met them outside the city and followed them to the Nauvoo Mansion House. . . . Mother took us children to view the bodies after they were prepared for burial."[1]

---

The parents of Mary Field were members of the United Brethren Church in Herefordshire, England, when Elder Wilford Woodruff taught them the gospel of Jesus Christ. They accepted baptism. The Fields, along with their children, including four-year-old Mary, voyaged to America to be with others of their faith in Nauvoo, Illinois. In that city of the Saints, Mary recalled, "My father did not have enough money to buy a home, so we rented a house from one of the saints." After his death, her family's poverty deepened. "We

---

1 Mary Field Garner as told to Harold H. Jenson, "The Last Leaf on the Tree," *LDS Church News*, August 17, 24, 1957; Mary Field Garner quote, in Bishop John D. Hooper remarks, Funeral Services for Mary Field Garner held at the Hooper Ward chapel, July 26, 1943, FamilySearch.

were very poor and had very little to eat, cornmeal being our main food," Mary said. "Oh! How hungry we were for something else to eat."[2]

In Nauvoo, Mary and her family listened to the Prophet Joseph Smith speak. "We marveled at his superior knowledge of the gospel and the simple way he could teach it to the saints," she said. "No greater words have ever been uttered by man, than the teachings of the Prophet Joseph." To her, Joseph was a "very dignified looking man, and in his uniform of a General he was noble and kingly looking. . . . We were proud to call him our leader at all times."[3]

A few weeks after the martyrdom of Joseph Smith, Mary and her "mother [were] present at the meeting . . . when the mantle of the Prophet Joseph fell upon Brigham Young." Mary said, "We heard the voice of Joseph and looked up quickly and saw the form of the Prophet [Joseph] standing before the congregation. It was, of course, Brigham Young, but he looked and talked so much like Joseph that for just a minute, we thought it was Joseph."[4] Mary was also present at the September 1846 Battle of Nauvoo when mobs tried to force Latter-day Saints from their homes and drive them across the Mississippi River:

> My mother was successful in hiding three guns in her feather beds and the mob did not find them. A sympathetic member of the mob offered to carry mother's baby down to the ferry, but Mother refused his kindness. Mother had some bread already in the kettles to bake. Of course she did not have time to bake it, so she hung it on the reach of our wagon and cooked it after we crossed the Mississippi River.[5]

Mary vividly remembered the "cries of hungry children, for food and shelter, and the groans of the sick and dying, the sadness of others for the loss of their loved ones" on the Iowa side of the Mississippi before "God sent a countless flock of quail to feed us." Of the quail, she said, "They were so tame we could catch them with our hands."[6]

Mary and her family journeyed across the Territory of Iowa to reach Council Bluffs. In that frontier settlement, she met William Garner, a champion heavyweight pugilist from England, who had forsaken his profession to gather with the Latter-day Saints in America.

2 "Last Leaf."
3 "Life of Mary Field Garner," FamilySearch.
4 "Life of Mary Field Garner."
5 "Life of Mary Field Garner."
6 "Life of Mary Field Garner."

In 1852, Mary helped drive a team of oxen to the Salt Lake Valley.[7] Most memorable on that journey was her encounter with Native Americans. "The Indians gave us considerable trouble, and especially me," Mary wrote. "You see, I had long red curly hair, hanging in ringlets down my back, which seemed to attract the Indians." An Indian Chief took a fancy to her and "wanted mother to give me to him as his white squaw, and he would give her many ponies [for me]."[8] Her mother refused. To keep Mary safe, she hid her between feather beds in the wagon. Mary recalled, "Sure enough, the Indian chief came back with his men. He asked for me. Mother told him I was lost. Not satisfied with this, he proceeded to look in every wagon to see if I was there. . . . He did not find me."[9]

Mary and her family settled in Slaterville, Utah. In that small settlement, Mary became reacquainted with William Garner. They were married on November 1, 1856, in Slaterville. They became the parents of ten children, five born in Slaterville and five in Hooper, a small town a few miles away. William supported his family as a farmer until he was called on a mission to England in 1882. "It was hard for the children and I to part with him," Mary wrote, "for he was always such a kind and loving father and husband, so considerate of his family."[10]

After the death of William in 1915, Mary spent decades alone. She liked to take her "daily exercise by walking around the yard and chopping a little kindling wood, and pulling a few weeds." She also liked "to do a little housework." As to why she had such a long life, she said, "I always eat good plain, wholesome foods and have plenty of sleep. I listen to the news broadcasts and especially the war news."[11]

By age ninety-five, Mary's mind was still sound. By age one hundred, her descendants numbered 465. At age 102, she said, "When a person is as old as I am the years drag."[12] Up until that advanced age, she had never worn glasses, a hearing aid, or been inside a hospital. She walked erect and never used a cane.

At age 105, Mary realized that she was the only living person to have seen and known the Prophet Joseph Smith. With that realization came a deep determination to share her testimony of Joseph's prophetic calling. Mary spoke

---

7   "Mary Field" in Utah Mormon Pioneer Travel Overland Database.
8   Jenson, "Last Leaf," *LDS Church News*.
9   Mary Field Garner, "Pioneer Vignette: The Indian and the Redhead," Newspaper clipping, FamilySearch.
10  Jenson, "Last Leaf," *LDS Church News*.
11  "Last Leaf."
12  "The Years Don't Fly when you're Age 102," newspaper clipping, FamilySearch.

often of "the truthfulness of the gospel, as revealed by the Prophet Joseph Smith, that Jesus Christ is the Savior of mankind, that Joseph Smith was a true and living prophet of God."[13] She liked to say to an older group of men, "Boys, I know that God lives; I know that Jesus is the Christ; I know that God spoke to Joseph Smith and I know that He has restored the Gospel and given back to mankind the priesthood."[14]

Mary lived ninety-nine years after the martyrdom of Joseph Smith. She saw the world go from steamboats, cotton gins, and the telegraph to the telephone, electric lights, and television. At age 107, she fell and broke her hip. Not long after, she died on July 20, 1943, in Hooper.

At her funeral, relatives were asked to move to the front of the chapel so that others could find a seat. "All of us are her descendants" was the response.[15] Speaking at her funeral, Bishop John D. Hooper said, "You all know as well as I that those eyes that are now closed in silent death were the last eyes in human heads to live upon this earth that had seen the Prophet Joseph and his brother Hyrum."[16]

**A Bridge to the Past**

When Mary was 105 years old, she found renewed purpose in life. She discovered that she was the only living person to have known the Prophet Joseph Smith. She now had a reason—a renewed purpose—to share her testimony of Joseph's prophetic calling. If we live long enough, we need to adapt and find renewed purpose. Don't withdraw from life and seek shelter in a quiet corner of the house. In that oppressive loneliness, thoughts turn negative, and interests in people and events that once held great value diminish. Find a renewed purpose, a cause—make a difference.

---

13   Jenson, "The Last Leaf," *LDS Church News*.
14   Funeral Services for Mary Field Gardner, FamilySearch.
15   Jenson, "The Last Leaf," *LDS Church News*.
16   Funeral Services for Mary Field Gardner, FamilySearch.

# Rachel Ridgeway Ivins Grant

(1821–1909)

---

"[Joseph Smith] was a fine noble looking man," Rachel wrote. "There were so few that he could trust or put confidence in. His life was so often sought that he had to be hid up. After he had been in hiding and had come out he was always so jolly and happy. He was different in that respect from Brother Hyrum, who was more sedate, more serious."[1]

---

When Rachel was four years old, her father suffered a sunstroke. For the next two years, "he was like a little child, and had to be fed and cared for like an infant."[2] He died when Rachel was six years old. Three years later, her mother died. In her youth, Rachel grew up in the homes of grandparents and cousins near Trenton, New Jersey. She was "religiously inclined but not of the long-faced variety" like her Quaker cousins. She said, "I thought religion ought to make people happier and that was the kind of religion I was looking for."[3] With the consent of her cousins, she joined the Baptists. "The singing pleased me and the prayers were somewhat inspiring," she wrote, "but the sermons were not much more satisfactory than the none-at-all of the Quakers."[4]

---

1 Mary Grant Judd, "Rachel Ridgway Ivins Grant," *Relief Society Magazine* 30, no. 4 (30 April 1943), 229.
2 Leonard J. Arrington, Susan Arrington Madsen, and Emily Madsen Jones, *Mothers of the Prophets* (Salt Lake City: Bookcraft, 2001), 114.
3 Arrington, Madsen, and Jones, 114.
4 Judd, "Rachel Ridgway Ivins Grant," 228.

In fall of 1837, Rachel listened to the preaching of twenty-three-year-old Jedediah Morgan Grant, a member of The Church of Jesus Christ of Latter-day Saints. After attending her first worship service, she wrote, "Upon returning home I went to my room, knelt down and asked the Lord to forgive me for thus breaking the Sabbath day."[5] But she continued to attend other meetings and read the Book of Mormon. "A new light seemed to break in upon me, the scriptures were plainer in my mind, and the light of the everlasting Gospel began to illuminate my soul," Rachel wrote. "I soon handed in my name for baptism."[6]

Following her baptism, at age twenty-one Rachel gathered with the Saints in Nauvoo, Illinois. Rather than experience peace in the "city beautiful," she knew much of turbulence. Her cousin Charles Ivins took part in the *Nauvoo Expositor* conspiracy. Her cousin James Ivins and family joined with apostate James Strang. Rachel was conflicted. She attended the August 8, 1844, meeting and heard Sidney Rigdon put forward his claim to lead the Church. She wrote, "Brigham Young jumped right up on the seat and spoke. If you had had your eyes shut you would have thought it was the Prophet Joseph. In face he looked like him, his very countenance seemed to change and he spoke like him."[7]

Yet still her future seemed uncertain. Rachel returned to her family in New Jersey, but in so doing never cast aside her faith in the Restoration. The internal conflict was real, and her choice had to be right. It was not until spring of 1853 that she knew the course she should follow. It was to reunite with The Church of Jesus Christ of Latter-day Saints. Although family members tried to dissuade her, she made the arduous trek to the Salt Lake Valley.

In the valley, Rachel received several offers of marriage. None suited her fancy until Jedediah Morgan Grant, the missionary she had first heard preach the gospel of Jesus Christ, asked her to marry him. At the time, Jedediah Grant was serving in the First Presidency of the Church. "Without a love story, but with mutual respect and common aspirations," Rachel married Jedediah on November 29, 1855, and became his seventh wife under the law of plural marriage.[8] At the time of their marriage, Rachel was age thirty-four and Jedediah thirty-nine.

---

5   Judd, 228.
6   Ronald Walker, "Rachel R. Grant: The Continuing Legacy of the Feminine Ideals," in Donald Q. Cannon, ed., *Supporting Saints: Life Stories of Nineteenth Century Mormons* (Provo, UT: Religious Studies Center, Brigham Young University, 1985), 17–42.
7   Walker, 17–42.
8   Frances Bennett Jeppson, "With Joy Wend Your Way: The Life of Rachel Ivins Grant, My Great-Grandmother," 10, typescript, 1952, Church Archives.

Only twelve months and two days after their marriage, Jedediah died of typhoid and pneumonia. Nine days later, Rachel gave birth to her only child, Heber Jeddy Grant. Rachel would marry again—George D. Grant, an older brother of Jedediah. The marriage ended in divorce. She seldom spoke of this trial in her life.

As for being raised by Rachel Ivins Grant, her son Heber wrote, "[My mother] was both father and mother to me; she set an example of integrity, of devotion and love, of determination, and honor second to none. I stand here today as the president of the Church because I have followed the advice and counsel and the burning testimony of the divinity of the work of God, which came to me from my mother."9

Rachel and her son, Heber, lived in a small adobe house at 14 South 200 East in Salt Lake City. To support herself and her son, Rachel did custom sewing for the Salt Lake Theater and took in boarders. "I never felt humiliated at having to work and support myself and [Heber]," penned Rachel, "and I thanked my heavenly Father for giving me the strength and ability to do it."10

Rachel was never prosperous. A relative said of her, "She could wear a dress longer than anyone I have seen and have it look fresh and nice. She always changed her dress in the afternoon and washed herself and combed her hair, and if at home put on a nice white apron."11

When Bishop Edwin D. Wooley visited her home and saw a half-dozen or so buckets on the floor to catch rain from the roof, he said, "Why, Widow Grant, this will never do. I shall take some of the money from the fast offering and put a new roof on this house." "Oh, no, you won't," said Rachel. "No relief money will ever put a roof on my house. I have sewing here, [and] I have supported myself and my son with a needle and thread for many years. . . . When I get through with this sewing that I'm doing now, I will buy some shingles and patch the holes in the roof."12

In 1868, when her son, Heber, was only twelve years old, Rachel lost most of her hearing. Her last forty years were spent in almost total silence. Of this affliction, she wrote, "I'm glad I can see. I feel blindness would be a great affliction."13 She contended that being deaf meant that "she missed a great deal

---

9 Heber J. Grant, Conference Report, April 1934.
10 Arrington, Madsen, and Jones, *Mothers of the Prophets*, 122.
11 Arrington, Madsen, and Jones, 121.
12 Bryant S. Hinckley, *Heber J. Grant: Highlights in the Life of a Great Leader* (Salt Lake City: Deseret Book, 1951), 13.
13 Arrington, Madsen, and Jones, *Mothers of the Prophets*, 124.

of unpleasantness, because people didn't bother to tell her scandal, while they always brought her any good news."[14]

For thirty-five of the forty silent years, Rachel was president of her ward Relief Society (1868–1903). In that capacity, she presided over meetings and supervised sewing projects, including the making of carpets for the Salt Lake Temple. As a tribute to her service, Susa Young Gates wrote, "For many, many years she meekly, grandly stood as leader of her sex in one small ward."[15] To perhaps cheer up her spirits, "she kept a hymn book under her pillow, and sometimes, when she couldn't sleep, she would turn on the light and read hymn after hymn."[16]

Although Rachel was often alone, she "had good books and pleasant memories to keep her company."[17] At times it appeared that death would be welcome. "I have far more friends and loved ones on the other side than I have here," she wrote.[18] Rachel died on January 27, 1909, at age eighty-six.

**A Bridge to the Past**

Rachel was a single parent. She made a living for herself and her son, Heber, by being a seamstress and renting a room in her house. For the last forty years of her life, she lived in silence, having lost her hearing. Yet she served for thirty-five of those silent years as a ward Relief Society president. Life doesn't have to be perfect for us to give service. Gratitude for being blessed with the strength and ability to give service is characteristic of a true leader among women.

---

14   Jeppson, "With Joy Wend Your Way," 13.
15   Susa Young Gates, "A Tribute to Rachel Ivins Grant," *Young Woman's Journal* (January 1910), 30.
16   Jeppson, "With Joy Wend Your Way," 19.
17   Jeppson, 19.
18   Arrington, Madsen, and Jones, *Mothers of the Prophets*, 124.

# Drusilla Dorris Hendricks

(1810–1881)

In writing of the martyrdom of Joseph and Hyrum Smith, Drusilla penned, "I could well bear witness to the feelings of the brethren, who were on missions at that time for my feelings were such that I prayed to the Lord to take them from me for it was more than I could stand."[1]

One of the earliest childhood memories of Drusilla was "saying Prayer after My Father. I was then about five years of age." Her parents were Baptists. Her neighbors were Methodists and Presbyterians. She recalled hearing "much talk concerning Religion" in her home and neighborhood. By age seven, Drusilla had enrolled in school. After completing a six-month term, she could read and write but little more. Her parents withdrew her from the classroom, believing she had all the schooling necessary for her to succeed. Her further "reading was confined to the Bible and the Hymn book." Of the Bible, she said, "I could recite pages of it without looking at the book." Her father said, "What a mind that child has got."[2] Hours of reading in the Bible led Drusilla to the conclusion that she was a sinner: "Lord have mercy on me and save me from that awful place I had heard so much about."[3]

At age seventeen, having learned all branches of housewifery, Drusilla married James Hendricks on May 31, 1827. Within a year of their marriage,

---

1 "Drusilla Dorris Hendricks—Her Own History," FamilySearch.
2 "Drusilla Hendricks—History."
3 "Drusilla Hendricks—History."

she gave birth to her first child. "It was then my troubles began," Drusilla wrote. "I found I was a Mother and the responsibilities of a mother were upon me. My husband came in and found me crying. He then asked if he had neglected me." Drusilla assured him that was not the case. "We had many serious hours over it and as it appeared to me then, so I found it. No small thing to be a mother."[4]

As she got a better grasp on motherhood, her attention once again turned to religion. She became a Baptist but confessed, "I was no better satisfied than before." It was not until Elders James Emmet and Peter Dustin came to Simpson, Kentucky, preaching the Restoration of the gospel of Jesus Christ that she heard something new. She wrote, "Those Elders brought the same light Jesus had in the days of John the Baptist." She very much wanted to be baptized, but her husband was decidedly against it. "I knew it was no use to ask him," Drusilla wrote. "I could only go by myself and ask the Lord to enlighten his mind that he might see the truth."[5]

Within days, James had seen the truth and also wanted to be baptized. When his brother learned of his desire, he threatened to "get two hundred men and tie him and the Elder and give them two hundred lashes each and see if they would stand that for Christ's sake." In spite of the threats, James and Drusilla were baptized. Drusilla wrote of her baptism, "I arose to walk in newness of life. That fear of death and Hell was all gone from me and I was a new creature. Such a feeling of calmness pervaded me for months and my husband had the same feelings."[6]

In the spring of 1836, James and Drusilla sold their property in Simpson, Kentucky, and moved to Missouri to be with others of their faith. They met many Saints who became wonderful friends and learned of their being driven from Jackson County a few years before, "not knowing that the same fate awaited" them.[7] Yet heightened fear of persecution led Drusilla and her family to move to Far West in Caldwell County. Drusilla penned, "We were to be let alone there so we were glad to go."[8] Of her experiences in Far West, she wrote, "I never lived happier in my life. I was always very sickly until now. I had quit taking snuff, tea and coffee and I became healthy and strong. Where before I could not walk half a mile, now I could walk three miles and not tire, for we kept the Word of Wisdom."[9] She described herself "like the old Nephite

---

4   "Drusilla Hendricks—History."
5   "Drusilla Hendricks—History."
6   "Drusilla Hendricks—History."
7   "Drusilla Hendricks—History."
8   "Drusilla Hendricks—History."
9   "Drusilla Hendricks—History."

women while they were traveling in the wilderness for they became strong like unto the men."[10]

Drusilla would need all the strength she could muster on October 25, 1838. At the Battle of Crooked River, James was shot in the neck "where it cut off all feeling of the body." As Drusilla rode toward where James lay in a small log home, she saw nine wounded brethren looking as "pale as death." When she reached James, "he could speak but could not move any more than if he were dead." In an attempt to revive his muscles, Drusilla "rubbed and steamed him but could get no circulation. He was dead from his neck down."[11]

It took several hours before James could be moved to their home. Drusilla paused to wonder aloud if she was sorry that she had become a Latter-day Saint. "I am not," she said. "I did what was right[.] If I die I am glad I was baptized, for the remission of my sins for I have an answer of a good conscience." She then heard a voice: "Hold on for the Lord will provide."[12]

The Lord provided for James and Drusilla. When Drusilla despaired over her seemingly impossible condition, the Lord sent someone, sometimes complete strangers, to provide for her needs. "I have just found out how the widow[']s crust and barrell [sic] held out through the famine," wrote Drusilla. "Just as it was out someone was sent to fill it."[13] To provide for the financial needs of her family, she took in washing and sewing. "I began to make beer and ginger bread and go out on public days," she said.[14] She also took in boarders, carpenters, and masons who came to Nauvoo to work on the temple.

Hoping to relieve some of the financial pressure on their family, on January 19, 1840, the Nauvoo High Council voted to donate a city lot to James Hendricks and encourage brethren to build a log house for his family. The security the home provided to Drusilla ended all too soon. The deaths of Joseph and his brother Hyrum were devastating and frightening to her. It was not until she saw the mantle of Joseph fall upon Brigham Young in August 1844 that she could be consoled. She wrote, "Pres. Brigham Young began to speak. I jumped up to look and see if it was not Brother Joseph for surely it was his voice and gestures. Every Latter-day Saint could easily see upon whom the priesthood descended for Brigham Young held the keys."[15]

---

10  "Drusilla Hendricks—History."; 1 Nephi 17:2.
11  "Drusilla Hendricks—History."
12  "Drusilla Hendricks—History."
13  "Drusilla Hendricks—History."
14  "Drusilla Hendricks—History."
15  "Drusilla Hendricks—History."

Willing to follow Brigham Young, James and Drusilla left their house and most of their belongings in 1846 to join the Latter-day Saint exodus to Iowa. They traversed through the Territory of Iowa to reach the Missouri River. "We were on our way to the mountains when the United States Officers came to our camp and told us their business," Drusilla wrote. Their business was to recruit Latter-day Saint men from ages eighteen to forty-five into a Mormon Battalion to fight in the Mexican War. Drusilla's overriding thought on recruitment was *not my son William*. "My son was all I had to depend on," Drusilla wrote, "his father being helpless and Joseph, my other son, being in his ninth year and my girls not healthy." Yet when Drusilla was alone, she heard the words, "Are you afraid to trust the God of Israel[?] Has he not been with you in all your trials[?] Has he not provided for your wants[?]" She also heard the voice ask "if I did not want the greatest glory." She answered, "Yes I did." "Then how can you get it without making the greatest sacrifice[?]" asked the voice. Upon answering, "Lord what lack I yet[?]" the voice said, "Let your son go in the Battalion."[16] Believing these words were from God, Drusilla encouraged William to join the epic march.

"I cannot tell the hardships we endured by his going," penned Drusilla.[17] William was gone from the family for fifteen months. During those months, the family journeyed with the Jedediah M. Grant wagon train to the Rockies, reaching the Salt Lake Valley on October 4, 1847. They settled temporarily in Fort Salt Lake before moving to Warm Springs to manage a twelve-room bathhouse, property of the Church. James was called to be the first bishop of the Salt Lake Nineteenth Ward. These proved to be happy days for Drusilla. "We made good gardens and the Lord blessed every move we made," she wrote. "I still wove, made gloves and rope, and kept boarders to gain a living."[18]

When James died in 1870, Drusilla viewed him as a "martyr for the cause of truth." Of her husband, she said, "I do not think he ever doubted the truth of the Gospel for one moment. I never heard him murmur nor speak against the authorities of the Church and he always gave good advice to his family. He laid five months in his illness. He often wanted the brethren to lay hands on him to ease him from pain but I could not ask the Lord to spare his life any longer for I thought he had suffered long enough."[19] As for Drusilla's testimony, it remained

---

16 "Drusilla Hendricks—History."
17 "Drusilla Hendricks—History."
18 "Drusilla Hendricks—History."
19 "Drusilla Hendricks—History."

sure: "The Gospel is true. I have rejoiced in it through all my trials for the Spirit of the Lord has buoyed me up or I should have failed."[20] Drusilla died eleven years after James Hendricks on May 20, 1881, at age seventy-one.

**A Bridge to the Past**
Drusilla had it tough. Being a mother did not come easy for Drusilla. Then her husband was shot in the neck and lost all feeling in his body. Due to his health condition, he was unable to support Drusilla and the children. Drusilla took in washing and sewing to have the means to provide shelter and food for her family. In the thick of her trials, she heard a voice from heaven say, "Hold on, for the Lord will provide." Trust in the Lord no matter the problem, for the Lord will provide. When dark clouds obscure the joys of life, the Lord will hear your prayers and buoy you up.

---

20 "Drusilla Hendricks—History."

# Mary Isabella Hales Horne

(1818–1905)

---

"I first met the Prophet Joseph Smith in the fall of 1837, at my home in the town of Scarborough, Canada West," Mary wrote. "When I first shook hands with him I was thrilled through and through and I knew that he was a Prophet of God, and that testimony never left me."[1]

---

Of her parents, Mary wrote, "My parents were honest, industrious people; and when very young I was taught to pray, to be honest and truthful, to be kind to my associates, and to do good to all around me."[2] Her parents were religious. Her father adhered to the Methodist faith and her mother to the Church of England.

"In the year 1832, when I was in my thirteenth year, there was great excitement in the town where I lived, over the favorable reports [of land in Upper Canada]," penned Mary. "My father and mother caught the spirit of going, and began to make preparations for leaving England." On April 16, 1832, the Hales family boarded a sailing vessel leaving English shores. After six weeks of sailing across the Atlantic Ocean, the vessel anchored at the town of York in Quebec. "To our dismay," wrote Mary, "we found that the cholera was

---

1  "The Prophet Joseph Smith: The Testimony of Sister M. Isabella Horne," *Relief Society Magazine* 38, no. 3 (March 1951), 158.
2  Mary Isabella Hale Horne Journal in Kenneth Glyn Hales, "From Windows: A Mormon Family in Three Autobiographies," FamilySearch.

raging fearfully in that region; but through all of those trying scenes the Lord preserved us in health."[3]

In spring of 1834, Mary attended a Methodist camp meeting in York. There she made the acquaintance of Joseph Horne. On May 9, 1836, Mary and Joseph were married. To their union were born fifteen children, eleven living to adulthood.

The newlyweds established their home one mile from Mary's parental house. "Although I had not been used to farm work," Mary wrote, "I milked cows, fed pigs and chickens, and made myself at home in my new situation, seeking to make my home pleasant for my husband, and working to advance his interests."[4]

In June 1834, the Hales learned that "a man professing to be sent of God to preach to the people would hold a meeting about a mile from [their] house." They went to the meeting and listened to Elder Orson Pratt speak of the Restoration of the gospel of Jesus Christ. "We were very much pleased with his sermon," Mary wrote. "My father was so delighted with the sermon that he left the Methodist Church and attended the 'Mormon' meetings altogether; and in a short time every member of his family had received and obeyed the gospel."[5] It was not until July 1836 that Mary was baptized by Orson Hyde.[6]

Following her baptism, her "house was open for meetings, and became a home for many of the elders." In the summer of 1837, she was privileged to host the Prophet Joseph Smith, Sidney Rigdon, and Thomas B. Marsh in her home. Of that sacred privilege, Mary wrote, "O Lord, I thank thee for granting the desire of my girlish heart, in permitting me to associate with prophets and apostles."[7]

In March 1838, Mary and Joseph and their children moved from Canada to Missouri to be with the Saints of God. They tarried for a season in Huntsville, Missouri, about a hundred miles from Far West. It was there Mary received a patriarchal blessing from Joseph Smith Sr., the father of the Prophet Joseph. In the blessing, she was told, "The Lord will bring you through six troubles, and in the seventh He will not leave you."[8] She and her family experienced many

---

3  "From Windows."
4  "From Windows."
5  "From Windows."
6  "From Windows."
7  "From Windows."
8  "From Windows."

trials in Missouri. Mary described it as a "full share of exposure, sickness and peril incident to the expulsion of the saints" from the state.⁹

While she was living in Quincy, Illinois, the Prophet Joseph stopped by her home. Mary wrote that Brother Joseph was in the best of spirits. He said, "Sister Horne, if I had a wife as small as you, when trouble came I would put her in my pocket and run."¹⁰ On another occasion, the Prophet said, "Sister Horne, the Spirit always draws me to your home." Seeing that his clothes needed to be washed, Mary offered to wash them. He said to her, "Indeed, Sister Horne, you do not look able to do it." Mary insisted, and he consented. She wrote, "I prepared his clothing that afternoon so that he was ready for his journey in the morning."¹¹

Mary and her family eventually settled in Nauvoo. When persecution raged in Nauvoo, they moved on to Winter Quarters. In June 1847, they began their journey to the Rocky Mountains. Mary wrote,

> Our family consisted of Mr. [Joseph] Horne, myself, and four children, one of whom had been born since we left our home in Nauvoo. We also brought a man and his wife with us, he driving one of the teams. We had three wagons, with two yoke of oxen to each, which contained farming implements, seed-grain, cooking utensils, a few necessary dishes, etc., clothing, and provisions that must last eight people for at least eighteen months; we also brought a small cooking stove, a very rare article in the pioneer camps, and a small rocking chair.¹²

As they journeyed along the Platte River, a band of Indians approached, wanting to trade buffalo robes for corn and provisions. Mary recalled that one Indian "took a fancy to my baby girl and wanted me to trade her for a pony. When I refused he brought another pony, and still another, until finally he went to get the fourth one, and seemed so determined to have her that I was afraid he would steal her from my arms."¹³ When the pioneer company reached the Black Hills, Mary wrote, "A large band of Indians placed themselves directly

---

9   "From Windows."
10  Lyneve Wilson Kramer and Eva Durant Wilson, "Mary Isabella Hales Horne," *Ensign*, Aug. 1982, 64.
11  "The Prophet Joseph Smith: The Testimony of Sister M. Isabella Horne," 159–60.
12  M. Isabella Horne, "Pioneer Reminiscences," *Young Woman's Journal* 13, no. 7 (July 1902), 292.
13  Horne, 292.

across our path, and would not allow us to pass; they demanded corn, sugar, and coffee. Some of the brethren went through the camp and collected as much as possible from our meagre supply, which the Indians accepted, and made no further trouble."[14]

At the Sweetwater River, their company met Brigham Young and others returning to Winter Quarters. A feast was held in their honor. Mary wrote, "Dishes were unpacked, and the sisters did the best possible to prepare a dinner worthy of the occasion. . . . The brethren cleared away the brush and improvised a rude table, and I can assure you we had a feast indeed, spiritual as well as temporal."[15]

Mary and her family arrived in the Salt Lake Valley the evening of October 6, 1847. Of reaching their destination, Mary wrote, "Only those who have had similar experience can realize how our hearts were filled with gratitude to our Heavenly Father that He had preserved our lives, and that we had met with no accident during our long and perilous journey of nearly four months through an unknown and uninhabited country."[16]

Mary and her family resided in Salt Lake City. Besides raising eleven of her fifteen children, Mary found time to give much service to the Church. She presided over the Salt Lake 15th Ward Relief Society for fourteen years before becoming president of the Salt Lake Stake Relief Society. She also served as treasurer of the Central Board of Relief Society and as a member of the Relief Society General Board. She presided over meetings of the Retrenchment Association in the Salt Lake 15th Ward, being called to the assignment by Brigham Young. She was a counselor to Zina D. Young in the Utah Silk Association and served on the Deseret Hospital board for twelve years. In addition, she was president of the Women's Co-op Mercantile and Manufacturing Institution and active in the women's suffrage movement, serving as the leader of the protest meeting held in the Salt Lake Theatre on March 6, 1886.

Mary died on August 25, 1905, at age eighty-seven. A large posterity mourned her death.

## A Bridge to the Past

Mary gave birth to fifteen children, raising eleven to maturity, and still had time to serve outside her home. She personified the words of the Lord to the

---

14  Horne, 292–93.
15  Horne, 293.
16  Kate B. Carter, *Our Pioneer Heritage* (Salt Lake City: Daughters of the Utah Pioneers, 1958), 1:121.

Prophet Joseph Smith, "Organize yourselves; prepare every needful thing; and establish a house, even a house of prayer, a house of fasting, a house of faith, a house of learning, a house of glory, a house of order, a house of God." and still had time to serve her neighbors.[17] If we strove to do as Mary did, how much improved would our lives be?

---

17  D&C 88:119.

## *Vienna Jacques*

(1787–1884)

As Vienna was picking up papers that had been strewn in the street by a mob who attacked the Latter-day Saint printing office in Independence, a mobber said to her,

> "Madam this is only a prelude to what you have to suffer. . . . There goes your Bishop [Edward Partridge], tarred and feathered"; she looked and saw a figure passing but did not recognize the Bishop and asked, where? The man replied, that he had first passed behind a house; she took two or three steps . . . and saw him going along, encircled in a bright light, surpassing the . . . Sun; She exclaimed Glory to God! For he will receive a crown of glory for tar and feathers.[1]

---

Vienna grew to maturity in Beverly, Massachusetts, the birthplace of the American Industrial Revolution. In that bustling suburb of Boston, Vienna knew much of crowded living and hope. Being religiously inclined, she attended Methodist services at the Bromfield Street chapel in Boston but too often found herself dissatisfied with the services. Wanting more

---

1  Vienna Jaques, "Statement," *Historian's Office Journal*, February 22, 1859, Church History Library.

than the preaching of Christlike living, she investigated other Christian denominations.

When Vienna learned of Joseph Smith and the Restoration, she wrote to Kirtland requesting a copy of the Book of Mormon.[2] When the book arrived, she casually glanced through the scripture and laid it aside. "A vision" convinced her to read the contents. As she read, her mind became "illuminated."[3] Convinced of the truthfulness of the book, at age forty-three Vienna cast "strict economy" aside to travel from Boston to Kirtland to meet the translator of the Book of Mormon, Joseph Smith.

Vienna traveled alone by canal boat and then by stage to reach Ohio. According to the *Boston Courier*, she "satisfied herself that the Mormon bible was a revelation from God, and the leaders true prophets. . . . She believed that the Mormonites could perform miracles. When asked if she had seen any miraculous operations, she replied that she had seen a person who was very sick suddenly restored to health."[4] Being a nurse, this had a profound effect upon her. She was baptized on July 12, 1831, by Emer Harris.

Vienna mingled with fellow believers for about six weeks in Kirtland before returning to Boston. In the port city, she visited family members and shared with them news of the Restoration of the gospel of Jesus Christ. Her missionary efforts led to conversions, yet she again journeyed to Kirtland alone. When she arrived in the city of the Saints, she was not penniless like so many new converts. She had $1,400, an enviable sum. On March 8, 1833, Joseph Smith directed Vienna to give her money to the Church. Without hesitation, Vienna offered the entire sum.

For her unselfish consecration, Vienna became one of only two nineteenth-century women named in the Doctrine and Covenants. The first was Emma Smith, the wife of the Prophet Joseph, and the second was Vienna Jacques. The Lord through His Prophet Joseph told Vienna,

> It is my will that my handmaid Vienna Jaques should receive money to bear her expenses, and go up unto the land of Zion.
>
> And the residue of the money may be consecrated unto me, and she be rewarded in mine own due time.

---

2  George Hamlin, "In Memoriam," *Woman's Exponent* 12, no. 19 (March 1, 1884), 152.
3  Hamlin, 152.
4  "Mormonites," *Boston Courier*, October 10, 1831, FamilySearch.

> Verily I say unto you, that it is meet in mine eyes that she should go up unto the land of Zion, and receive an inheritance from the hand of the bishop;
>
> That she may settle down in peace inasmuch as she is faithful, and not be idle in her days from thenceforth.[5]

Vienna journeyed with William Hobart to Missouri. As promised, she was given an inheritance in Zion.

On September 4, 1833, the Prophet Joseph wrote to Vienna:

> I have often felt a whispering since I received your letter, like this: "Joseph, thou art indebted to thy God for the offering of thy Sister [Vienna], which proved a Savior of life as pertaining to thy [pecuniary] concern[s]. [Therefore] she should not be forgotten of thee, for the Lord hath done this, and thou shouldst remember her in all thy prayers and also by letter, for she oftentimes calleth on the Lord, saying, O Lord, inspire thy Servant Joseph to communicate by letter some word to thine unworthy handmaid."[6]

In the same letter, Joseph told of being forewarned of the struggles that she would face in Missouri: "When you left Kirtland [I knew] that the Lord would chasten you, but I prayed fervently in the name of Jesus that you might live to receive your inheritance. . . . I am not at all astonished at what has happened to you."[7]

As religious persecution raged in Independence, Vienna fled with other Latter-day Saints to Clay County, Missouri. She was residing near Fishing River in 1834 when Joseph Smith and members of Zion's Camp reached the river. Vienna was among the first to greet them and offer help. Heber C. Kimball penned, "I received great kindness . . . from sister Vienna Jaques, who administered to my wants and also to my brethren—may the Lord reward [her] for [her] kindness."[8]

In Missouri, Vienna married widower Daniel Shearer. The marriage ended in separation in Nauvoo. In 1847, at age sixty and without Daniel, Vienna

---

5  D&C 90:28–31.
6  Letter to Vienna Jacques, September 4, 1833, *The Joseph Smith Papers* [punctuation added].
7  Letter to Vienna Jacques.
8  Heber C. Kimball, "Extract from Journal," *Times and Seasons* 6 (March 15, 1845), 839–40.

drove a wagon across the plains in the Charles C. Rich Company, arriving on October 2, 1847, in the Salt Lake Valley. Daniel did not journey across the plains until 1852. There is no record of Vienna and Daniel living together in the valley.

Vienna lived in a wagon during her first winter in the valley. Not wanting to repeat the experience, she wrote to Brigham Young on October 16, 1848:

> You told me to hold on, respecting my lot, but you did not say how long I must wait. Now if you think I am worthy to have a lot or a part of a lot if you will let me know where to live so that I can have my adobes hauled on to the same place I will endeavor to build as neat a house as others do so as not to disgrace your city. All the choice I have is to have my place of residence so that I can walk to the place of worship.[9]

Vienna was given a city lot in the Salt Lake 12th Ward. She viewed the lot as her new inheritance. She lived on the lot the remainder of her days. She was self-sufficient. Vienna milked her own cow and made her own butter. She gave the butter to the needy. She did "her own housework, including washing, ironing and cooking, [wrote] many letters, and [did] a great deal of reading. Sister Vienna [was] very familiar with the Scriptures."[10]

When she was age ninety-four, it was reported, "The erectness of her carriage is sufficient to fill many of the Misses of the nineteenth century with envy."[11] The next two years her "mental facilities were clouded and her speech quite incoherent." Vienna died on February 7, 1884, in her home at age ninety-six. Her faithfulness was extolled in her obituary: "She was true to her covenants and esteemed the restoration of the Gospel as a priceless treasure."[12]

## A Bridge to the Past

Gifts of the Spirit prevailed in Vienna's life. For example, a vision illuminated her mind with the truthfulness of the Book of Mormon. The Spirit of the Lord whispered to the Prophet Joseph Smith telling him to remember Vienna in his prayers. And Vienna saw a bright light

---

9   "Letter of Vienna Jacques to Brigham Young," October 16, 1848, FamilySearch.
10  "Home Affairs," *Woman's Exponent* 7, no. 3 (July 1, 1878), 21.
11  "Birthday Anniversary of One of our Oldest Veterans," *Woman's Exponent* 9 (June 15, 1880), 13.
12  Hamlin, "In Memoriam," 152.

surrounding Bishop Partridge after he had been tarred and feathered. Gifts of the Spirit follow those who believe and keep the commandments of God. The gifts are a blessing from the Lord.

# *Jane Elizabeth Manning James*

(1822–1908)

---

WHILE STAYING AT THE MANSION House in Nauvoo, Jane recalled,

> On the morning that my folks all left to go to work, I looked at myself clothed in the only two pieces I possessed; I sat down and wept. Brother Joseph came into the room . . . and said, "Good morning. Why—not crying, [are you]?" "Yes sir," [I said] "the folks have all gone and got themselves homes, and I have got none." He said, "Yes you have, you have a home right here if you want it. You mustn't cry, we dry up all tears here." . . . Brother Joseph went out and brought Sister Emma in and said "Sister Emma, here is a girl that says she has no home. Haven't you a home for her?" "Why yes, if she wants one." He said, "She does," and then he left us.[1]

---

"When a child only six years old, I left my home and went to live with a family of white people; their names were Mr. and Mrs. Joseph Fitch," Jane recalled. "They were aged people and quite wealthy. I was raised by their daughter [in Connecticut]. When about fourteen years old, I joined the

---

1   James Goldberg, "The Autobiography of Jane Manning James: Seven Decades of Faith and Devotion," December 11, 2013.

Presbyterian Church. Yet I did not feel satisfied; it seemed to me there was something more that I was looking for."[2]

Within eighteen months of joining the Presbyterian Church, Jane learned that Elder John Wesley Randall and his companion would soon be preaching in her town. Although "the pastor of the Presbyterian Church forbid me going to hear them—as he had heard I had expressed a desire to hear them," she went anyway. Jane was "fully convinced" that the elders preached the "true gospel."[3] She was baptized and confirmed a member of The Church of Jesus Christ of Latter-day Saints.

"One year after I was baptized I started for Nauvoo," Jane said. In October 1842, she and eight members of her family left Wilton, Connecticut, and traveled by canal boat to Buffalo, New York. In Buffalo, fares were demanded before the family could proceed to Ohio. Unable to meet the demand, Jane and her family "left the boat and started on foot to travel a distance of over eight hundred miles" to join the Saints in Nauvoo. "We walked until our shoes were worn out, and our feet became sore and cracked open and bled until you could see the whole print of our feet with blood on the ground," Jane said. "We stopped and united in prayer to the Lord; we asked God the Eternal Father to heal our feet and our prayers were answered and our feet were healed forthwith."[4]

When Jane and her family reached Peoria, Illinois, a government official threatened to put them in jail if they did not show "free papers." Jane explained, "We didn't know at first what he meant, for we had never been slaves." After much discussion, a disgruntled official let her and her family pass on. "We traveled on until we came to a river and as there was no bridge, we walked right into the stream. When we got to the middle, the water was up to our necks, but we got safely across." When night fell, Jane was unable to see her hands due to the darkness, but she still moved forward. After sleeping in a forest, she and her family awoke to find that frost had fallen heavy in the night, and there was "a light fall of snow." Jane recalled that they walked "through that frost with our bare feet, until the sun rose and melted it away." In recalling these trials, she remarked, "We went on our way rejoicing, singing hymns, and thanking God for his infinite goodness and

---

2   Goldberg, "Autobiography of Jane Manning James."
3   Goldberg, "Autobiography of Jane Manning James."
4   Goldberg, "Autobiography of Jane Manning James."

mercy to us in blessing us as he had, protecting us from all harm, answering our prayers and healing our feet."[5]

In due course, Jane and her family reached the beautiful city of Nauvoo. Emma Smith saw them approaching her house and exclaimed, "Come in. Come in!" That evening, several listened as the Prophet Joseph said to Jane, "You have been the head of this little band haven't you?" She answered, "Yes, sir!" He then said, "God bless you!" before inviting Jane to share incidents of her journey with his guests. When she finished her recitation, Joseph turned to his guest Dr. John Bernhisel and said, "What do you think of that, doctor: isn't that faith?" Dr. Bernhisel replied, "Well, I rather think it is. If it had been me, I fear I should have backed out and returned to my home!" Turning to Jane and her family, Joseph said, "God bless you. You are among friends now and you will be protected."[6]

For several months, Jane resided in the Smith home. She took occasion in the home to learn from Joseph Smith. She viewed him as one of the finest men she had ever known. After the martyrdom of Joseph, Jane resided in the Brigham Young home until her marriage to Isaac James, a free black man from rural Monmouth County, New Jersey.

In 1847, Jane and Isaac journeyed with the Ira Eldredge Company to the Salt Lake Valley. In the valley, Isaac obtained employment with Brigham Young. The pay was commensurate with the work, and Jane said, "We got along splendid, accumulating horses, cows, oxen, sheep, and chickens in abundance. I spun all the cloth for my family clothing for a year or two, and we were in a prosperous condition—until the grasshoppers and crickets came along, carrying destruction wherever they went." It was after the destruction that Jane said, "Oh how I suffered of cold and hunger, and the keenest of all was to hear my little ones crying for bread and I had none to give them. But in all, the Lord was with us and gave us grace and faith to stand it all."[7]

For over sixty years, Jane resided in the Salt Lake Valley. She wrote, "I have seen Bro. Brigham, Bros. Taylor, Woodruff and Snow rule this great work and pass on to their reward."[8] She participated in ward Relief Society events and contributed to the building funds of the St. George, Manti, and Logan Temples.

---

5   Goldberg, "Autobiography of Jane Manning James."
6   Goldberg, "Autobiography of Jane Manning James."
7   Goldberg, "Autobiography of Jane Manning James."
8   Goldberg, "Autobiography of Jane Manning James."

In the Salt Lake Tabernacle, a seat was reserved for her in the front center of the building during general conferences.

At age eighty, Jane was nearly blind. She confessed that blindness was "a great trial to me. It is the greatest trial I have ever been called upon to bear." She then told of seeing her "husband and all of my children but two laid away in the silent tomb."[9] But through it all she testified:

> The Lord protects me and takes good care of me in my helpless condition, and I want to say right here that my faith in the gospel of Jesus Christ as taught by the Church of Jesus Christ of Latter-day Saints is as strong today, nay, it is, if possible, stronger than it was the day I was first baptized. I pay my tithes and offerings [and] keep the Word of Wisdom. I go to bed early and rise early. I try in my feeble way to set a good example to all.[10]

The *Deseret News* of April 16, 1908, reported her death:

> Jane Manning James, an aged colored woman familiarly known as "Aunt Jane," passed away about noon today at her late residence, 529 Second East Street, after a lingering illness. She was in her ninety-fifth year. . . . Her brother Isaac Manning, two years her junior . . . tenderly cared for [her] during the last 15 years. . . . Few persons were more noted for faith and faithfulness than was Jane Manning James, and though of the humble of earth she numbered friends and acquaintances by the hundreds. Many persons will regret to learn that the kind and generous soul has passed from earth.[11]

**A Bridge to the Past**

Although Jane endured many trials on her journey from Connecticut to Nauvoo, she said, "We went on our way rejoicing, singing hymns, and thanking God for his infinite goodness and mercy to us." How's that for attitude? No wonder Jane was so beloved by the Prophet Joseph and her hundreds of acquaintances. What happens to you isn't as important as your attitude

---

9   Goldberg, "Autobiography of Jane Manning James."
10  Goldberg, "Autobiography of Jane Manning James."
11  *Deseret News*, April 16, 1908, as quoted in Susan Easton Black and Mary Jane Woodger, *Women of Character* (Salt Lake City: Covenant Communications, Inc., 2011), 149.

about what happens. Jane chose to rejoice and thank God on her arduous journey when others facing a similar journey might have chosen to murmur and complain. There is precious little joy in murmuring; whereas, there is an abundance of joy in rejoicing.

(1818–1898)

THE RELIEF SOCIETY, ONE OF the largest organizations of women in the world—nearly six million women in over 170 countries—can be traced to Sarah Granger Kimball. In remembrance of Sarah's contributions to the Relief Society, her home in Nauvoo was restored and opened to the public on March 17, 1982, exactly 140 years after the Female Relief Society of Nauvoo was organized by the Prophet Joseph Smith.[1] Barbara B. Smith, General President of the Relief Society at the time, said at the dedication ceremonies of the Kimball home: "We want the world to know that something big can come of something small. We hope women will understand that within their own homes things can happen that can have great significance in the Church and in the world."[2]

Sarah's father, Oliver Granger, was the first in her family to become a member of The Church of Jesus Christ of Latter-day Saints. Sarah wrote of his conversion:

---

1. The Hiram Kimball home is known today as the "Sarah Granger Kimball Home" although Sarah's name was not on the property deed. See Susan Easton Black, Harvey B. Black, and Brandon Plewe, *Property Transactions in Nauvoo, Hancock County, Illinois and Surrounding Communities (1839–1859),* 7 vols. (Wilmington, DE: World Vital Records, 2006), 4:2188–2191.
2. Barbara B. Smith, "Dedication of Sarah Granger Kimball Home," as cited in *Serving in Nauvoo*, knudsensgmission.blogspot.com.

My father, Oliver Granger, had an interesting experience in connection with the coming forth of the Book of Mormon. He obtained the book a few months after its publication, and while in the city of New York at Prof. Mott's eye infirmary, he had a "heavenly vision." My father was told by a personage who said his name was Moroni that the Book of Mormon, about which his mind was exercised, was a true record of great worth, and Moroni instructed him (my father) to testify of its truth and that he should hereafter be ordained to preach the everlasting Gospel to the children of men.[3]

When Sarah was fifteen years old, her family moved to Kirtland, Ohio, where they became closely associated with the Prophet Joseph Smith. From Kirtland, Sarah and her family moved with the Saints to Missouri and then on to Nauvoo. In Nauvoo, Sarah attracted the attention of Hiram Kimball, a prosperous merchant in town who was not a Latter-day Saint. At the time, Sarah was age twenty-one and Hiram was thirty-four. They were married on September 22, 1840, by Warren Cowdery, a brother of Oliver Cowdery. To their union were born three sons—Hiram, Oliver, and Franklin.

Three days after the birth of her firstborn son, Hiram Kimball Jr., Sarah asked her husband:

"What is the boy worth?"
He replied, "O, I don't know, he is worth a great deal."
Sarah asked, "Is he worth a thousand dollars?"
Hiram replied, "Yes more than that if he lives and does well."
Sarah then declared, "Half of him is mine, is it not?"
"Yes, I suppose so," said Hiram.
"Then I have something to help on the Temple," she replied.
"You have?" said Hiram.
"Yes and I think of turning my share right in as tithing," said Sarah.
"Well, I'll think about that," said Hiram.[4]

When Hiram shared this conversation with Joseph Smith, the Prophet said, "You now have the privilege of paying $500 and retaining possession [of your son], or receiving $500 and giving possession." A financial agreement was reached. Sarah gave one of the largest donations to the building of the

---

3 "Auto-biography of Sarah M. Granger Kimball," *Woman's Exponent*, 12:52.
4 "Auto-biography of Sarah Kimball," 12:52.

Nauvoo Temple. Joseph Smith said to her, "You have consecrated your first born son, for this you are blessed of the Lord."[5]

Sarah was generous in other ways too. The most remembered example occurred in 1842. "A maiden lady (Miss [Margaret] Cook) was seamstress for me, and the subject of combining our efforts for assisting the Temple hands came up in [our] conversation," Sarah wrote. "She desired to be helpful, but had no means to furnish. I told her I would furnish material if she would make some shirts for the workmen." Sarah believed "some of our neighbors might wish to combine means and efforts with ours, and we decided to invite a few to come and consult with us on the subject of forming a Ladies' Society. The neighboring sisters met in my parlor [March 4, 1842] and decided to organize" a society patterned after a benevolent society to look after the poor.[6]

Wanting to ensure that the organization was founded on a firm base, Sarah asked Eliza R. Snow to create a constitution and bylaws for the society. After writing the constitution, Eliza showed her efforts to the Prophet Joseph Smith. He said to Eliza, "Tell the sisters their offering is accepted of the Lord, and he has something better for them than a written Constitution. . . . I will organize the women under the priesthood after the pattern of the priesthood."[7]

On March 17, 1842, twenty women met in the upper room of Joseph Smith's Red Brick Store in Nauvoo. Joseph proceeded to organize the Female Relief Society of Nauvoo. Joseph said of that society, "The Church was never perfectly organized until the women were thus organized."[8] Sarah attended weekly meetings of the society, some meetings held in her own home.

Her goodness and kindness to the less fortunate in Nauvoo led to her husband's baptism on July 20, 1843, by Eli John Smith. Yet his faithfulness has been questioned, for when Sarah fled from persecution and mobs in Nauvoo to the safety of Iowa, Hiram was not by her side. The reason—he was on an extended business trip in New York City. Not waiting for him to return to Nauvoo, Sarah and her two sons, Hiram W. and Oliver, and her widowed mother journeyed to the Salt Lake Valley in 1852. Hiram joined them the next year. "He came to me financially ruined and broken in health," Sarah wrote.[9]

---

5 "Auto-biography of Sarah Kimball," 12:52.
6 "Auto-biography of Sarah Kimball," 12:52.; see "Record of the Relief Society from First Organization to Conference, April 5, 1892, Book II," catalogued as "Relief Society Record, 1880–1892," 29–30, Church History Library.
7 "Auto-biography of Sarah Kimball," 12:52.
8 "Auto-biography of Sarah Kimball," 12:52.
9 "Auto-biography of Sarah Kimball," 12:52.

Sarah taught school in the Salt Lake 14th Ward under trying circumstances. When Hiram recouped his financial standing, she left the classroom. In 1857, she was called to be the Relief Society president of the Salt Lake 15th Ward. She served as president for a decade, long after the tragic death of her husband: On March 1, 1863, Hiram was set apart as a missionary to labor in the Sandwich Islands (Tahiti) by Elders John Taylor and Wilford Woodruff. One day later, on March 2, 1863, he left Salt Lake City to begin his mission with Elder Thomas Atkinson. On April 27, 1863, at San Pedro, California, the two missionaries boarded the *Ada Hancock*, a small steamer employed as a tender to carry passengers from the wharf to the steamship *Senator*, anchored in deep water five miles distant. The steamship boiler exploded, killing forty passengers on board, including the two missionaries. Elders Hiram Kimball and Thomas Atkinson were the first elders of the Church to lose their lives in such an accident.[10]

As for Sarah, life went on but not without change. Her last years were more public than private. If she were "seated in a railway carriage with parties on one hand discussing fashions, and politics to be heard on the other, she would turn to the discussion on politics."[11] In 1882, she was an active participant in the Utah Constitutional Convention. In 1891, she was a leader in the Woman Suffrage Association of Utah. As such, she petitioned the US Congress for help in stopping abuse inflicted upon Utah women by federal deputies. In 1895, she was named an honorary vice president of the National American Woman's Suffrage Association. She was best known for her speeches, or as one biographer wrote, "As a public speaker she was concise and always to the point, never made long speeches, but said what she felt forcibly and always with effect."[12] Sarah died on December 1, 1898, in Salt Lake City at age seventy-nine. Literally thousands mourned her passing.

## A Bridge to the Past
An idea born in a generous heart should not be discarded. In Sarah's case, whether it was donating to the building fund of the Nauvoo Temple or helping

---

10  Andrew Jenson, *Latter-day Saint Biographical Encyclopedia: A Compilation of Biographical Sketches of Prominent Men and Women in the Church of Jesus Christ of Latter-day Saints*, 4 vols. (Salt Lake City: Andrew Jenson History Company, 1914), 2:372; "Auto-biography of Sarah M. Granger Kimball," 12:52.
11  Augusta Joyce Crocheron, *Representative Women of Deseret: A Book of Biographical Sketches* (Salt Lake City: J. C. Graham & Co., 1884), 28.
12  Jenson, *LDS Biographical Encyclopedia*, 2:373–374.

the less fortunate who worked on the temple, Sarah wanted to help and believed her neighbors and others wanted to help too. We can help also.

> I have wept in the night
> At my shortness of sight
> That to others' needs made me blind,
> But I never have yet
> Had a twinge of regret
> For being a little too kind.[13]

---

13  Poem by C. R. Gibson.

SEAGULL BOOK (0250)
1114 NORTH MAIN STREET LOGAN
435 755-0370

* * Where you Never pay full price * *
* * for Anything * *

CASHIER: Brittney          02 Apr 2021
RECEIPT: 2500680302        03:10PM

TITLE                              PRICE

GLORIOUS TRUTHS ABOU  1304343    13.59
                                 -----
1225040        SUB TOTAL:        13.59
7.0000         SALES TAX:         0.95
               TOTAL:            14.54
XXXXX5527      :                 14.54
               CHANGE:            0.00

STEPHANIE LITTLE
YOU SAVED $2.40

Exchanges/Returns accepted within 30
days for unopened unused merchandise.
--- THIS RECEIPT IS REQUIRED ---

Seagull Clothing Return Policy
No cash refunds on credit or debit
cards. Merchandise not washed or worn
may be exchanged or returned within
30 days of original purchase date.
Original tags and receipt are required
on all cash, debit or credit card
returns. Original tags are required on
all exchanges.

----------------------------------------

CASHIER: Brittney         04-02-21 03:10PM
RECEIPT: 2500680302

# Vilate Murray Kimball

(1806–1867)

---

VILATE WROTE OF A VISION the Prophet Joseph Smith had concerning the "twelve apostles of this dispensation, for whose welfare his anxiety had been very great. He saw the twelve going forth, and they appeared to be in a far distant land; after some time they unexpectedly met together, apparently in great tribulation, their clothes all ragged, and their knees and feet sore. They formed into a circle, and all stood with their eyes fixed on the ground. The Saviour appeared and stood in their midst and wept over them, and wanted to show himself to them, but they did not discover him. . . . The impression this vision left on Brother Joseph's mind was of so acute a nature, that he never could refrain from weeping while rehearsing it."[1]

---

Vilate was raised to womanhood in Montgomery County, New York. She met Heber C. Kimball on her father's farm in Victor, New York. "One hot day, during the summer of 1822 . . . Heber became thirsty and stopped at a farmhouse on the south side of the road. Jumping from his wagon he asked for a drink of water." Heber was given water by sixteen-year-old Vilate Murray. Heber's biographer, Stanley B. Kimball, wrote, "As soon as decently possible, Heber arranged to become thirsty again in the same neighborhood and repeated his request. As [Roswell] Murray went to draw the water, Heber

---

1 "Selections from the Autobiography of Vilate Kimball," in Edward W. Tullidge, *The Women of Mormondom* (New York, 1877), 110.

blurted out, 'If you please, I'd rather Milatie [as he understood the daughter's name] would bring it to me.'"[2] This led to a second meeting of Vilate and Heber. On November 7, 1822, they were married. To their union were born ten children, seven reaching maturity.

After their marriage, Vilate and Heber settled in Mendon, New York. They became caught up in the religious revival taking place in Mendon. "About three weeks before we heard of the latter-day work we were baptized into the Baptist Church," wrote Vilate. The message of the Restoration was shared with them at the home of Phineas Young, brother of Brigham Young. "Hearing of these men, curiosity prompted Mr. Kimball to go and see them," penned Vilate. Heber was baptized on April 15, 1832, by Elder Eleazer Miller. "Just two weeks from that time I was baptized by Joseph Young," Vilate wrote.[3]

Soon after their baptisms, the Kimballs moved from New York to Kirtland, Ohio. In Kirtland, they found members of the Church

> in a state of poverty and distress. It appeared almost impossible that the commandment to build the temple could be fulfilled, the revelation requiring it to be erected by a certain period. The enemies were raging, threatening destruction upon the saints; the brethren were under guard night and day to preserve the prophet's life, and the mobs in Missouri were driving our people from Jackson county.[4]

In this time of crisis, Zion's Camp, a quasi-army, was organized to fight the wrongs done to Latter-day Saints who had lived in Jackson County. "Heber being one of the little army," Vilate penned. On May 5, 1834, the march toward Jackson County began. "It was truly a solemn morning on which my husband parted from his wife, children and friends, not knowing that we should ever meet again in the flesh," Vilate wrote.[5] In his absence, she provided for herself and children and assisted in making clothing for men working on the Kirtland Temple. When Zion's Camp was disbanded and Heber returned to Kirtland, he joined those who "labored night and day to build the house of the Lord."[6]

---

2   Stanley B. Kimball, *Heber C. Kimball: Mormon Patriarch and Pioneer* (Urbana, IL: University of Illinois Press, 1981), 10–11.
3   Tullidge, *Women of Mormondom*, 104–6.
4   Tullidge, *Women of Mormondom*, 109.
5   Tullidge, *Women of Mormondom*, 109.
6   Tullidge, *Women of Mormondom*, 109.

In February 1835, Heber was called to the Quorum of the Twelve Apostles. In 1837, he was called to serve a mission in England. Of her husband's receiving that call, Vilate wrote, "One day while Heber was seated in the front stand in the Kirtland Temple, the prophet Joseph opened the door and came and whispered in his ear, 'Brother Heber, the spirit of the Lord has whispered to me, let my servant Heber go to England and proclaim the gospel, and open the door of salvation.'"7

In a January 1838 letter to Heber, Vilate wrote,

> I want your advice and assistance more than I ever did before in my life, yet the painful thought occurs to my mind that thousands of miles separate us and the Great Atlantic rolling between.... But O: the scenes that have transpired in Kirtland.... Some have suggested the [idea] to me whether or not I would go [to Missouri] before you return, providing there should be a door open for me.... Me thinks you would say, be calm, my dear Vilate, and trust in the Lord. That is what I have resolved to do.... I have no one to depend upon but the Lord, but I have ever found it good to trust in him.3

Vilate waited until Heber returned from England to move to Far West, Missouri. In the spring of 1838, they lived in a cowshed measuring eight feet by eleven feet in Far West. They remained in the Latter-day Saint city until government-sanctioned persecution forced them to flee from the state. It took another move and swamp fever before Heber received a second call to serve a mission in England. As he and Brigham Young were beginning their journey, Heber felt as though his "very inmost parts would melt" at the thought of leaving his family who were sick. Asking the teamster to pull up on the reigns, he said to Brigham, "This is pretty tough, isn't it; let's rise up and give them a cheer." They did so, swinging their hats three times over their heads and shouting, "Hurrah, hurrah for Israel!" Vilate, hearing their shouts, called out, "Good bye, God bless you."9

A week later, Vilate sent a letter to Heber:

> As to my feelings I don't know but I am perfectly reconciled to your going, but I must say I have got a trial of my faith as I never had before. The day you left home was as sick a one as

---

7   Tullidge, *Women of Mormondom*, 111.
8   Letter of Vilate Kimball to Heber C. Kimball, January 19, 1838.
9   Orson F. Whitney, *Life of Heber C. Kimball* (Salt Lake City: Kimball Family, 1888), 276.

I ever experienced. The pain in my back and head was almost intolerable. No doubt the pain in my head was worse on the account of my much weeping.[10]

She then wrote, "All that I can ask of you is to pray that I may have patience to endure to the end whether it be long or short."[11]

As Vilate waited for Heber to return, she penned,

> No being round the spacious earth
> Beneath the vaulted arch of heaven,
> Divides my love, or draws it thence,
> From him to whom my heart is given.
>
> . . .
>
> The gift was on the altar laid;
> The plighted vow on earth was given;
> The seal eternal has been made,
> And by his side I'll reign in heaven.[12]

When Heber completed his second mission to England, he returned to Nauvoo and built a brick home for his family. It was not long, however, before he and his family were forced to abandon their home and flee from religious persecution. They crossed the mighty Mississippi River to reach the Territory of Iowa and then trekked on to Winter Quarters. From there, Heber journeyed with the vanguard company to the Salt Lake Valley in 1847. He returned to Iowa to get Vilate and their children. Together they entered the valley in 1848. Eliza R. Snow penned a poem on the trail west for Vilate to bolster her spirits:

> Thou much belov'd in Zion,
> Remember, life is made
> A double-sided picture,
> Contrasting light and shade.
>
> Our Father means to prove us:
> And here we're fully tried,
> He will reverse the drawing,
> And show the better side.

---

10  Vilate Kimball to Heber C. Kimball, September 21, 1839, in Richard E. Turley Jr. and Brittany A. Chapman, *Women of Faith in the Latter Days, Volume One, 1775–1820* (Salt Lake City: Deseret Book, 2011), 139.

11  Turley and Chapman, *Women of Faith in the Latter Days,* 140.

12  Whitney, *Life of Heber C. Kimball,* 346.

> Whatever seems forbidding,
> And tending to annoy,
> Will, like dull shadows, vanish,
> Or turn to crowns of joy.[13]

For the next twenty years, Vilate lived in Salt Lake City. She struggled with health issues for many years. She died on October 22, 1867, at age sixty-one. Her funeral was held in her home with President Brigham Young giving the sermon. He said that "if anyone had ever found fault with Sister Kimball, he had never heard of it." As her body was being taken to the cemetery, Heber said, "I shall not be long after her."[14] Heber died within the year.

**A Bridge to the Past**
Vilate loved her husband. It was a trial of her faith when Heber was called to serve missions and was gone from her for great lengths of time. Putting personal discomforts aside, she supported him in his callings. No wonder Heber loved her. Be grateful if you have a husband, father, brother, son, or other man in your life who loves the Lord and is willing to accept a calling to serve.

---

13  Eliza R. Snow, "To Miss V. Kimball," *Ensign*, July 1977.
14  "Vilate Murray Kimball," in *Pioneer Women of Faith and Fortitude*, 4 vols. (Salt Lake City: International Society Daughters of Utah Pioneers, 1998), 2:1668–1669.

(1812–1884)

"Many were the curious glances that I cast at this strange man [Joseph Smith] who dared to call himself a prophet," Lydia wrote. "I saw a tall, well-built form, with the carriage of an Apollo; brown hair, handsome blue eyes, which seemed to dive down to the innermost thoughts with their sharp, penetrating gaze; a striking countenance, and with manners at once majestic yet gentle, dignified yet exceedingly pleasant."[1]

Lydia grew to womanhood in the states of Massachusetts and New York. In 1828, at age sixteen, she married Calvin Bailey, a young man she had known in school. Two children were born to their union before Calvin deserted Lydia. Distraught over her circumstance, Lydia returned home to her parents who "wept at her sorrow, but gladly took her to their arms once more."[2] By the time Lydia was age twenty-one, both of her children had died.

In sorrow and wanting to start life anew, Lydia moved to Mount Pleasant, Canada, and resided with the Moses Nickerson family. In mid-October 1835, the Prophet Joseph Smith and his counselor Sidney Rigdon came to Mount

---

1   Lydia Knight and Susa Young Gates, *Lydia Knight's History* (Salt Lake City: Juvenile Instructor's Office, 1883), 14, as quoted in Mark L. McConkie, *Remembering Joseph: Personal Recollections of Those Who Knew the Prophet Joseph Smith* (Salt Lake City: Deseret Book, 2003), 31.
2   McConkie, 145.

Pleasant with news of the Restoration. Lydia heard the Prophet speak and said, "His face became white and a shining glow seemed to beam from every feature."[3] She was baptized a few days later. Upon coming out of the baptismal waters, Lydia cried aloud, "Glory to God in the highest! Thanks be to His holy name that I have lived to see this day and be a partaker of this great blessing."[4]

The seventh day of the Prophet Joseph's stay in Mount Pleasant, he was seated near a fireplace in the Nickerson home when Moses Nickerson said, "I would be so glad if some one who has been baptized could receive the gift of tongues as the ancient Saints did and speak to us." Joseph Smith replied, "If one of you will rise up and open your mouth it shall be filled, and you shall speak in tongues." Lydia arose and "her mouth was filled with the praises of God and His glory."[5]

A few days later, the Prophet Joseph said to her,

> I have been pondering on Sister Lydia's lonely condition, and wondering why it is that she has passed through so much sorrow and affliction and is thus separated from all her relatives. I now understand it. The Lord has suffered it even as He allowed Joseph of old to be afflicted, who was sold by his brethren as a slave into a far country, and through that became a savior to his father's house and country. Even so shall it be with her, the hand of the Lord will overrule it for good to her and her father's family.[6]

Joseph then proceeded to place his hands on the head of Lydia and give her a blessing. In the blessing he pronounced,

> Sister Lydia, great are your blessings. The Lord, your Savior, loves you, and will overrule all your past sorrows and afflictions for good unto you. Let your heart be comforted . . . You shall yet be a savior to your father's house. Therefore be comforted, and let your heart rejoice, for the Lord has a great work for you to do. Be faithful and endure unto the end and all will be well.[7]

In 1835, Lydia moved from Canada to Kirtland, Ohio, to be with the Saints. In Kirtland, she met and fell in love with widower Newel Knight. On

---

3   McConkie, 146.
4   McConkie, 146.
5   Hyrum L. Andrus and Helen Mae Andrus, *They Knew the Prophet* (Salt Lake City: Bookcraft, 1974), 456.
6   McConkie, 146.
7   McConkie, 146–47.

November 23, 1835, Lydia and Newel were married by the Prophet Joseph Smith, the first marriage performed by him. A few months later, Lydia was given a patriarchal blessing by Joseph Smith Sr. In the blessing, Lydia was told,

> Thou shalt be a mother of many children, and thou shalt teach them righteousness and have power to keep them from the power of the destroyer; and thy heart shall not be pained because of the loss of thy children; for the Lord shall watch over them and keep them and they shall be raised up for glory. . . . The Lord loves thee and has given thee a kind and loving companion for thy comfort and your souls shall be knit together.[8]

Lydia and Newel moved with the Saints from Kirtland to Missouri to escape religious persecution. Instead of finding peace in Missouri, they faced an extermination order against the Latter-day Saints. Once again, the Knights moved on, eventually settling in Nauvoo, Illinois. Lydia was very sick in Nauvoo and suffered greatly. She lamented not being able to attend the funeral of Joseph and Hyrum Smith in June 1844. Later that summer, when Lydia was healthier, she and Newel went to Carthage Jail. Lydia wanted to see for herself the ball holes in the walls and the bloodstains on the floor.

On April 17, 1846, Lydia and her family left Nauvoo and joined other Latter-day Saints journeying across Iowa. In the winter of 1847, in a Latter-day Saint encampment, Newel died. As his remains were being carried to a burial site, Lydia was heard to whisper, "God rules!" The loss of Newel caused Lydia great sorrow. She cried, "Oh Newel, why hast thou left me!" In answer to her cry, Lydia claimed Newel appeared to her and said, "Be calm, let not sorrow overcome you. It was necessary that I should go. I was needed behind the vail [sic] to represent the true condition of this camp and people. . . . Dry up your tears. Be patient, I will go before you and protect you in your journeyings."[9] With seven children and pregnant with her eighth child (her oldest was age twelve and her youngest eighteen months old), Lydia prepared to continue her journey to the Salt Lake Valley. She wrote,

> I felt I must make every possible effort to go to the valley the home of the Saints but what should I do or where to begin I did not know. I told the Lord all my trouble and asked him

---

8   H. Michal Marquardt, *Early Patriarchal Blessing of The Church of Jesus Christ of Latter-day Saints* (Salt Lake City: The Smith-Pettit Foundation, 2007), 126.
9   McConkie, 150.

to give me wisdom and open up the way for I felt the time had come and I must go. . . . I laid in provisions all I could and the necessary things and called my fit out [preparations] complete although many would not have thought it a fit out at all for such a family and journey but I had done the best I could and trusted in God.[10]

Lydia and her children crossed the plains and arrived in the Salt Lake Valley on October 3, 1850, about four years after departing from Nauvoo.

In 1850, Lydia became the plural wife of John Dalton. The marriage ended in divorce. In 1864, she married James McClellan. After his death in 1880, Lydia moved to St. George. She spent much of her time in the St. George Temple performing proxy ordinance work for her kindred dead. Lydia died on April 8, 1884, in St. George.

**A Bridge to the Past**
Lydia was a savior in her father's house just as Joseph Smith prophesied. When her husband, Newel, died, she brought her children to the westward Zion and taught them the gospel. Lydia spent the last years of her life participating in proxy ordinances for her ancestors and, in her own way, gathered her family on the covenant path. Gather your families together on both sides of the veil. Rejoice in the opportunity to be a savior on Mount Zion to your kindred dead.

---

10   McConkie, 151.

# Mary Alice Cannon Lambert

(1828–1920)

---

"I first saw Joseph Smith in the spring of 1843," Mary wrote. "When the boat in which we came up the Mississippi River reached the landing at Nauvoo, several of the leading brethren were there to meet the company of saints that had come on it. Among those brethren was the Prophet Joseph Smith. I knew him the instant my eyes rested upon him, and at that moment I received my testimony that he was a Prophet of God, for I never had such a feeling for mortal man as thrilled my being when my eyes first rested upon Joseph Smith. He was not pointed out to me. I knew him from all the other men, and, child that I was (I was only fourteen), I knew that I saw a Prophet of God."[1]

---

Mary spent most of her childhood in Liverpool, England, except for five years when she lived with her maternal grandmother in the quaint town of Peel on the Isle of Man. At age eleven, she was introduced to Elder John Taylor, who had come from America to preach the gospel of Jesus Christ on English shores. Her father, George Cannon, a brother of Elder Taylor's wife, Leonora, embraced the gospel message and was baptized a member of The Church of Jesus Christ of Latter-day Saints. Mary "earnestly prayed to the Lord for a testimony as to its truth." She received "a strong assurance from the Lord of its truth." But it was not until June 1840, after Elder Parley P. Pratt and Elder

---

1 "Joseph Smith, the Prophet," *Young Woman's Journal* 16, no. 12 (December 1905), 554.

John Taylor had finished eating breakfast at their home, that Elder Pratt asked, "Elder Taylor, have you preached the Gospel to these children? Some of them want to be baptized now. Don't you?" Elder Pratt asked, looking at Mary. "Yes, sir," she promptly replied. Mary and her siblings were baptized that June.[2]

Desiring to gather with Latter-day Saints in Nauvoo, Illinois, the Cannon family boarded a sailing vessel in Liverpool bound for America in September 1842. During their eight-week voyage, Mary's mother died and was buried at sea. After the vessel docked at New Orleans, the Cannon family took passage aboard a steamboat going up the Mississippi. When the steamer grounded on a sandbar and the river froze, the captain announced the voyage was over. The Cannon family spent the winter of 1842 to 1843 in St. Louis. They didn't reach Nauvoo until April 1843, seven months after their departure from England.

Unfortunately, the Cannons arrived in Nauvoo at a time when disaffection was rife and the allegiance of many to the Prophet Joseph was uncertain. Apostates, secret and outspoken, conspired with enemies to overthrow the work of the Lord. In these trying times, the Cannons remained faithful. Mary's father helped care for the bodies of the martyrs, Joseph and Hyrum Smith, when they were returned to Nauvoo. With the assistance of Ariah Brower, George Cannon made plaster casts of the prophet's and patriarch's faces.

In August 1844, tragedy struck the Cannon family when Father George Cannon died. After this, and without a mother to care for the children, George Q. Cannon and his sister Ann were taken into the home of John and Leonora Taylor. Mary, though two weeks shy of being sixteen years old, married Charles Lambert, age twenty-six. The newlyweds took into their home Mary's younger siblings—Angus, David, and Leonora Cannon.

Charles supported his bride and her siblings as a mechanic and provided them with a comfortable home and a farm. He and his family were in Nauvoo when the city was attacked in September 1846. Charles played a key role in defending the city, operating a cannon created from an old steamboat shaft. During the battle, an "old gentleman . . . whose anxiety to see how the battle waged led him to ascend to the top of the roof of the [Charles] Lambert house to get a good view, was so alarmed by a cannon ball passing close by his head that he rolled from the roof to the ground."[3]

---

2   "Life Sketch of Mary Alice Cannon Lambert by her Children," FamilySearch.
3   "Life Sketch of Mary Lambert."

When a flag of truce was raised and a treaty signed, the Lamberts quickly loaded a few possessions into a wagon and drove to the river. A mob member demanded that Mary give up any firearms stowed in the wagon. She told him that "the weapons had already been surrendered, and that she did not have the keys to unlock the boxes in the wagon." The mob member used a hammer to break open the boxes and ransack their possessions, taking a sword and a bowie knife. He accused Mary of lying and threatened "to cut her head off."[4]

In spite of his threats, the Lamberts were able to ferry across the river to reach safety in Iowa. Preferring to walk rather than ride in the wagon, Mary crossed the hilly countryside on foot. Unfortunately, when the family approached Soap Creek, Mary stumbled and fell in front of the wagon. Before the ox team could be halted, two wagon wheels passed over the small of her back. Mary was given a priesthood blessing. Her life was miraculously spared. However, she suffered the rest of her days from the effects of the accident.

The Lambert family reached Winter Quarters in late November 1846. By spring 1847, they had moved to St. Joseph, Missouri, where opportunities for work were plentiful. By February 1849, the family had accumulated means to continue their journey to the Salt Lake Valley. They arrived in the valley in the fall of 1849.

The Lamberts experienced their full share of hardship and privation in the valley, but "no family ever bore privation with less complaining." Mary became a "dress-maker and tailoress for the family even to the carding and spinning of the wool."[5]

In addition to giving birth to fourteen children, Mary served as secretary and then president of the Relief Society of the Salt Lake Seventh Ward. She honorably fulfilled a mission to England with her husband, Charles, in 1882 to 1883. Upon their return to Salt Lake City, she became the caretaker of Charles, who suffered from inflammatory rheumatism and partial loss of eyesight. Charles died in May 1892.

In 1906, Mary spent several months visiting countries in Europe to obtain genealogical data about her kindred dead. Upon her return to the States, she served as proxy for hundreds of her relatives and friends in the Salt Lake Temple. A biographer wrote of Mary, "If happiness is at all dependent on the love of kindred, she ought to be supremely happy; for she has a numerous posterity, who almost idolize her."[6] Mary died on September 7, 1920, in Salt Lake City at age ninety-two.

---

4   "Life Sketch of Mary Lambert."
5   "Life Sketch of Mary Lambert."
6   "Life Sketch of Mary Lambert."

## A Bridge to the Past

Life has many twists and turns, whether sickness or health, prosperity or privation. Mary experienced it all and in so doing gained the wisdom to know what was really important to her. Paramount in her life was family and the gospel. She did not let less important things take precedence. Take charge of your life by taking charge of your time. There is no better place to start than ordering your priorities. Given the demands of the "to dos" of the day and the pervasiveness of technology, you inevitably face multiple professional and personal demands. Multitasking is a way of life. By multitasking, you can stay on top of day-to-day matters but unknowingly miss opportunities to brighten your life. Guard your free time for what matters most. It was famed Latter-day Saint artist Minerva Teichert who said, "I do not make calls or play bridge. That is the 'spare time' in which I glory."[7]

---

[7] Minerva Teichert to Professor B. F. Larsen, undated. Museum of Art at Brigham Young University Files, in Susan Easton Black and Mary Jane Woodger, *Women of Character: Profiles of 100 Prominent LDS Women* (American Fork, UT: Covenant Communications, Inc., 2011), 326.

## Sarah Studevant Leavitt

(1798–1878)

---

IN HER AUTOBIOGRAPHY, SARAH WROTE,

> We knew they had Joseph in prison [Carthage Jail] and threatened to take his life, but that was nothing new or strange, for his enemies always did that, but we did not believe they could have power to murder him. . . . The law could have no power over him, but powder and balls could, so they shot him in Carthage jail. When the news came the whole city of Nauvoo was thunderstruck; such mourning and lamentation was seldom ever heard on the earth. There was many, myself among them, that would gladly have died if his life could have been spared by doing so. I never had spoken to the man in my life, but I had seen him and heard him preach and know that he was [a] Prophet of God, sent here by the Almighty to set up his kingdom, no more to be thrown down.[1]

---

"My parents were very strict with their children, being descendants of the old Pilgrims," Sarah wrote. "They taught [us] every principle of truth and honor as they understood it themselves. . . . My father had many books that treated

---

1 Juanita Leavitt Pulsipher Brooks, ed. "Sarah Studevant Leavitt Autobiographical Sketch, April 19, 1875," 1919, FamilySearch.

on the principle of Man's salvation and many stories that were very interesting, and I took great pleasure in reading them. He was Dean of the Presbyterian Church."[2]

From her childhood through her youth, Sarah "desired very much to be saved from that awful hell I heard so much about."[3] It was not until she married Jeremiah Leavitt on March 6, 1817, that she began to reconsider her religious thinking. Yet when the newlyweds moved to Canada, she grew anxious when seeing men drink and play cards on Sunday. After the birth of her second daughter, Sarah had

> a vision of the damned spirits in hell, so that I was filled with horror more than I was able to bear, but I cried to the Lord day and night until I got my answer of peace and a promise that I should be saved in the Kingdom of God. . . . That promise has been with me through all the changing scenes of life ever since.[4]

Sarah joined the Baptist church in Canada and subscribed to their newspaper. One day, she read in the paper of "a prophet that pretended he talked to God."[5] She was curious:

> I read the Book of Mormon, The Doctrine and Covenants, and all the writings I could get from the Latter-Day Saints. It was the book of Doctrine and Covenants that confirmed my faith in the work. I knew that no man, nor set of men, that could make such a book or would dare try from any wisdom that man possessed. I knew it was the word of God and a revelation from Heaven and received it as such.[6]

In 1835, Sarah and her family moved to Kirtland, Ohio, to learn more about Joseph Smith and the Church. "I had no chance to be baptized and join the church until I got there," Sarah wrote.

> We stayed at Kirtland about a week and had the privilege of hearing Joseph preach in that thing the Baptist said they called a meeting house, which proved to be a very good house.

---

2 Brooks, "Sarah Leavitt Autobiographical Sketch."
3 Brooks, "Sarah Leavitt Autobiographical Sketch."
4 Brooks, "Sarah Leavitt Autobiographical Sketch."
5 Brooks, "Sarah Leavitt Autobiographical Sketch."
6 Brooks, "Sarah Leavitt Autobiographical Sketch."

We went into the upper rooms, saw the Egyptian mummies, the writing that was said to be written in Abraham's day, Jacob's ladder being pictured on it and lots more wonders.[7]

Wanting to be close to the Prophet Joseph, Sarah and Jeremiah settled in Mayfield, about ten miles from Kirtland, before moving on to Twelve Mile Grove in Illinois. At each locale, Jeremiah supported his family as a farmer. The Leavitts eventually joined the Saints in the Nauvoo vicinity. Sarah wrote,

> My husband bought a place three miles from the city and [built] a house. There was some land plowed which he sowed to wheat. He had to work very hard for a living provisions were scarce and high and the most of the saints poor. . . . We all had to work hard for a living, but with the blessing of God and our exertions we soon began to get a good living. We swapped farms with a man, got one by the big mound, seven miles from the city, a fine pleasant place.[8]

In June 1844, Sarah mourned the deaths of Joseph Smith and his brother Hyrum. She supported Brigham Young and the Twelve as having the keys to lead the Church. She wrote, "He was the man clothed with all the power and authority of Joseph." Due to her religious stance, she faced opposition and persecution. "But there was no fear in my heart, for I knew we were in the hands of God, and He would do all things right," she wrote.[9]

Sarah and her family abandoned their farm in Illinois to seek safety in Iowa. When they reached the Latter-day Saint encampment at Mt. Pisgah, their provisions were low. Jeremiah turned back to Bonaparte, Iowa, to gather supplies. This was the last time Sarah and her children saw him. On his journey, Jeremiah contracted chills and died.

Becoming a widow with children to care for and having no visible means of support was almost more than Sarah could bear. Yet she wrote, "I have never complained or looked back, for I was sure that there was better days coming. I knew that Mormonism was true and better days would surely come."[10]

Sarah moved from Mt. Pisgah to Trader's Point near the Missouri River. She took in washing to support herself and her children. By 1850, she and her family had crossed the plains to reach the Salt Lake Valley. During the

---

7   Brooks, "Sarah Leavitt Autobiographical Sketch."
8   Brooks, "Sarah Leavitt Autobiographical Sketch."
9   Brooks, "Sarah Leavitt Autobiographical Sketch."
10  Brooks, "Sarah Leavitt Autobiographical Sketch."

remainder of her life, Sarah stayed very close to her children. She moved with them to southern Utah in response to a prophetic call. Sarah died in Gunlock, Utah, at age eighty.

**A Bridge to the Past**
Sarah moved forward to new vistas following her husband's death. She did not languish in Iowa, lost in self-pity and sorrow. Although she knew little to nothing about driving a team of oxen or crossing the plains, she turned her face to the West and, in some sense, began life anew. There is more than one note to play on a keyboard and more than one club in a golf bag, and there is more than one way to solve a problem. There is a new world to explore. For those willing to start anew, opportunities await.

# Mary Elizabeth Rollins Lightner

(1818–1913)

---

When news reached Far West that the "militia [and hundreds of men] were marching to destroy our city and its inhabitants. . . . They sent in a flag of truce, demanding an interview with John Cleminsen and wife, and Adam Lightner and wife [John Clemensen's wife was my husband's sister]. We went a short distance to meet them," wrote Mary. "I asked [General Clarke] if he would let all the Mormon women and children go out? He said, 'No.' 'Will you let my mother's family go out?' He said, 'The Governor's orders were that no one but our two families should go but all were to be destroyed.' [I said,] 'Then, if that is the case, I refuse to go; for where they die, I will die, for I am a full-blooded Mormon, and I am not ashamed to own it.' 'Oh,' said he, 'you are infatuated, your Prophet will be killed with the rest.' Said I, 'If you kill him today, God will raise up another tomorrow.' [He answered,] 'But think of your husband and child.' I then said that [my husband] could go and take the child with him, if he wanted to, but I would suffer with the rest. Just then a man kneeling down by some brush, jumped up and stepping between the Governor and myself, said, 'Hold on, General,' then turned to me and said, 'Sister Lightner, God Almighty bless you, I thank my God for a soul that is ready to die for her religion.'"[1]

---

1  Heber C. Kimball quote in "Autobiography of Mary E. R. Lightner," 3, Church History Library.

When Mary was two years old, her father died in a shipwreck on Lake Ontario. Following his death, she and her mother and siblings moved into the home of her uncle Algernon Sidney Gilbert in Ohio. In 1828, the extended family moved to Kirtland. It was in Kirtland that Mary first heard of the Book of Mormon. In October 1830, news of the book was confirmed by Oliver Cowdery.

Upon learning that Isaac Morley, another resident of Kirtland, had a copy of the Book of Mormon, Mary went to his house to see the book. "I felt such a great desire to read it, that I could not refrain from asking [Brother Morley] to let me take it home and read it. . . . He had hardly had time to read a chapter in it himself, and but few of the brethren had even seen it, but I pled so earnestly for it." Upon seeing her enthusiasm, Morley said, "Child if you will bring this book home before breakfast tomorrow morning, you may take it." Mary said, "If any person in this world was ever perfectly happy . . . I was." She ran home. Upon entering the house, she said, "Oh, Uncle, I have got the 'Golden Bible.'"[2] That night, she and her family stayed up late to read the book.

"As soon as it was light enough to see, I was up and learned the first verse in the book," she wrote. Mary then took the book back to Brother Morley. "I guess you did not read much in it," he said. "I showed him how far we had read. He was surprised and said, 'I don't believe you can tell me one word of it.' I then repeated the first verse, also the outlines of the history of Nephi. He gazed at me in surprise, and said, 'Child, take this book home and finish it, I can wait.'"[3]

Just before Mary finished the last chapter, the Prophet Joseph Smith arrived in Kirtland. Upon seeing that copy of the Book of Mormon in Uncle Gilbert's home, he asked about Mary. "He came and put his hands on my head," she recalled, "and gave me a great blessing, the first I ever received, and made me a present of the book, and said he would give Brother Morley another."[4]

With such love of the scriptures, is it any wonder that Mary would be willing to risk her life to save another scripture—the Book of Commandments?

In fall 1831, Mary and her family moved to Independence, Missouri, where her Uncle Gilbert opened a dry goods and grocery store. Their circumstances were prosperous for a time, before tensions between Latter-day Saints and the old settlers erupted. "One night, a great many got together and stoned our house, part of which was hewed logs, the front was brick. After breaking

---

2 "Autobiography of Mary Lightner," 1.
3 "Autobiography of Mary Lightner."
4 "Autobiography of Mary Lightner," 2.

all the windows, they commenced to tear off the roof of the brick part amidst awful oaths and howls that were terrible to hear," Mary wrote. More extreme difficulties followed. "I saw Bishop Partridge tarred and feathered, and also Brother Charles Allen."[5]

But for Mary, it was on the night that the "mob renewed their efforts again by tearing down the printing office" that she risked her life to save the word of God. Recalling the circumstances, she penned, "My sister Caroline and myself were in a corner of a fence watching them." It was when the sisters saw the mob bring out a pile of large sheets of paper and heard them say, "Here are the Mormon Commandments" that Mary knew what she had to do. She was "determined to have some of" the papers even though it put her life in grave danger. Her sister Caroline agreed to help her, but said, "They will kill us." The sisters waited until the mob turned to pry "out the gable end of the [printing] house." They then "got our arms full, and were turning away, when some of the mob saw us and called on us to stop," Mary recalled. "But we ran as fast as we could . . . into a large cornfield, laid the papers on the ground, and hid them with our persons."[6]

The corn was about five or six feet tall and "very thick." Mobs "hunted around considerable and came very near us but did not find us," Mary penned. After the sisters were satisfied that the men were gone, they came out of the cornfield and ran to safety. The pages they saved were later "bound in small books." Of the book given her, Mary wrote, "I prized [it] very highly."[7]

On August 11, 1836, Mary was wed to Adam Lightner Jr. in Liberty, Missouri. To their union were born ten children, six living to adulthood. Soon after their marriage, Mary and Adam moved to Far West. In that predominately Latter-day Saint community, Adam built a store and worked as a carpenter, merchant, and farmer. Due to the extermination order issued by Governor Lilburn W. Boggs, they were forced to leave their property.

Instead of joining the Saints on their trek to Quincy, Illinois, Mary and her husband moved to Louisville, Kentucky, and then Montrose, Iowa Territory, before joining the Saints in Nauvoo, Illinois. Their series of moves continued but not to the West. They lived in Marine Township, Minnesota, in 1860 and then in Hannibal, Missouri. In each locale, Adam struggled to support his family and refused to enter baptismal waters. Yet he was supportive of Mary. In 1863, when Mary wanted to unite with the Saints in the Rocky Mountains,

---

5   "Autobiography of Mary Lightner," 4.
6   "Autobiography of Mary Lightner," 4.
7   "Autobiography of Mary Lightner," 4.

Adam agreed to venture west with her. The Lightners arrived in the Salt Lake Valley on September 4, 1863. Mary wrote, "We were truly thankful to find a home and friends, after an arduous journey."[8]

Mary and Adam settled in Minersville, Utah. Adam died at age seventy-five in Minersville of tuberculous and congestion. Mary lived until December 1913. To support herself, she taught school and sewed men's suits. Mary shared her testimony often with loved ones and strangers. She wanted it known that she was a friend of Joseph Smith, a prophet of God.

**A Bridge to the Past**
In her youth, Mary risked her life to save the pages of the Book of Commandments. Although she did many wonderful things after, it was her youthful courage that is remembered. What in your youth did you risk to keep on the covenant path? Blessings await those who let the Lord prevail in their lives.

---

8 "Autobiography of Mary Lightner," 4.

(1827–1888)

---

As a teenager, Mary worked in the Mansion House for Joseph Smith and his wife, Emma. She helped care for their children and did light housework. In that process, Mary became well acquainted with the Prophet Joseph and learned to love his family. She bore a strong testimony that Joseph Smith was a prophet of God from her days in Nauvoo to her final days in Lehi, Utah. The testimony she gained while associating with the Prophet Joseph never dimmed.[1]

---

Mary Elizabeth Lott was the third of eleven children born to Cornelius and Permelia Lott.[2] In her childhood, an accident left her impaired and in pain each day. The back pain she suffered made it hard to do even menial chores. Yet she never complained.[3]

On December 1, 1837, Mary and her family were baptized members of The Church of Jesus Christ of Latter-day Saints. Mary expressed being "thrilled with the gospel message."[4] She and her family gathered with the Saints in Kirtland, Ohio. When religious persecution reared in Ohio, they moved on to Missouri and settled near Hawn's Mill. After the massacre at the mill, Mary and her family fled from the state of Missouri to the Mississippi River.

1 "Personal History of Mary Elizabeth Lott," FamilySearch.
2 "Personal History of Mary Lott."
3 "Personal History of Mary Lott."
4 "Personal History of Mary Lott."

Within a few months, they had moved to Nauvoo.[5] It was in Nauvoo that the Lott family became close friends with the Prophet Joseph Smith. Mary worked in the Smith home, helping care for his children and doing light housework. It was in this employ that she met Abraham Losee, a young convert from Canada working as a farmhand at the Joseph Smith farm. Abraham stood five feet eight inches, weighed 175 pounds, and had grey eyes and black hair. He spoke often of the Prophet Joseph and of working on the farm side by side with him. When his father died, Abraham brought his mother and siblings into his home to care for them. To Mary, he seemed nearly perfect.

But her thoughts soon turned elsewhere. The Prophet Joseph and his brother Hyrum had been killed in Carthage Jail. She lamented their deaths and could not be consoled until August 8, 1844, when Brigham Young stood transfigured in the image of Joseph Smith before a large assembly of Latter-day Saints and proclaimed that the Quorum of the Twelve held the keys for leading the Church.[6] Mary's sister Alzina Lott was sitting next to her mother at the August meeting and said, "Mama, I thought the Prophet was dead."[7]

As persecution intensified in Nauvoo, Mary and her family fled from the city across the Mississippi River to the Territory of Iowa and then on to Winter Quarters.[8] Perhaps by more than coincidence, on June 7, 1848, Mary and Abraham Losee departed from Winter Quarters with the Heber C. Kimball Company to journey over 1,100 miles to reach the Salt Lake Valley.[9] Two months after Mary and Abraham arrived in the Salt Lake Valley, they were wed on November 12, 1848, in Salt Lake City. They were sealed for time and all eternity on July 3, 1853, in the Endowment House on Temple Square. To their union were born eight children, each living to adulthood.

In 1848, Abraham supported his young bride by working at the Church farm in Salt Lake City. Two years later, Brigham Young called Abraham and his family to settle in the Utah Valley. The first winter in the valley, the Losees lived in a covered wagon. By spring, Abraham had built a house for his family in Lehi. He supported the family by laboring as a farmer and a cooper. Civically, he served as an alderman in the community.

---

5 "Personal History of Mary Lott."
6 "Personal History of Mary Lott."
7 "Personal History of Mary Lott."
8 Clara Goates Beus, "Mary Elizabeth Lott (Losee) Chronological Timeline," FamilySearch.
9 "Mary Elizabeth Losee," Mormon Pioneer Overland Travel Database.

As for Mary, her life was crowded with responsibilities for children and home industry. She spent one full day each week making candles. It was reported that she kept a clean house, cooked delicious food, sewed, made soap, and did other chores for her family, nursing them when ill. Few things could interrupt her routine. But when David Hyrum Smith, the son of Joseph and Emma Smith, made a surprise visit, the routine didn't matter. Mary hadn't seen David since he was a baby. According to family tradition, David told Mary and Abraham that he believed The Church of Jesus Christ of Latter-day Saints to be the true church and that he intended to be baptized. Later, Mary learned that he was hospitalized in an asylum for the insane in Illinois.

In 1878, at age sixty-four, Abraham, in the presidency of the 20th Quorum of the Seventies, accepted a mission call to Canada. He was set apart for the assignment by Elder Charles C. Rich.[10] He left his family believing that his Father in Heaven would watch over Mary and the children in his absence.

Abraham died of a kidney disorder on October 25, 1887, at age seventy-three. His biographer wrote, "He was loved and respected by all who knew him. His life was one of service to his family and his fellowmen."[11] Mary lived seven months after Abraham's death, dying at age sixty-nine on May 18, 1888, in Lehi.[12]

**A Bridge to the Past**
Mary worked in the household of Joseph and Emma Smith and was well acquainted with them and their children. Of the women in Nauvoo who shared their testimonies of the Prophet, Mary may have known him better than most. She would have seen Joseph relaxing, playing with his children, eating dinner, etc. Her testimony of him and his prophetic calling never wavered. Few of us can have experiences with prophets like Mary. Yet we can strengthen our testimony of living prophets and the restored gospel of Jesus Christ by study and faith. Study and faith work.

---

10   "Abraham Losee," Missionary Database.
11   Glade Powell, "Abraham Losee, Personal History," FamilySearch.
12   "Mary Elizabeth Lott Losee," Find A Grave.

# Permelia Darrow Lott

(1805–1882)

---

PERMELIA WAS THE "LANDLADY" OF the Joseph Smith farmhouse in Nauvoo, Illinois. One day, the Prophet Joseph Smith came rushing into the farmhouse and said to her, "They are after me," meaning a mob was hunting him. According to family tradition, Permelia, always ready to act no matter the urgency, took a feather tick off a bed, opened the straw tick in the center and pushed the straw to either side, making an opening for Joseph to crawl in. She then made the bed. When a mob searched the farmhouse, they never found the Prophet.[1]

---

Permelia was born in Susquehanna County, Pennsylvania, and may have known Emma Hale in her youth before Joseph Smith made her acquaintance. Permelia received a better-than-average education and was described as a "very quiet, well mannered and educated young woman."[2] She became a schoolteacher, riding her horse twenty miles a day in order to teach her assigned students.

On April 27, 1823, at age seventeen, Permelia married twenty-four-year-old Cornelius Peter Lott in Bridgewater Township, Pennsylvania. To their union were born eleven children, eight living to adulthood. It was said of Permelia that she "was a good mother, teaching her daughters the art of

---

1 "History of Permelia Darrow Lott," FamilySearch.
2 "Cornelius Peter Lott—Personal History," FamilySearch.

homemaking and all her children the importance of education."³ Until 1838, the Lott family raised their children in various townships in Pennsylvania—Bridgewater, Springville, Tunkhannock, and Susquehanna. In each locale, Cornelius labored on a farm while Permelia attended to cooking, washing, and other chores that were the common lot of a farmer's wife.

Permelia and Cornelius embraced the teachings of the gospel of Jesus Christ as preached by missionaries and were baptized members of The Church of Jesus Christ of Latter-day Saints on December 13, 1833. They were the only members of the Darrow and Lott extended families to enter baptismal waters.

Three years later, they packed up their possessions and moved to Kirtland, Ohio, to be with the Saints of God. On August 1, 1836, in Kirtland, Cornelius received a patriarchal blessing from Joseph Smith Sr. and was promised,

> Thou shalt see the Savior if faithful, and angels shall minister unto thee. And I seal upon thee the father's blessing, even long life and eternal life. Thou shalt receive the blessings of the Priesthood in all its fullness, also thou shalt bless thy family and teach them righteousness. Thou shalt stand when the heavens shall rend and thou shalt have the riches of the earth and of eternity. This for thee and for thy posterity to all generations. Thou art sealed up unto eternal life, even so, Amen.⁴

In 1837, when religious persecution raged in Kirtland, the Lotts fled to Missouri in hopes of finding peace and safety. They settled near Hawn's Mill. Unfortunately, religious persecution intensified in Missouri. Governor Lilburn W. Boggs issued an extermination order against Latter-day Saints residing in the state. Rather than deny their faith, Cornelius and Permelia and their family fled to the banks of the Mississippi River and then to safety in Pike County, Illinois. It wasn't until 1842 that the Lotts moved upriver to Nauvoo. In the city, the family lived in the Joseph Smith farmhouse. Cornelius was appointed the farm manager.

Permelia was faithfully supportive of Cornelius's service as a farm manager, his service as a missionary in Kentucky, his entering the law of plural marriage, and her daughter Melissa Lott being sealed as a plural wife to the Prophet Joseph

---

3   "Permelia Darrow Lott," *Pioneer Women of Faith and Fortitude*, 4 vols. (Salt Lake City: International Society Daughters of Utah Pioneers, 1998), 2:1813.
4   H. Michael Marquardt, *Early Patriarchal Blessings of The Church of Jesus Christ of Latter-day Saints* (Salt Lake City: The Smith-Pettit Foundation, 2007), 128.

Smith. Permelia was among the second company to receive her endowment in the Nauvoo Temple on December 11, 1845. She was in Nauvoo when Joseph and his brother Hyrum were martyred in Carthage Jail.

Following the lead of Brigham Young, Permelia and her family fled from religious persecution in Nauvoo to the Territory of Iowa. They crossed Iowa to reach the banks of the Missouri River. Cornelius was selected to journey with Brigham Young in the Vanguard Company to the Salt Lake Valley in 1847. This left Permelia to care for their children until he returned. In his absence, she buried two children at Winter Quarters. When he returned in 1848, Cornelius and Permelia joined the Heber C. Kimball Company to trek across the plains toward a western Zion.

Of all the stories told of Cornelius Lott, none is repeated more often than his encounter with Mary Fielding Smith. At age forty-nine, Cornelius was selected as the Captain of the Third Ten in the Heber C. Kimball Company. Mary Fielding Smith, a single mother and widow of Hyrum Smith, was a member of his company. According to the Smiths, Cornelius told Mary that she should stay back until she gathered others to help her and her children make the journey west, indicating that she would be a burden on the company. She refused to follow his advice. According to her son Joseph F. Smith, Cornelius humiliated her.[5] Not everyone felt the same as Joseph F. Smith, especially Permelia.

Less than two months after their arrival in the Salt Lake Valley, Permelia gave birth to her last child, Benjamin Smith Lott.[6] The Lotts lived in a two-room cabin with a dirt floor at the southwest corner of Third South and State Street in Salt Lake City. The cabin was typical of starter homes in Salt Lake and described in verse by Joel Wilde:

> Of logs we built our houses,
> Of shakes we made the doors,
> Of sod we built the chimneys,
> Dirt we had for floors.[7]

Cornelius supported his family as the superintendent of a Church farm in the Forest Dale area of Salt Lake until his death from consumption in July 1850. Left a widow with six children, one being a babe in arms, Permelia needed help.

---

5   Joseph F. Smith Reminisces, "Cornelius Peter Lott" in Mormon Pioneer Overland Travel, 1847–1868.
6   "History of Permelia Darrow Lott," FamilySearch.
7   Joel Wilde poem, as quoted in Rhea L. Vance, "From Descendants of Cornelius Peter Lott" (1972), FamilySearch.

The absence of a father required new arrangements. She was allotted twenty acres of farm and prairie land in Utah County. She moved to Lehi in Utah County to be near her daughter Mary and to claim the land. She lived on 200 South and 300 West in an adobe house with two rooms downstairs and two upstairs in Lehi. She had apple trees, currant bushes, raspberry bushes, and a lovely garden. But better than that, she had a loving, attentive family.

By 1880, Permelia was living in the household of her son-in-law Abram Hatch in Heber, Wasatch County.[8] She died on January 6, 1882, in Lehi at age seventy-seven and was buried in the Salt Lake City Cemetery next to her husband, Cornelius Lott. A grandchild wrote of Permelia:

> Grandma Lott, as an old lady, impressed one with her quiet dignity and sweet unassuming manners, and all who knew her loved her. She never sought publicity of any kind, but was ever ready with a helping hand for the sick or needy. She died . . . as she had lived, "faithful to her trust."[9]

**A Bridge to the Past**

Permelia did not know much of comfort and ease. She had many trials, including being a widow with six children to rear. Permelia did not shrink from her responsibilities. With quiet dignity, she raised her children in a modest home and taught them to love the Lord. When unexpected disappointment and sorrow strikes, reach up to the Lord, find your familiar surface, and face life head-on with "quiet dignity."

---

8   US Federal Census, 1880.
9   "Permelia Darrow Lott," *Pioneer Women of Faith and Fortitude*, 2:1813.

# Sophronia Smith Stoddard McCleary

(1803–1876)

SOPHRONIA, THE ELDEST DAUGHTER OF Joseph Smith Sr. and Lucy Mack, was living in Lima, Illinois, when she saw her brothers Joseph and Hyrum after they escaped imprisonment in Missouri. Wandle Mace recorded, "Their sister . . . hurried to and fro pressing them to partake of refreshments at the same time telling them how anxious they had been and how fearful they were lest the mob would take their lives." Brother Mace heard the Prophet Joseph tell Sophronia, "You were much troubled about us but you did not know the promise of God to us."[1]

When Sophronia was age nine, she was living with her family in Lebanon, New Hampshire. For three months in 1813, she suffered from typhoid fever. The attending physician pronounced her "so far gone, it was not for her to receive any benefit from medicine." She lay "motionless with her eyes wide open, and with that peculiar aspect which bespeaks the near approach of death." Her parents prayed to the Lord, asking that her life be spared. They received an answer—"a testimony that she should recover."[2]

---

1   *Wandle Mace, 1809-1890*, 36–37, L. Tom Perry Special Collections, Harold B. Lee Library, Brigham Young University, Provo, UT.
2   Lucy Mack Smith, *Biographical Sketches of Joseph Smith the Prophet and His Progenitors for Many Generations* (Liverpool: S. W. Richards, 1853), 60–61.

Sophronia did recover and moved on with her family from the eastern states to Palmyra, New York. When she was age seventeen, her brother Joseph had his First Vision, and when she was age twenty, he recounted to the family his first interview with the angel Moroni. In fall 1827, when Joseph received the golden plates from the angel Moroni, Sophronia was age twenty-three, a "tall and delicate-looking young lady with soft brown hair and big dark-brown eyes that seemed to look into one's very soul."[3] She was being courted by Calvin Stoddard, "a young bible student [who] . . . was well-educated and of exemplary habits. He often visited the Smith home and was much interested in Joseph's visit with the angel."[4] Sophronia married Calvin Stoddard on Christmas Day in 1827. To their union were born two children. Their daughter, Maria Stoddard, lived to adulthood.

Sophronia and Calvin resided in Macedon, New York, in a "frame house with unpainted weather-boarding."[5] They were both early believers of the prophetic calling of Joseph Smith and willingly responded to his call to gather to Ohio. They settled in Chardon, Ohio, about ten miles from Kirtland. The Prophet Joseph recorded in his journal, "This day I road [sic] from Kirtland to Chardon to see my sister Sophronia."[6] Unfortunately, Joseph found her husband, Calvin, was wavering in his faith. Hyrum believed his lack of religious commitment was "in consequence of his open rebellion against the laws of God."[7]

Calvin repented but never fully committed to the faith again. He accepted a mission call to labor with Jared Carter in 1832 but did not complete the mission, confessing that "he had not magnified his office, but had transgressed and been out of the way."[8] This was most difficult for Sophronia, who was ill at the time. Mother Smith wrote, "She became so weak that we could not

---

3   Mary Salisbury Hancock, "The Three Sisters of the Prophet Joseph Smith," *Saints' Herald* 101, no. 2 (January 11, 1954), 35, as cited in Kyle R. Walker, *United by Faith: The Joseph Smith Sr. and Lucy Mack Smith Family* (American Fork, UT: Covenant Communications Inc., 2005), 165.
4   Walker, *United by Faith*, 168–69.
5   Thomas Gregg, *The Prophet of Palmyra* (NY: John B. Alden, 1890), 48.
6   Joseph Smith Journal, 1832–1834, 2, as cited in Walker, *United by Faith*, 171.
7   Hyrum Smith Diary, November 18, 1831–February 21, 1835, 16–17, as quoted in Jeffrey S. O'Driscoll, *Hyrum Smith: Life of Integrity* (Salt Lake City: Deseret Book, 2003), 64.
8   Fred C. Collier and William S. Harwell, eds., *Kirtland Council Minute Book* (Salt Lake City: Collier's Publishing, 1996), 3.

turn her in bed for several days. She did not speak and many thought that she was dying."⁹ Sophronia regained her health, however.

On December 9, 1834, Sophronia received a patriarchal blessing from her father, Joseph Smith Sr. In the blessing she was told,

> The Lord has seen fit in his providence, to afflict you with much sickness, and much sorrow, because of the conduct of thy husband; but I pronounce the blessing of thy father Jacob upon thee, and thou shalt have a name and a place in thy father's family, because of thy tears and prayers, for thou hast prevailed unto the obtaining this blessing: Thou shall yet be comforted, for the days of thy tribulation shall have an end, and the time of thy rejoicing shall come; and thou shalt be blessed with an abundance of the good things of this life. Thou art blessed and shall be blessed, and saved in the kingdom of heaven. Amen.¹⁰

This blessing was a comfort to Sophronia as she continued to suffer because of the actions of her husband. In 1835, Calvin brought a lawsuit against her brother Joseph, which led to threats and a scuffle. Joseph wrote in his journal, "My heart is pained within me, because of the difficulty that exists in my father's family. The devil has made a violent attack on . . . Calvin Stoddard . . . the powers of earth and hell seem combined to overthrow us and the Church, by causing a division in the family."¹¹ Calvin died shortly after Joseph's journal entry in November 1836 at age thirty-five.

As a widow with a young daughter, Sophronia was dependent on her parents for temporal support until February 11, 1838, when she married William McClearly, eleven years her senior. In marked contrast to Calvin Stoddard, William was unwavering in his support of the Prophet Joseph Smith. He was a strong support for Sophronia during the religious persecution in Ohio and Missouri. After William and Sophronia moved to Nauvoo, he continued to provide faithful strength.

---

9   Smith, Preliminary Manuscript, as cited in Lavina Fielding Anderson, ed., *Lucy's Book: A Critical Edition of Lucy Mack Smith's Family Memoir* (Salt Lake City: Signature Books, 2001), 586.
10  H. Michael Marquardt, *Early Patriarchal Blessings of The Church of Jesus Christ of Latter-day Saints* (Salt Lake City: The Smith-Pettit Foundation, 2007), 13.
11  Joseph Smith, *History of the Church of Jesus Christ of Latter-day Saints*, 7 vols. (Salt Lake City: Deseret Book Company, 1948), 2:352.

Sophronia was with her father, Joseph Smith Sr., in the last moments of his life. He gave her a blessing on that occasion and said,

> Thou didst see trouble and sorrow, but thy trouble shall be lessened, for thou hast been faithful in helping thy father and thy mother in the work of the Lord. And thou shalt be blessed, and the blessings of heaven shall rest down upon thee. Thy last days shall be thy best. . . . Thou shalt live as long as thou desirest life.[12]

The McClearys moved on to Ramus, Illinois. While seated at Sophronia's dinner table in Ramus, her brother Joseph gave instructions and corrections that are contained in the Doctrine and Covenants, Section 130.

After Joseph's martyrdom, Sophronia embraced the leadership of Brigham Young. She received her endowment in the Nauvoo Temple on December 23, 1845. She and her husband, William, made plans to journey to the Rockies. Priddy Meeks wrote, "I had been working with William McCleary, brother-in-law to the Prophet, making each of us a wagon to cross the plains in."[13]

William crossed the Mississippi River to Iowa and then traveled across the territory to reach Winter Quarters. Sophronia was not with him. He returned to Nauvoo, hoping to encourage her to join him. William W. Phelps wrote, "Brother McCleary came with me to take his wife, and Mother Smith . . . on to the camp."[14]

Sophronia and her daughter, Maria, did not go west. They remained in Illinois. In 1873, Sophronia affiliated with the Reorganized Church of Jesus Christ of Latter Day Saints. She died three years later, on July 22, 1876, at age seventy-three. Notice of her death appeared in the *Saints' Herald* on October 1, 1876:

> She was the oldest sister of Joseph Smith the martyr, and she was a member of the church from the time it was established. She was ever ready to bear her testimony to the truth of the work, and she fell asleep in Christ without a struggle with full hope in being raised in the first resurrection.[15]

---

12   Smith, *Biographical Sketches of Joseph Smith the Prophet*, 268.
13   J. Cecil Alter, "Journal of Priddy Meeks," *Utah Historical Quarterly* 10, nos. 1–4 (1942), 154.
14   Letter of W. W. Phelps to Reuben Miller, May 30, 1847, as cited in Anderson, *Lucy's Book*, 779.
15   Jessie Salisbury, "Died," *True Latter Day Saints' Herald* (October 1, 1876), 607, as cited in Walker, *United by Faith*, 194.

**A Bridge to the Past**
Although Sophronia suffered from bouts of illness, it was not health concerns that caused her great sorrow. It was the conflict between her husband and her brother Joseph. A blessing from her father proved a comfort to her, especially his promise that her last days would be her best days. Priesthood blessings bring comfort. The Lord has promised, "I, the Lord, am bound when ye do what I say" (D&C 82:10). What is He bound to do? He is bound to take you by the hand and lead you through life. Cast your burdens upon Him, and He will sustain you.

# Lucy Smith Millikin

(1821–1882)

---

IN 1840, LUCY RECEIVED A blessing from her father, Joseph Smith Sr. In the blessing, she was told,

> Lucy, thou art my youngest child, my darling. And the Lord gave thee unto us to be a comfort and blessing to us in our old age, therefore, thou must take good care of thy mother. . . . If thou wilt continue faithful, thou shalt be blessed with a house and land; thou shalt have food and raiment, and no more be persecuted and driven, as thou hast hitherto been. Now continue faithful, and thou shalt live long and be blessed, and thou shalt receive a reward in heaven.[1]

---

Lucy was born in 1821 when her father, Joseph Smith Sr., was age fifty and her mother, Lucy Mack Smith, was forty-six. Lucy's early years revolved around the Restoration—her brother Joseph's visitations from the angel Moroni, his translation of the gold plates, the coming forth of the Book of Mormon, and the organization of the Church.

Her most-recounted childhood experience was when her brother Alvin was on his deathbed in November 1823. Lucy Mack Smith wrote,

---

1  Lucy Mack Smith, *Biographical Sketches of Joseph Smith the Prophet and His Progenitors for Many Generations* (Liverpool: S. W. Richards, 1853), 288.

I went to [my daughter], and said, "Lucy, Alvin wants to see you." At this, she started from her sleep, and screamed out, 'Amby, Amby'; (she could not yet talk plain, being very young). We took her to him, and when she got within reach of him, she sprang from my arms and caught him round the neck, and cried out, "Oh! my Amby!" and kissed him again and again.[2]

Alvin told his sister Lucy, "You must be the best girl in the world, and take care of mother; you can't have your Amby any more. Amby is going away; he must leave little Lucy." After kissing her goodbye, Alvin requested, "Take her away I think my breath offends her." Lucy clung to him. It was "with difficulty we succeeded in disengaging her hands."[3] After his death, Lucy could not be consoled.

As a youth, Lucy witnessed changing dynamics within her family—marriages of her siblings and their resettling in Kirtland, Ohio. On December 9, 1834, at age thirteen, Lucy received a patriarchal blessing from her father. In the blessing, she was told,

> Thou hast been a comfort to my heart, and I have besought the Lord for blessings for thee in much prayer and fasting, for thou art a child, even a youth, surrounded with the follies and vanities of the Gentiles; therefore thou needest those to watch over thee who are experienced and wise. . . . Thou shalt be spared to a good old age, and rise up to call thy father blessed, and so shall thy children bless thee: thou shalt be blessed with my other children, with an inheritance in the land of Zion. . . . Thou shalt have dreams and visions: the holy angels shall minister unto thee. My child, I seal a father's blessing upon thee: thou art the fruit of my loins, even in my old age, and thou art numbered among the chosen seed. Thou art sealed up to eternal life; even so. Amen.[4]

As Lucy matured to womanhood, she met Arthur Millikin, a convert from Saco, Maine. Arthur was not a model Latter-day Saint. He was

---

2  Smith, *Biographical Sketches of Joseph Smith the Prophet*, 93.
3  Smith, *Biographical Sketches of Joseph Smith the Prophet*, 93.
4  H. Michael Marquardt, *Early Patriarchal Blessings of The Church of Jesus Christ of Latter-day Saints* (Salt Lake City: The Smith-Pettit Foundation, 2007), 18–19.

reprimanded by the Kirtland High Council for inappropriate behavior.⁵ He was disfellowshipped from the Church for his actions. Within a few weeks, he confessed his follies and was forgiven. His fellowship was reinstated.

Nothing much came of the friendship between Lucy and Arthur in Kirtland, but when the Smith family moved on to Missouri, the friendship between Lucy and Arthur blossomed into courtship after the Battle of Crooked River, when Arthur was shot above both knees. He was taken to the home of the Prophet Joseph to convalesce. Lucy was often at his side.

When Arthur's wounds were healed, he and his friend Benjamin F. Johnson fled from Missouri to Kansas, seeking refuge from religious persecution. Both young men ended up in Illinois. As for Lucy, she left Missouri too. On her journey to Quincy, Illinois, it was reported that she "lost her shoes several times and her father had to thrust his cane into the mud to ascertain where they were because they were so completely covered with mud and water."⁶

On June 4, 1840, Lucy and Arthur were married by the Prophet Joseph Smith. Lucy was age eighteen and Arthur was twenty-three. The Prophet Joseph wrote of Arthur, "He is a faithful, an honest, and an upright man."⁷ To their union were born eight children.

In 1843, Lucy and Arthur visited extended family members in Saco, Maine. While on their visit, Lucy gave birth to her first child in the same home that Arthur was born in about twenty-six years earlier.

By May 1844, the Millikins had returned to Nauvoo. A month later, Lucy's brothers Joseph and Hyrum Smith were assassinated in Carthage, Illinois. Lucy and Arthur greatly mourned their deaths, especially since Arthur had served as a clerk to the Prophet Joseph. The Millikins willingly took the grieving Lucy Mack Smith into their home and cared for her.

In 1845, Lucy and Arthur joined with others of the Smith family in rejecting the leadership of Brigham Young. When the Saints moved West, the Millikins remained in Nauvoo. When the Battle of Nauvoo erupted in September 1846, they fled to Knoxville, Illinois, sixty-five miles northeast of Nauvoo. Upon learning that violent disruptions in Nauvoo had subsided, they returned to the city. Their stay in Nauvoo was brief. They soon moved on to Ramus and then Fountain Green, Illinois.

---

5   Fred C. Collier and William S. Harwell, eds. *Kirtland Council Minute Book* (Salt Lake City: Collier's Publishing, 1996), 196–201.
6   Lavina Fielding Anderson, *Lucy's Book: A Critical Edition of Lucy Mack Smith's Family Memoir* (Salt Lake City: Signature Books, 2002), 686.
7   Histories, Volume D-1: Joseph Smith Histories, 1838–1856, 1373, The Joseph Smith Papers.

In these locales, Arthur supported his family as a saddle and harness maker. When they moved to Colchester, Illinois, he worked in the mines. According to George A. Smith, he also "spent his time weighing coal for a railroad company." Elder Smith added, "I did not fail to tell [the Millikins] that they ought to be in the Mountains striving to build up Zion."[8]

Lucy and Arthur never moved to the Rockies or united again with The Church of Jesus Christ of Latter-day Saints. They remained in Illinois and united with the Reorganized Church of Jesus Christ of Latter Day Saints. Arthur died of pneumonia and rheumatism in 1882 at age sixty-four. Seven months later, Lucy died on December 9, 1882, of a respiratory disease. At her funeral, nephew Solomon Salisbury said of the Millikins,

> Their lives have been taken, mobbed, hated and reviled, because they feared God more than man. Few have loved them, many have hated them. The world to come certainly will be for them a rest: for here there was none found.[9]

**A Bridge to the Past**
Lucy loved her family, and they loved her. Though her life was not a carefree one, she always strove to care for those who needed her most. When we show love to those around us and serve them with all our hearts, we will find that rest and peace that only the Spirit can bring.

---

8   June Moon, *Story of Colchester, Illinois* (Colchester, IL: Colchester Chronicle, 1956), 14–15, as cited in Kyle R. Walker, *United by Faith: The Joseph Sr. and Lucy Mack Smith Family* (American Fork, UT: Covenant Communications Inc., 2005), 420–21.
9   S. J. Salisbury, "Died—Millikin," *Saints' Herald*, January 13, 1883, as cited in Walker, *United by Faith*, 422–23.

# Mary Adeline Beman Noble

(1810–1851)

---

IN SPRING OF 1834, THE Prophet Joseph Smith preached in Mary's neighborhood of Avon, New York. Mary wrote,

> This was the first time I ever beheld a prophet of the Lord, and I can truly say at the first sight that I had a testimony within my bosom that he was a man chosen of God to bring forth a great work in the last days. His society I prized, his conversation was meat and drink to me. The principles that he brought forth bind the testimony that he bore of the truth of the Book of Mormon and made a lasting impression upon my mind.[1]

---

Mary grew to maturity in Western New York. Her father, Alvah Beman, was "a prosperous farmer and through hard work and frugality [he] acquired a good home, and much land." Mary was known as his "bright child." She wrote, "I did not, like most of the children idle away my time. But my time was devoted to books. At the age of ten and twelve I had a very good understanding of Geography and Grammar. At the age of fourteen I boarded out and attended a select school."[2]

---

1 "A History of Mary A. Noble," 18–19, as cited in Mark L. McConkie, *Remembering Joseph: Personal Recollections of Those Who Knew the Prophet Joseph Smith* (Salt Lake City: Deseret Book, 2003), 106.
2 "Journal of Mary Adeline Beman," FamilySearch; "The Life Sketch of Mary Adeline Beman Noble," FamilySearch.

Religion was important to Mary and her family. The Beman family were early converts of the Church of Jesus Christ in the New York area. Her father became an early believer even before the Book of Mormon was published. Elder Parley P. Pratt recalled being hosted in his home: "Among those whose hospitality we shared in that vicinity (Genesse Co., New York) was Old Father Beman and his amiable and interesting family. He was a good singer and so was [sic] his daughters."3

At age eighteen, Mary earned a certificate qualifying her to be a schoolteacher. For four winters, she taught school. "The summer seasons my time was employed in the domestic affairs of my father's family. . . . My time together with my sisters was spent in manufacturing [cloth] and attending to the dairy."4

While teaching school in Avon, New York, Mary became acquainted with Joseph Noble, a boarder at the home of Mr. Knowls. Mary wrote,

> The same place I made my home when I did not go to my father['s]. . . . At this time Mr. Noble was paying attention to Mr. Knowls['s] daughter. She was a fine girl; she was my intimate acquaintance; she was also a school teacher. We were frequently in each other's society. She was naturally rather a proud spirited girl and did not care much for religion, but was naturally very lively but I was rather of a different turn. I always had respect to the principles of truth and righteousness, and sought the happiness of others as well as my own. I did not much expect at this time ever to be united to Mr. Noble. Still, it would have been a matter of my choice, could I have been permitted to have made it, but I unbosomed my feeling to no one. I held sacred the feelings of my heart. My mind was employed in school and I attended my own business, trusted in the Lord, believing he would rule all [things] for my own good and for the glory of God.5

About this time, Joseph Noble entered baptismal waters and became a member of The Church of Jesus Christ of Latter-day Saints. Mary highly approved of his religious commitment and wrote, "His [course], conduct, and conversations were highly gratifying to me. He was a person of good habits, good principles and a fine intelligent young man. In his society, I was happy."6

---

3 "The Life Sketch of Mary Adeline Beman Noble," FamilySearch.
4 "Life Sketch of Mary Noble."
5 "Life Sketch of Mary Noble."
6 "Life Sketch of Mary Noble."

In 1834, Joseph made plans to join Zion's Camp and made preparations to journey to Missouri to assist the Saints who had lost lands of inheritance in Jackson County. "On the first of May (1834) he called in the evening to take his leave," wrote Mary. "He said he was going to start the next morning for Missouri. We bid adieu for a season but under the most solemn engagement. At his return in the fall, if our lives were spared, we were to be united in the bonds of matrimony. For that cord of filial affection that was existing between us was not easily broke."7

With Joseph moving ever closer to Missouri with Zion's Camp, Mary greatly lamented his absence. "Almost every night after school I would bow before the Lord and in my supplications I would remember Zion Camp," she confessed. Upon his return, Joseph and Mary were wed without delay on September 11, 1834. Many people attended the ceremony and the dinner that followed. In honor of her daughter, Mary's mother, Sally Beman, wrote,

> My love for thee must ever be
> fond as in years gone by,
> While to the heart it shall be like a dream of memory,
> Dearest, farewell, may angel hosts
> Their vigils o'er thee keep.
>
> How can I speak that fearful word?
> Farewell and yet not weep,
> Go dearest one, my selfish love
> Shall never pale thy cheek
> Not even a mother's fears for thee
> Will in sadness speak.8

To support his bride, Joseph worked as a miller in the greater Kirtland area. In spare moments, he attended the School of the Prophets and learned a little Hebrew but felt hampered by his lack of a formal education. As for Mary, she knew much of sorrow. Out of the nine children born to her, only three lived to adulthood.

The Nobles moved from Kirtland just as religious persecution was beginning to rage. They settled in Missouri until being driven from the state. Seeking safety, they took refuge in an abandoned log barrack in Montrose, Iowa. It was not until 1841 that the Nobles moved to Nauvoo. Joseph built a home in

---

7  "Life Sketch of Mary Noble."
8  Sally Brutts Beman poem to her daughter Mary Adeline Beman, 1834, as quoted in biographies submitted to the Daughters of Utah Pioneers, FamilySearch.

Nauvoo that was later purchased by Church agents and given to Lucy Mack Smith.

Within six weeks of receiving their endowments on December 15, 1845, the Nobles fled from religious persecution in Nauvoo to safety in the Territory of Iowa. When the family reached Winter Quarters, Joseph became bishop of the Winter Quarters 13th Ward. He relinquished his ecclesiastical position to continue his journey to the Salt Lake Valley, arriving on October 2, 1847.

Joseph Bates Noble built three homes for his family in the Salt Lake area before Mary died on February 14, 1851, at age forty-one. Her funeral was held in the bowery on Temple Square. President Brigham Young preached at her funeral. Joseph Bates lived to be ninety years old. He was ordained a patriarch in his later years.

**A Bridge to the Past**

When it came to marital matters, Mary trusted in the Lord "believing he would rule all things for my own good." Turn to the Lord and wait to see what He has in store for you. Waiting upon the Lord is action-packed. It begins with kindness. Mary discovered this great truth.

## Louisa Barnes Pratt

(1802–1880)

---

Louisa wrote,

> The sisters even resolved to pay fifty cents each towards buying the nails and glass [for the Nauvoo Temple]. By strict economy I obtained the amount. I started in good faith to go to the Temple office and bestow my offering.... A temptation came over me. I paused. I turned over in my mind, how many things I needed for family use, and that money would relieve my present necessities. In an instant more I resisted. Said I, "If I have no more than a crust of bread each day for a week, I will pay this money into the treasury."[1]

---

Louisa, daughter of Willard and Dolly Barnes, was a timid child who hated being reprimanded. She wrote,

> Going to a neighboring house on an errand, I had leave to stay half an hour, but told the lady two hours were permitted me. She was suspicious, and dispatched her little girl to inquire into the truth of my statements. I was called home and

---

[1] Louisa Barnes Pratt, *The History of Louisa Barnes Pratt: The Autobiography of A Mormon Missionary Widow and Pioneer*, S. George Ellsworth, ed. (Logan, UT: Utah State University Press, 1998), 72–73.

reprimanded severely, and felt the greatest contrition of heart, while mother painted my crime in its strongest colors, and rehearsed the threatenings of scripture. . . . My age then did not exceed five years. I am not conscious of having told after this occurance, [sic] but one lie, which was not to my mother.[2]

Other childish failings caused Louisa to be sent to live with an aunt. Her aunt took an immediate liking to Louisa and her immature pranks and incessant talking. Louisa remained under her aunt's care until her father sold his farm and took her and the rest of his family to Canada in July 1810.

"I was of a religious turn when young," Louisa wrote. "At the age of seven, if left at home alone, on the Sabbath the time was passed not idly, but in the exercise of devotion, singing principally."[3]

In Canada, Louisa was known as the smartest girl in her class. At age fourteen, she was baptized a member of the Episcopal Church. Soon thereafter, she left her parental home again, this time to live with a sister-in-law who taught her the art of tailoring. It was not long, however, before she was attending the Female Academy at Winchester, New Hampshire. There she befriended Rebekah J. Pratt and learned of her adventurous brother Addison, who sailed the high seas. More than a little curious about the whaler, Louisa wrote to Addison Pratt. When he sailed into the Boston Harbor, the letters gave him reason to visit Louisa.

When Louisa met Addison, she found him to be "rough and unpolished, but . . . frank and ingenuous . . . mirthful in the extreme, fond of singing and telling wonders."[4] Addison and Louisa were married on April 3, 1831, in Dunham, Canada.[5] The newlyweds lived near Lake Erie in Ripley, New York. It was not until 1838 that Addison and Louisa learned of The Church of Jesus Christ of Latter-day Saints from Louisa's sister Caroline and Caroline's husband, Jonathan Crosby.

Addison and Louisa soon entered baptismal waters and made plans to gather with the Saints in Missouri. Upon learning of religious persecution in Missouri, they journeyed on to Illinois.[6] In Nauvoo, Illinois, Addison was paid a dollar a day plus board to work on the temple. In this way, Addison and Louisa

---

2 Pratt, 5.
3 Pratt, 10.
4 Pratt, 29.
5 Pratt, 35.
6 Pratt, xv.

prospered. But a mission call to serve in the Society Islands changed their circumstances. Addison accepted the call even though it meant that he would not be with Louisa and their four daughters for several years. Of this separation and others that followed, Louisa wrote, "More than half the years of my married life I have stood alone. Created the means to sustain myself and children: and although I had kind friends around me I had no one immediately interested to supply my daily wants. My cares often weighed heavily upon me, yet for the most part I have been cheerful."[7]

Louisa wrote of her remaining days in Nauvoo,

> I was subject to severe fits of melancholy. I felt a loneliness indescribable! . . . My belief in the gospel was my secret joy. . . . Thus was my life made up of a mixture of joys and sorrows. Notwithstanding the appearances I kept up I sometimes felt very helpless and inadequate to the burden that was laid upon me. I felt like an orphan child.[8]

Extended time away from her husband led Louisa to become self-sufficient. "I am not amenable to man['s direction]," she said. "Neither will I suffer man to judge me." Alpheus Cutler of the Nauvoo Temple Committee said of Louisa, "If all the sisters were as enterprising like Sister Pratt we should not see so many ragged men about the streets." Yet inwardly, Louisa struggled: "My domestic sorrows I forbear to mention. I carry them in my own bosom, and bear my injuries in silence."[9]

Louisa brought her four daughters across the plains to the Salt Lake Valley. In the valley, she was reunited with her husband after a five-year separation. Within a short time, Addison was again called to serve a mission to Tahiti. This time, Louisa and her daughters were asked to join him. Before leaving the valley, Louisa received a blessing from Brigham Young. Louisa wrote of that blessing, "He said I was called, set apart, and ordained, to go to the Islands of the sea, to aid my husband in teaching the people . . . that I should do a good work, and return in peace."[10] Their mission was cut short when the French Protectorate government enforced a law forbidding foreign missionaries to live and work among the Tahitians.[11] After leaving Tahiti, the Pratt family settled

---

7   Pratt, xxi.
8   Pratt, 67–68.
9   Pratt, xxi–xxii, 67.
10  Pratt, 108–9.
11  Pratt, xvi.

in San Francisco before making their home in San Bernardino, a Latter-day Saint settlement.

Addison, who was used to presiding over Church matters in the islands, found it difficult to accept direction from Latter-day Saint leaders in San Bernardino. He also had trouble at home. He liked his independence and often left home to hunt and fish, neglecting household matters. Louisa was frustrated: "O how have I involved myself, by taking upon me the support of my family and my husband [who] by being separated from us for seven years in fourteen has nearly lost all the ability he once had."[12]

Addison was called back to Tahiti in 1854 but did not go because the government of the French Protectorate refused to lift their policy toward foreign missionaries. He did return to the Pacific in 1856, but was not allowed to preach. On April 12, 1856, Louisa penned—

> Again you go far far from home
> A foreign shore to greet,
> And little do you know the ills
> Of fortune we may meet.
> No father brother husband friend
> May faithful prove to me,
> And yet I trust that to the end
> God will remembered be
> A friend in time, and in eternity.[13]

Addison returned to San Bernardino and his family. When Brigham Young called for all the Saints to come to Utah and prepare to fight Johnston's Army, Addison refused to follow counsel. Louisa took the opposite stance. She left her husband and moved with two of her daughters to Beaver, Utah, hoping that Addison would soon follow. He remained in California. In 1862, Louisa visited a daughter in California and brought Addison back to Utah. Before long, he returned to California, claiming the climate was better. Addison and Louisa separated but did not divorce.

Although Louisa was tried and tested through many marital separations, her faith never wavered. She was the secretary and counselor of the Female Relief Society in Beaver, Utah. Addison died in California on October 14, 1872. Louisa died eight years later on September 8, 1880, of pneumonia.

---

12  Pratt, xvi.
13  Pratt, 393.

**A Bridge to the Past**
Louisa's husband, Addison, had adventures before and during their marriage. Half of Louisa's married life was spent alone. She was subjected to fits of melancholy and loneliness. If we are to learn anything from Louisa, maybe it should be that joy will come when we reach out to those who feel lonely and that God will always be our companion, even when others abandon us.

# Elizabeth Hancock Redd

(1798–1853)

---

WHEN ELIZABETH AND HER HUSBAND, John Redd, learned that the Prophet Joseph Smith had said, "It was not right for one human being to be in bondage to another," they freed their slaves and made financial provisions for each of them.[1] A few of their former slaves had entered baptismal waters and pled to remain in Elizabeth and John's service. They journeyed with the Redds to Nauvoo to meet a prophet of God.

---

Elizabeth was raised along the Atlantic coast in North Carolina like generations of her ancestors before her. Her father, Zebedee Hancock, was a wealthy tobacco farmer. He had a ready market for his product with merchants along the coastal shoreline and sea captains trafficking between the states and the Caribbean Seas. As a wealthy Southern gentleman, Zebedee provided well for his family, having slaves attend his fields, his home, and his children.

Growing up in similar circumstances as Elizabeth was John Hardison Redd. His home was in the fishing village of Sneads Ferry on Stump Sound, a key village on the post road linking Suffolk, Virginia, with Charleston, South Carolina. Travelers often stopped at Sneads Ferry for shrimp, flounder, clams, and oysters. His father, a merchant, made a handsome profit off the travelers.

---

1 "Story of Historic Utah Family told in New Book," *Sunday Herald* [Provo, UT], September 29, 1968.

John received an education from private tutors. Later on, he was known as a "man of unusual learning" and a "man of letters." His handwriting and grammatical construction in extant letters and papers evidence his educational training.[2] John, like his father, became a successful merchant in Sneads Ferry. He was known as Captain Redd, an honorific title that had as much to do with the fish industry in the village as the growing trade between coastal Carolina and islands in the Caribbean.

On May 7, 1821, at age twenty-two, John owned a farm in Onslow County, North Carolina, debt-free. Due to his financial position, he was considered one of the most eligible bachelors in the county. John and Elizabeth grew up in the same social circle, but it took time for their acquaintance to blossom into courtship.

On March 2, 1826, at age twenty-eight, Elizabeth married twenty-six-year-old John Hardison Redd in Onslow County, North Carolina. To their union were born eight children, six living to adulthood. Elizabeth brought to the marriage two slaves—Venus, age ten, and Chaney, age seven. Although her slaves were mere children, much of the cares that normally would have fallen on the shoulders of Elizabeth were given to Venus and Chaney. For sixteen years, Elizabeth enjoyed an opulent lifestyle at Sneads Ferry surrounded by luxury and social occasions with family and friends.

Yet in 1838, John and Elizabeth were ready for a change. An expansive plantation in Tennessee was available for purchase. When the family migrated from North Carolina to Middle Tennessee, John purchased the plantation located nine miles from Murfreesboro, the county seat of Rutherford County. The Redds lived in a large two-story house with a veranda on both levels. In the back of their home were rows of servants' quarters. Once again, John and Elizabeth were considered the upper crust of society. But not all was pleasant in their situation:

> One day a neighboring slave ran away from his plantation to hide from his cruel master. Great-grandfather Redd was away, but his master came and found him and beat him unmercifully. When [John Redd] came home he was very angry to have had such a thing happen, and he said, "Powell knew I was away or he never would have dared to whip a slave on my plantation."[3]

---

2 Ellen Redd Bryner, "Sketch of John Hardison Redd and his wife, Elizabeth Hancock," FamilySearch.

3 Luella Adams Dalton, "Incidents about John Hardison Redd," January 18, 2014, FamilySearch.

After four years of opulent living in Tennessee, John and Elizabeth met missionaries from The Church of Jesus Christ of Latter-day Saints. One of the missionaries was John D. Lee, later infamous for the Mountain Meadows Massacre. The Redds recognized the truth of the gospel message shared by Elder Lee, and in 1843, Elizabeth and her family and two slaves entered baptismal waters.

After their conversion, Elizabeth and John wanted to gather with those of their faith. Their desire to meet the Prophet Joseph Smith and other Latter-day Saints superseded their desire to remain in Tennessee. The Redds packed up their belongings, sold their plantation, and with six freed slaves, moved to Nauvoo.

In Nauvoo, Elizabeth and John met the Prophet Joseph Smith. John received a patriarchal blessing on April 3, 1844, from Hyrum Smith, the brother of the Prophet Joseph. In his blessing, John was told,

> You are of the lineage of Jacob and of the tribe of Levi or in other words You are of that descent and of that origin and from that lineage cometh Your blessings . . . seek first the Kingdom of God and his righteousness all others things shall be added—now therefore I say unto You John You shall be blessed with the priesthood and it shall be a blessing unto You and Your house and Your name shall be perpetuated from Generation to Generation and You shall be blessed in Your house and habitation and in the covenant of Grace.[4]

Elizabeth and John were in Nauvoo when Joseph Smith helped "a colored man named Anthony" who had been "arrested for selling liquor on Sunday." Anthony claimed the "reason he had done so was that he might raise the money to purchase the liberty of a dear child held as a slave in a Southern State." The Prophet Joseph "presented Anthony with a fine horse, directing him to sell it, and use the money obtained for the purchase of the child."[5]

When religious persecution mounted against Latter-day Saints in Nauvoo, Elizabeth and her family fled to Iowa. In 1850, the Redds joined the James Pace Company and journeyed to the Rocky Mountains. On the journey, John kept a diary. In the diary, he expressed gratitude to the Lord for His mercy.

After arriving in the Salt Lake Valley on September 23, 1850, the Redd family was called to settle in Provo by Brigham Young. Near the Spanish Fork

---

4   H. Michael Marquardt, *Early Patriarchal Blessings of The Church of Jesus Christ of Latter-day Saints* (Salt Lake City: The Smith-Pettit Foundation, 2007), 228.
5   Mary Frost Adams, *Young Woman's Journal*, 538, as quoted in blacklds.org.

River, John helped build the first sawmill south of Provo. More importantly, a small Church branch—Upper Settlement—was formed with Stephen Markham as president and John as clerk. John's reports of branch meetings were sent to Brigham Young. On August 11, 1852, John was invited to come to the office of the president—meaning the office of Brigham Young—and receive his endowment.[6]

In 1853, a series of battles broke out between the Indians and settlers living near Spanish Fork. The small settlement that the Redds called home was destroyed. Before the fighting ended, John lost $6,000 worth of property.

John and Elizabeth started over again in a new settlement. It was said of Elizabeth,

> [She] was a courageous pioneer mother. She had been reared with slaves to jump to her every whim. What a change it was when she took a life of a frontier woman; Indian troubles, the hard work of reclaiming the soil, the struggle to bring water to the land, quest for lumber to build the fort, caring for her children in often dangerous times.[7]

But between the Indian uprising and the death of two of her teenage children, it was more than Elizabeth could endure. A few descendants claim it was heartache that caused Elizabeth's death on November 28, 1853 at age fifty-five. Others disagree and point to the fact that Elizabeth had stopped eating and gone to bed. Still others claim that she was ill, for within three days, her skin looked yellow. Elizabeth was buried next to her two children—Catherine and John—in the Pioneer Heritage Cemetery in Spanish Fork.

In 1856, John married Mary Lewis, a native of Cardiff, Wales. To their union was born one daughter. A year after the marriage, John was kicked by a horse. He never recovered. He died on June 15, 1858, in Spanish Fork at age fifty-eight. He was buried the next day in the Pioneer Heritage Cemetery in Spanish Fork near his wife Elizabeth and two of their children.

## A Bridge to the Past

Elizabeth knew much of Southern opulence and hospitality as a child and a young married woman. When presented with a decision to accept the Restoration message and gather with the Saints in Nauvoo or remain on her

---

6 "John Hardiman Redd," Ordinances, FamilySearch.
7 "Elizabeth Hancock Redd," *Pioneer Women of Faith and Fortitude*, 4 vols. (Salt Lake City: International Society Daughters of Utah Pioneers, 1998), 3:2507.

plantation with slaves attending to her every whim, Elizabeth chose to unite with the Saints. Her decision proved pivotal as it changed Elizabeth's life from comfort to persecution, hardship, and privation. She never again lived in wealth. What sacrifice is worth making sacred covenants with God? The lyricist Hannah Last Cornaby asked,

> Who's on the Lord's side? Who?
> Now is the time to show.
> We ask it fearlessly;
> Who's on the Lord's side? Who?[8]

---

8   "Who's on the Lord's Side?" *Hymns*, no. 260.

(1814–1893)

---

OF HER DAYS IN NAUVOO, Sarah recalled,

> The Prophet Joseph would also call on us from time to time, he took great interest in the welfare of the families of those that were off on missions, to see that they did not want for the comforts of life. We then, as a people were united and were more like family than like strangers. And as there were many sick the Prophet Joseph Smith would go from house to house with others of the brethren and administer to the sick, and see that they had the necessary comforts that the sick needed, and many were healed and raised up from a bed of sickness.[1]

---

As she matured to womanhood, Sarah lightened the burdens of her parents. "I did all in my power while I was young to help my dear father and mother to get along in days of poverty and hardships," she wrote.[2]

When Sarah was age twenty-one, Latter-day Saint missionaries preached in her home—

> The two elders came and held a meeting and preached on the first principles of the gospel, and related to the people

---

1  Sarah D. Rich, "Autobiography," FamilySearch.
2  Rich, "Autobiography."

> about their [sic] being a prophet in their church, and told us about the Book of Mormon, and about an angel appearing to the prophet and others; all of which was new doctrine . . . I felt anxious to see the Book of Mormon they had told us about and I asked one of the elders if I could see the book and read some in it that evening. . . . I truly was greatly astonished at its contents that it left an impression upon my mind not to be forgotten.[3]

About six weeks after the missionaries left, Sarah had a dream that they returned and she met them on the porch of her home. The next morning, Sarah asked her father

> if he would not try to come home early that evening. He answered, "Why are you so particular, is your young man coming?" I said, "No, father, but those two Mormon elders will be here tonight." "Why," said my father, "have you heard from them?" I said, "No, but I dreamed last night that they would be here, and I feel sure it will be so." Father said I must be crazy for those men were hundreds of miles away. I said, "Father, hurry home this evening for I am sure they will come." He only laughed at me, and he and mother went off to town.[4]

That very day, the elders came to her home. Sarah met them on the front porch. One elder told her, "We had a vision that we were to return here and baptize you and build up a Church in this region." When her father neared home, he asked Sarah, "Where are your Mormon elders?" To his surprise, the elders stepped out of the house to greet him. Sarah and her family were baptized members of The Church of Jesus Christ of Latter-day Saints.

For the next three years, several elders visited with the family. More than one elder told Sarah that he had recommended her to Charles C. Rich. On March 23, 1837, Sarah received a letter from Elder Rich:

> Miss Sarah Pea,
>
> It is with pleasure that I at this time pen a few lines to you, although a perfect stranger to you. However, I trust that this few lines may be received by you and may be the beginning of a happy acquaintance with you. I will now let you know the

---

3   Rich, "Autobiography."
4   Rich, "Autobiography."

reason of my boldness in writing to you. It is because Elder George Hinkle and others have highly recommended you as a Saint of the Last Days as being worthy of my attention . . . I should be happy to get a good companion. Such a one as I could take comfort with through life and such a one as could take comfort with me. As you have been recommended to me as such, I should be very happy to see you and converse with you on the subject.

Six months after receiving his letter, Sarah and her family moved to Far West, Missouri. Sarah wrote,

> It was in a public meeting that our eyes first rested on each other and without anyone pointing us out to each other, we knew each other at sight; and in four months from the time we first met, we were married . . . we were the happiest couple in all the land. My husband had a beautiful prospect for a nice farm with plenty of timber and water and our plans were laid for a comfortable and happy home in the near future. . . . we never once dreamed what was in store to break up our happy anticipations.[5]

In a violent clash between Latter-day Saints and the Missouri Militia at Crooked River, Charles took command of the Latter-day Saint forces when Captain David W. Patten was mortally wounded. Due to his leadership in battle, the Missouri militia sought his life. "Little did I think the time was so near that [Charles] would be compelled to flee for his life," Sarah wrote, "and leave me as it were in the midst of a howling mob with no one to look to for protection but my Father in Heaven."[6] Sarah was robbed of her riding horse, chickens, and cows before she, too, fled from the state.

At the Mississippi River, she was united with Charles after a three-month separation. He took her across the river to safety in Quincy, Illinois, where she gave birth to the first of their eight children. Sarah was in Nauvoo when news of the martyrdom of Joseph and Hyrum Smith reached her. She wrote, "I cannot describe the sorrow the Church was thrown into at this time, men, women, and children wept and cried aloud when the news came in that our

---

5   Sarah D. Rich Autobiography, 2 vols. (1885), as cited in Kenneth W. Godfrey, Audrey M. Godfrey, and Jill Mulvay Derr, *Women's Voices: An Untold History of the Latter-day Saints, 1830–1900* (Salt Lake City: Deseret Book, 1982), 98.
6   Godfrey, Godfrey, and Derr, *Women's Voices*, 99.

brethren were killed. . . . Many of our enemies said now Mormonism is at an end, and we would all be scattered to the four winds."[7]

Sarah and Charles served in the Nauvoo Temple until it closed in February 1846. They then joined other Latter-day Saints fleeing across the Mississippi River to safety in Iowa. From Iowa, they moved on to Winter Quarters and then to the Salt Lake Valley.

Charles was ordained an Apostle of the Lord Jesus Christ. To fulfill his responsibilities, he was often gone from home. Sarah wrote, "To be left alone in those days with a sick family was rather trying to me, but I realized that unless I passed through trials in this life I could not expect to gain the reward hereafter that is promised those that are faithful through tribulations in this life."[8]

When Charles presided for seven years over the Latter-day Saint settlement in San Bernardino, California, Sarah wrote, "I did the best I could in his absence. My children were small; I tried to teach them what was right, and worked hard myself to try to help along while their father was gone. I turned my attention part of the time to start a little orchard. Mr. Rich sent me some fruit seed from California."[9] Charles next served in England for two years. During his absence, Sarah penned, "This was another lonely time for me, and I truly had many cares and responsibilities resting upon me. I now had five sons to look after, all under sixteen years of age; also, two girls and one grandchild. I braved the storm and did the best I could, and tried to teach my children what was right."[10] Then came his calling to build up a settlement in Bear Lake Valley, Utah. Sarah joined him but was "sick nearly all the time." After three years, Charles moved Sarah back to Salt Lake City. He remained in Bear Lake.[11]

At age seventy-eight, Sarah described herself as "getting old and feeble." Shortly before her death in 1893, she wrote to her children,

> I know, dear children, that the principles of Mormonism, as it is called, are true. I know that Joseph Smith was a prophet of God. How do I know it you may ask? I know it by hearing him prophesy what was coming, and have lived to see the things prophesied about come to pass. I have seen the sick healed by his administration; and in answer to his prayers, I have seen many miracles performed in this Church. . . . The

---

7 Rich, "Autobiography."
8 Rich, "Autobiography."
9 Rich, "Autobiography."
10 Rich, "Autobiography."
11 Rich, "Autobiography."

Lord has established His work and His Church on the earth now in the last days never to be taken from the earth until He comes Himself to dwell with the Saints.[12]

**A Bridge to the Past**
Sarah was blessed with many gifts of the Spirit. From her first reading of the Book of Mormon, she knew it was true. She recognized her husband-to-be without anyone pointing him out to her. From an inspired dream, she knew the exact day the missionaries would be at her home. She was healed of health issues by the administration of the priesthood. She was prepared to receive gifts of the Spirit and to be the wife of an Apostle of the Lord Jesus Christ. The seventh Article of Faith reads, "We believe in the gift of tongues, prophecy, revelation, visions, healing, interpretation of tongues, and so forth." Having gifts of the Spirit is one of the signs that "follow them that believe."[13] Gifts of the Spirit include knowledge, wisdom, faith to be healed, the working of miracles, discernment of spirits, and a witness of Jesus Christ and His Atonement.

---

12  Rich, "Autobiography."
13  Mark 16:17.

# Jane Snyder Richards

(1823–1912)

---

Jane wrote of the first time she saw Joseph Smith:

> The first time I ever saw Joseph Smith I recognized him, from a dream I had had. He had such angelic countenance as I never saw before. He was then thirty-seven years of age, of ordinary appearance in dress and manner, a child-like appearance of innocence. His hair was of a light brown, blue eyes and light complexioned. His natural demeanor was quiet, his character and disposition was formed by his life['s] work, he was kind and considerate, taking a personal interest in all his people, considering every one his equal. We were regular in our attendance at the meetings, and [I] was always anxious to hear Brother Joseph.[1]

---

Jane was the last in her family to be baptized. Her reason for waiting to be baptized was that she couldn't think of any serious sins she needed to be forgiven of. It wasn't until she became bedridden and feared death that she changed her mind. Jane wrote,

---

1 "Reminiscences of Mrs. F. D. Richards," as cited in Mark L. McConkie, *Remembering Joseph: Personal Recollections of Those Who Knew the Prophet Joseph Smith* (Salt Lake City: Deseret Book, 2003), 34–35.

> At this time my brother Robert [Snyder] had fasted for days on my account; he asked me if he could lay his hands on me and pray for me. I could not speak but nodded to him, he did so. I could then see for the first time that he had received the Gospel of the Lord Jesus and that God had blessed him with the gift of healing. I could then see it was my duty to be baptized.[2]

In 1841, at age eighteen, Jane met Franklin Dewey Richards. He was "a talented, faithful young Elder about twenty years old, about two years older than myself," Jane wrote. They were married on December 18, 1842, in Nauvoo. When she reflected on her days in Nauvoo, memories of Joseph Smith were second only to thoughts of her husband and the children who blessed her home. Jane wrote,

> As Prophet he seemed to understand, and was able to foretell the mysteries of the future with a marked degree of accuracy. . . . As Seer and Revelator he was fearless and outspoken, yet humble, never considering that he was more than the mouthpiece through whom God spoke. As the leader of his people he was ever active and progressive but always modest and considerate of them and their trying circumstances. Socially he was an ideal of affability and always approachable to the humblest of his acquaintances.[3]

With her first child in arms, Jane attended the August 8, 1844, meeting in which Brigham Young stood transfigured before the congregation. It was reported,

> [Jane] was sitting in the meeting and had bent over to pick up a small plaything dropped by her little daughter, when President Young uttered the first words of his address. His voice was that of the Prophet. On hearing it, she was so startled that she dropped the article she had just taken from the floor, and on looking up beheld the form and features of the martyred Seer.[4]

---

2  Jane S. Richards, "Autobiography," FamilySearch.
3  Jane S. Richards, "Joseph Smith, the Prophet," *Young Woman's Journal* 16, no. 12 (December 1905), 550.
4  "Jane Snyder Richards," in Orson F. Whitney, *History of Utah*, 4 vols. (Salt Lake City: G. Q. Cannon & Sons Company, 1904), 582.

Jane fled from religious persecution in Nauvoo to the Territory of Iowa. She then journeyed across Iowa to reach Winter Quarters. From that Latter-day Saint outpost, she traveled with the Willard Richards Company to the Salt Lake Valley in 1848. "I can't here undertake to describe the great sufferings and privation of food and cold for want of a comfortable house that I passed through after three months sickness on the way," she wrote.[5]

Due to poor health, in 1849, Jane received a priesthood blessing from Willard Richards of the First Presidency of the Church. "From that moment I began to recover," she wrote. In a later priesthood blessing administered by her husband and Daniel Spencer, Jane was promised, "Sister Richards, you shall live, and I say unto you arise and walk and leave your sickness in this bed, it shall not come out of the bed with you." She "walked about the room, and the happy feeling which I enjoyed is impossible for me to describe. From this time I gained my strength right along and had no more sickness."[6]

Her husband, Franklin, a member of the Quorum of the Twelve Apostles, was often away from her for long periods of time, serving missions and helping with Church matters. During his absences, Jane was filled with loneliness and struggles.

By 1869, she had moved to Ogden, Utah, to be with Franklin, who was presiding over Church branches in that area. Unfortunately, Jane was ill most of the time, being confined to bed. She wrote, "I was so very low for months that my life was despaired of and many times during this period my husband and children stood round the bed in tears, as it seemed to me that my time had come and I must leave them. Medicine and doctors afforded me no relief."[7]

After another miraculous recovery, Jane was called to preside over the Relief Society in Ogden. She wrote,

> This I attempted to decline but their answer was, "The Lord has raised you from a bed of sickness to do us good, and we want you to accept the office." After being entreated in this manner for weeks I accepted the office with reluctance, feeling my inability to fill such a responsible position. I entered upon my duties with fear and trembling and trusted in the Lord to aid me in the arduous duty, whose assistance I fully realized. Having left my home many times feeling weak and feeble to

---

5 Richards, "Autobiography."
6 Richards, "Autobiography."
7 Richards, "Autobiography."

attend my meetings, I have returned home feeling the strength of a Samson.

> I can say in regard to all of my Society duties, that I have been blessed more than I have power to express, and have felt it a pleasure to do what little good I could knowing that it was my Heavenly Father in whom I trusted that gave me the ability.[8]

At age fifty-eight, Jane wrote of her children and their faithfulness to the Lord—

> I had my children all blessed and named when eight days old. . . . They were also baptized when eight years old and confirmed members of the Church of Jesus Christ of Latter Day Saints. They also received their endowments in the House of the Lord at an early age and were all married by the Celestial Law, they are firm believers in the gifts of the Gospel, have great faith in administration by laying on of hands for the healing of the sick. . . . I rejoice greatly with my children and my earnest prayer is that they will keep the faith and live and die in the faith of this Gospel.[9]

Jane died in 1912 at age eighty-nine, having been "one of the best known women of Utah."[10]

## A Bridge to the Past

In spite of years of poor health, through the administration of the priesthood, Jane was raised up from her bed of sickness to do much good. Are you willing to abandon your bed of nails? It isn't always easy, but it is worth it—for opportunities to serve await. As lyricist Will L. Thompson asked,

> Have I done any good in the world today?
> Have I helped any one in need?
> Have I cheered up the sad and made someone feel glad?
> If not, I have failed indeed.

---

8   Richards, "Autobiography."
9   Richards, "Autobiography."
10  "Sterling Tribute to Jane S. Richards," *Deseret Evening News*, February 1, 1910.

Has anyone's burden been lighter today?
Because I was willing to share?
Have the sick and the weary been helped on their way?
When they needed my help was I there?[11]

---

[11] "Have I Done Any Good," *Hymns*, no. 223.

## *Katharine Smith Salisbury*

(1813–1900)

---

IN A PATRIARCHAL BLESSING GIVEN to Katharine by her father Joseph Smith Sr., she was promised, "Thy name shall be had in remembrance among the pure in heart; for thou shalt live to a good old age, and depart to rest with thy Redeemer when thou art satisfied with this life."[1]

---

Katharine was the daughter of Joseph Sr. and Lucy Mack Smith. She was the last survivor of Joseph Smith's siblings. She was age six in the spring of 1820 and age ten when her brother Joseph had his first interview with the angel Moroni. She was age fourteen when Joseph brought the gold plates home on September 22, 1827. She recalled that event and the persecution that followed:

> We got a chest and locked the records up in the house. From that time on our house was searched all around; and our field and our wheat stacks were searched. The mob was around our house nearly every night, and one night they went into father's cooper shop and tore up his floor and dug the

---

[1] H. Michael Marquardt, *Early Patriarchal Blessings of The Church of Jesus Christ of Latter-day Saints* (Salt Lake City: The Smith-Pettit Foundation, 2007), 18.

earth up. And from that time until we went to Pennsylvania we had to keep watch for the enemy.²

Although her recollection is questioned, it shows Katharine's awareness of the gold plates and problems faced by her family in Palmyra. According to her grandson Herbert S. Salisbury, Katharine spoke of seeing "a package on the table containing the gold plates. . . . She said she hefted those plates and found them very heavy like gold and also rippled her fingers up the edge of the plates and felt that they were separate metal plates and heard the tinkle of sound that they made."³

These early recollections evidence Katharine's great interest and faith in the coming forth of the Book of Mormon.

As a teenager, Katharine moved with her family from Palmyra/Manchester to Waterloo near Fayette, New York. It was in Fayette that Katharine met Wilkins "Jenkins" Salisbury, a lawyer and a blacksmith by trade. Katharine attended worship services with Jenkins at the Fayette Branch.

She and Jenkins responded to the prophetic call to gather in Ohio. Soon after their arrival in Kirtland, Ohio, they were married on June 8, 1831, by Sidney Rigdon. Unfortunately, their marriage was fraught with difficulties. George A. Smith wrote of one difficulty on the march with Zion's Camp to Missouri: "I put [my musket] into the baggage wagon. When I arrived at camp in the evening my gun could not be found . . . my gun was pawned for whisky by one of our company, and have always believed that Jenkins Salisbury was the culprit."⁴ His assumption was not without merit. Jenkins was later expelled from the Church for intemperance.

In a patriarchal blessing given to Katharine by her father, Joseph Smith Sr., he spoke of problems in her marital relationship: "My heart mourns for thee in consequence of the transgression of thy husband; yea, my soul is grieved that he should suffer himself to be led away from his holy calling."⁵ Jenkins mended his ways and was called to the First Quorum of the Seventy. Unfortunately, his

---

2  "An Angel told Him: Joseph Smith's Aged Sister tells about Moroni's Talk," *Kansas City Times*, April 11, 1895, as cited in Kyle R. Walker, ed., *United by Faith: The Joseph Sr. and Lucy Mack Smith Family* (American Fork, UT: Covenant Communications, Inc., 2005), 310–11.
3  "Prophet's Sister testifies She lifted the B of M Plates," *Messenger* [Berkeley, CA], October 1954, in Larry E. Morris, "Empirical as Witnesses of the Gold Plates," *Dialogue: A Journal of Mormon Thought* 52, no. 2 (Summer 2019), 63.
4  George A. Smith, "History of George Albert Smith: Zion's Camp," May 16–May 22, 1834, as cited in Walker, *United by Faith*, 316.
5  Marquardt, *Early Patriarchal Blessings*, 18.

repentance was short-lived. In 1836, he was charged with "unchristian like conduct." At a Church trial held to examine the charge, his brothers-in-law Joseph and Hyrum Smith reported Jenkins neglected his family and ill-treated Katharine. Others spoke of strong liquor. Jenkins was excommunicated and listed on Church records as an "apostate."6

Although Jenkins faltered in faithfulness and personal responsibilities, he and Katharine continued to live near the faithful in the Kirtland area and later in Missouri. They were among those who fled with the Saints from Missouri to the banks of the Mississippi River. Katharine, like her sister-in-law Emma Smith, carried small children in her arms across the frozen Mississippi to reach Quincy, Illinois.

Katharine and her family settled in Plymouth, Illinois. Jenkins supported the family as a blacksmith. Katharine recalled that he "often received coon skins and maple sugar in exchange for work at the anvil."7 She also recalled the kindness of her brothers Joseph and Hyrum: "Whenever there was a church celebration or any big doings at Nauvoo they would always send for me."8 In January 1843, the Prophet Joseph and Willard Richards visited Katharine in her home at Plymouth. Willard Richards wrote of her poverty: "While there my heart was pained to see a sister of Joseph's almost barefoot and four lovely children entirely so, in the middle of a severe winter."9

By spring of 1845, Katharine and her family were destitute. They were also dissenters from The Church of Jesus Christ of Latter-day Saints. In September 1845, Katharine said, "We were considered by Brigham apostates. . . . Myself and husband did not believe in Brigham taking Joseph's place."10 When the Saints moved west, she and her family remained in Illinois.

Jenkins died of typhoid fever in October 1853. Four years later, Katharine married Joseph Young, whose faith wavered much like Jenkins Salisbury's had. Their marriage was brief. Young moved on to Iowa. As for Katharine, she put down deep roots in Fountain Green, Illinois, where she was known as Katharine Salisbury.

---

6   Journal History, April 9, 1837, as cited in Walker, *United by Faith*, 317.
7   Herbert S. Salisbury, "Reminiscences of Joseph Smith: As told by His Sister, Catherine Smith-Salisbury, to Her Grandson, Herbert S. Salisbury," as cited in Walker, *United by Faith*, 321.
8   "A Sister of the Prophet," *Carthage Republican*, May 16, 1894, 5, as cited in Walker, *United by Faith*, 321.
9   Smith, *History of the Church*, 5:247.
10  Letter of Katharine Salisbury, February 26, 1889, as cited in Walker, *United by Faith*, 325.

On April 29, 1871, Katharine wrote to Brigham Young, asking for $200 to help defray the cost of building a home. Brigham Young sent the money along with expressions of concern for any Smith who remained in Illinois. (Word had been received by Brigham that Katharine and other Smith relatives were being persecuted because of their familial relationship to the Prophet Joseph.) Katharine wrote to Brigham informing him that his generosity had "created a great desire within me and Some of my family to come out there and make you all a visit. I would like very much to See you all once more before we depart this life. May the blessings of heaven rest upon you and all the church."[11]

As to her improved circumstance, a granddaughter wrote,

> Our grandmother Catherine lived very comfortably on her little farm with her youngest son Frederick to do the farming. She always kept a cow or two for her milk & butter and a few chickens for eggs, selling the surplus eggs with which she bought the extra groceries needed, such as tea, sugar, flour etc. She also had a great carpet loom on which she wove carpet & rugs for her floors & for her neighbors which brought in the needed change [money] for clothing etc.[12]

When her children and grandchildren expressed interest in religion, they attended worship services of the Reorganized Church of Jesus Christ of Latter Day Saints. By the summer of 1872, Katharine had joined them. On June 17, 1873, she was baptized and confirmed a member of the Reorganization by Joseph Smith III. Katharine died of pneumonia on February 2, 1900.

## A Bridge to the Past

Katharine had a difficult marriage. In her patriarchal blessing, Father Smith said, "My heart mourns for thee in consequence of the transgression of thy husband." Katharine remained with her husband and was ill-treated and lived in abject poverty. Through it all, Katharine persevered and was well-loved for her efforts. Brigham Young was concerned about her and sent Katharine $200 to defray the cost of building a home. Through her experiences, we know being proactive in relieving sorrow is better than watching sorrow from the sidelines. As to when to relieve sorrow, I recall the story of parents

---

11  Katharine Salisbury to Brigham Young, May 28, 1871, as cited in Walker, *United by Faith*, 333.
12  Autobiography of Mary Salisbury Hancock (1963), 2, as cited in Walker, *United by Faith*, 338.

who took their young son to his first symphony concert. He was fascinated by the musician who played the cymbals. After the performance, the parents took the little boy backstage to speak with the cymbal player. The boy asked him, "What do you have to know to play the cymbals?" The musician said, "The one thing you must know is when."[13] When to be proactive in relieving sorrow is now.

---

13  Binford Winston Gilbert, *The Pastoral Care of Depression: A Guidebook* (NY: Haworth Pastoral Press, 1998), 57.

# *Patty Bartlett Sessions*

(1795–1892)

---

Patty found inspiration in reading the scriptures: "I have been reading [the] book of Mormon and the spirit of the Lord rests upon me. Although alone by myself I am happy." As she closed the scriptures, she often pondered their message: "My meditation is sweet and my prayer is that the Holy Ghost will be poured out upon the servants of God that they may ferret out evil until we become a just people." She also found joy in reading her journal entries: "I am here alone. I have been reading my journal and I feel to thank the Lord that I have passed through what I have. I have gained an experience I could have gained no other way."[1]

---

On February 4, 1795, Patty was born in the small township of Bethel, Maine. Her father, Enoch Bartlett, toiled as a cobbler, and her mother, Anna, worked as a weaver. At age seventeen, Patty was married to David Sessions in the Methodist church in Newry, Maine. Of the eight children born to their union, five died as infants from epidemics that swept through their small town. The children who survived to adulthood were Perrigrine, Sylvia, and David.

Patty made many sacrifices for her religious beliefs after being baptized a member of The Church of Jesus Christ of Latter-day Saints in 1834. By 1837,

---

[1] Patty Sessions, as quoted in Elizabeth Willis, "Voice in the Wilderness: The Diaries of Patty Sessions," *Journal of American Folklore* 101, no. 399 (1988), 43–45.

she, her husband, and their three children had left the quiet familiarity of Maine to reside in Kirtland, Ohio, among the Saints of God. Within a year, the Sessions were brutally forced from their home by mobs. In 1838, they faced the same thing in Far West, Missouri, where again they were confronted with religious hostility. An extermination order issued by Governor Lilburn W. Boggs of Missouri against all Latter-day Saints within the state's borders brought the horrors of war to Patty's doorstep. She and her family were forced to abandon their holdings in Missouri—an estimated loss of $1,200 in land and $400 in livestock and corn.

As religious exiles, Patty and her family suffered for want of shelter and food. For fourteen days, they had nothing to eat but parched corn. Their appetites were not satisfied until they crossed the Mississippi River and found people in Quincy, Illinois, anxious to minister to their needs. After a brief sojourn in Quincy, the Sessions family settled in Nauvoo. In beautiful Nauvoo, they found a brief haven of peace, a refuge from the storms of hate and bigotry experienced in Ohio and Missouri.

However, as threats of extermination loomed again, Elder Orson Pratt advised, "Brethren awake! . . . Let every branch in the east, west, north, and south, be determined to flee out of Babylon either by land or by sea."[2] The call to move on was familiar to Patty, but this move was particularly painful for her. Her husband, David, was asked to go ahead of her and build bridges across rivers in the Territory of Iowa. She was to bring her children and follow in a few weeks. Her children refused to leave Nauvoo when she was ready to move on. Throughout the terrors she had faced in Ohio and Missouri, Patty had been comforted by a solicitous husband and obedient children. The decision to journey with the Saints to the uncharted West entailed a greater sacrifice of saying goodbye to loved ones. Although the choice was difficult, she followed her convictions. "I desire to do right and live my religion that I may enjoy the light to see as I am seen and know as I am known. O my Father, help me to live my religion, this is my greatest desire."[3]

For Patty Sessions, it was an Abrahamic test with all the emotional ramifications of refining fire and fuller's soap to leave Nauvoo and head west without her children. Although her youngest child was an adult, nearly twenty-three years of age, her decision was not easy. She was handed a simple parting gift— a small notebook from her daughter Sylvia. The inscription on the notebook read, "A Day Book, given to me, Patty Sessions, by Sylvia . . . this 10th day of

---

2   Orson Pratt quote in Smith, *History of the Church*, 7:516.
3   Willis, "Voice in the Wilderness," 45.

February, 1846. Patty Sessions, her book. I am now fifty-one years six days old. February 10, 1846, City of Joseph, Hancock County, Illinois."[4]

As Patty made entries in her daybook, she revealed sorrow and joy, unwavering faith, and unselfish deeds. Although her literary talents pale in comparison to those of her friend and poetess Eliza R. Snow, they led historian Leonard J. Arrington to label Patty as "a remarkable blend of things temporal and spiritual."[5] Her day-to-day notations evidence the Lord's promise that "by small means the Lord can bring about great things."[6]

Although Patty disregarded proper spelling, grammar, and punctuation, her brief entries weave a tale of courageous adventure as a pioneer traveling from the Mississippi River to the Rocky Mountains. One journal entry reveals her joy at receiving letters "from my children in Nauvoo. I read them with joy and gratitude to God for the privilege of hearing from them. Have read Perrigrine's letter to Brigham. He says they will all get away soon."[7]

By centering her life on Jesus Christ, Patty found abiding happiness in months of familial loneliness. "I am happy all the time," she penned.[8] When her happiness was tested, she wrote, "I have been in the cold and in the mud. There is no food for our teams but browse. I never have felt so bad as now, but I am not discouraged yet."[9] When she penned, "My health's poor, my mind weighed down," she concluded the entry with, "but my heart is in God."[10]

On the arduous trek, Patty found the answer to the question philosophers and sages have pondered through the centuries—what is the secret to a happy life? On the trek west, she wrote, "About six o-clock in the morning I was called for to go back two miles. It then snowed. I rode behind the men through mud and water, some of the way belly deep to the horse. I found the sister that I was called to see in an old log cabin."[11] In her journal entry of March 6, 1846, she penned, "I go back ten miles this morning to see Sarah Ann. She

---

4   Patty Bartlett Sessions, Daybook, as quoted in Claire Augusta Wilcox Noall, *Guardians of the Hearth: Utah's Pioneer Midwives and Women Doctors* (Bountiful, UT: Horizon Publishers, 1974), 22.
5   Leonard J. Arrington, "Persons for All Seasons: Women in Mormon History," *BYU Studies* 20 (Fall 1979), 44.
6   1 Nephi 16:29.
7   Noall, *Guardians*, 25.
8   Noall, *Guardians*, 37.
9   Noall, *Guardians*, 26.
10  Noall, *Guardians*, 26.
11  Noall, *Guardians*, 25.

was sick. Sent for me. I rode horseback."[12] She later recorded, "Was sent for to go back two miles to a sick woman, Sister Stewart. I asked her [for] no pay."[13] She also wrote of helping men who complained of blistered feet, ague, and muscle cramps:

        Mar. 9, Ezra Benson . . . . . . . . 2.00

        Mar. 11, A. P. Rockwood . . . . . 1.00/1.50

        Oct. 1, Erastus Snow . . . . . . . . paid 2.00

        Dec. 8, Wilford Woodruff . . . . paid 2.00

        Feb. 6, Newel K. Whitney . . . . paid 2.00[14]

Of her medical service, none brought her more notoriety than delivering babies. Two days after entering the Salt Lake Valley, she assisted in the birth of a son to Harriet Page Young. She believed caring for that mother and son was the fulfillment of a prophetic promise given her in Nauvoo: "It was said to me more than five months ago that my hands should be the first to handle the first-born son in the place of rest for the Saints, even in the City of God." She recorded, "I have come more than one thousand miles to do it since it was spoken."[15]

It is estimated that Patty Sessions delivered fourteen babies in the Salt Lake Fort that first winter. Near the end of the year, Thomas Bullock reported, "'Mother Sessions' has had a harvest of 138 little cherubs since living in the valley. Many cases of twins; in a row of seven houses joining each other, eight births in one week."[16] Death was a painful reminder to Patty of her limited medical knowledge, especially the death of her husband, David, in 1850.

In her later years, she founded the Patty Sessions Academy to provide children with an education at no cost. She also pursued her talents as a seamstress—from the basics of carding, spinning, and weaving to the more sophisticated process of creating clothes, rugs, and comforters. She also spent time reading: "I take 3 papers: *Deseret News*, *Juvenile Instructor* and *Woman's Exponent*. I read them all."[17] On December 18, 1892, Patty died at age ninety-seven. The

---

12   Noall, *Guardians*, 23.
13   Noall, *Guardians*, 26–27.
14   Noall, *Guardians*, 35–36.
15   Noall, *Guardians*, 40.
16   Noall, *Guardians*, 42.
17   Noall, *Guardians*, 51.

*Deseret Evening News* printed, "She has gone to her grave, ripe in years, loved and respected by all who knew her."[18]

## A Bridge to the Past
Patty enjoyed her own company. She was happy when circumstances dictated another emotion would be more appropriate. The scriptures tell us that the tree of life has fruit that "was desirable to make one happy,"[19] and those who keep commandments unto the end shall "dwell with God in a state of never-ending happiness."[20] Patty didn't discover a 24/7 giddy happiness but a happiness found in blessedness—a confidence that her life was worthwhile and that she was on the right path.

---

18  "A Remarkable Woman," *Deseret Evening News*, December 22, 1892.
19  1 Nephi 8:10.
20  Mosiah 2:41.

## Amanda Barnes Smith

(1809–1886)

"The journey [from Kirtland to Missouri] lasted about six months as we were forced to stop at time and work to get food and clothes," wrote Amanda. "We were often threatened on the way and sometimes traveled at night and laid over during the day to avoid mobs. . . . We were stopped by a mob; they told us that if we went another step, they would kill us all. They took our guns from us. . . . They took us back five miles, placed a guard around us, kept us three days and then let us go. I thought—Is this our boasted land of liberty?"[1]

---

Amanda's father was an honorable man but not religious. Her mother was a devout Presbyterian. Amanda was a Campbellite, having been baptized by Sidney Rigdon. When she was married at age eighteen to Warren Smith, he tolerated her religious choice but was not pleased. It was not until Latter-day Saint missionary Simeon Carter preached the gospel of Jesus Christ in April 1831 that the young couple found commonality in religion. Soon after their baptisms, they moved to Kirtland, Ohio. Amanda wrote of her husband, "He enjoyed himself well, done all he could to establish the bank and build the temple." With the failure of the Kirtland bank, Warren and Amanda lost their financial base and property but not their faith. They packed up their meager belongings and stopped in Amherst, Ohio, to bid family farewell as they were

---

1 "Highlights in the Life of Amanda Barnes Smith," FamilySearch.

moving on to Missouri to be with the Saints of God. Amanda wrote, "The treatment we received will never be forgotten. . . . My mother said she hoped she should never see me, hear of me nor hear my name mentioned in the world again."[2]

Amanda and her family left Ohio and ventured toward Missouri, settling in Hawn's Mill. On the morning of October 30, Warren pitched a tent next to the blacksmith's shop, not knowing that a mob of some 240 men were marching toward Hawn's Mill. At about 4:00 p.m., Amanda saw the men and ran to the blacksmith shop to warn those inside. But as balls began to pierce the air, she was too late. She grasped the hands of her daughters and ran to the woods. "I ran down the bank and crossed the mill pond on a [wood] plank, ran up the hill on the other side into the bushes and bullets whistled by me like hailstones and cut down the bushes on all sides of me," she wrote.[3] Although bullets passed through her clothing, Amanda was not harmed. For two hours, she and her daughters hid from the mob.

As for her sons Sardius and Alma, when the mob opened fire on the blacksmith shop, the boys crawled under the bellows for protection. Sardius survived the first attack on the shop but not the second. During the second attack, one man put a rifle to his head and fired, killing him instantly. Amanda's husband, Warren, was shot in the initial attack and dragged across the floor by a man trying to yank off his boots. He died a few moments later.

Unaware of these horrific events, when gunfire ceased, Amanda went back to Hawn's Mill to search for her sons and her husband. When she saw her oldest son, Willard, come out of the blacksmith shop carrying the body of his six-year-old brother, Amanda cried, "O! my Alma is dead!" Her son exclaimed, "No, mother; I think Alma is not dead. But father and brother Sardius are killed!"[4]

"My husband and son murdered; another little son seemingly mortally wounded; and perhaps before the dreadful night should pass the murderers would return and complete their work! But I could not weep then," wrote Amanda.[5] She prayed, "O, Thou who hearest the prayers of the widow and

---

2   Journal of Amanda Barnes Smith, FamilySearch.
3   *Heroines of "Mormondom": The Second Book of the Noble Women's Lives Series* (Salt Lake City: Juvenile Instructor Office, 1884), 88.
4   Edward W. Tullidge, *The Women of Mormondom* (New York: Tullidge and Crandall, 1877), 122.
5   Tullidge, *Women of Mormondom*, 122–23.

fatherless, what shall I do? Thou knowest my inexperience, Thou seest my poor, wounded boy, what shall I do? Heavenly Father, direct me!"[6]

Amanda heard a voice tell her to go to the smoldering fire, take warm ashes, and make lye, then pour the lye into a cloth and put it on the boy's wound. In faith, Amanda prepared the cloth and pressed it into the wound again and again until the wound was clean. "Having done as directed I again prayed to the Lord and was again instructed as distinctly as though a physician had been standing by speaking to me."[7] She was told to make a poultice of slippery elm. This she did and placed the poultice on the wound. After being assured that her little boy was out of danger, she began to look for the dead. Upon finding her son Sardius, she wrapped him in a sheet and, with the help of her eldest son, placed his body down an open well to protect it from further mutilation by the mob.

Amanda then returned to her injured son. By this point, she had determined to remain in Hawn's Mill until her son was well enough to travel. In the days and weeks that followed, Amanda faced further harassment. During this most turbulent time, she talked with her son about faith.

> "Alma, my child," I said, "you believe that the Lord made your hip?"
>
> "Yes, mother."
>
> "Well, the Lord can make something there in the place of your hip, don't you believe he can, Alma?"
>
> "Do you think that the Lord can, mother?" inquired the child, in his simplicity.
>
> "Yes, my son," I replied, "he has shown it all to me in a vision."[8]

Alma survived the ordeal and was walking within weeks. Amanda believed that a flexible cartilage had grown in the place of the missing joint. His recovery remained a marvel to all, especially physicians. Alma was never a cripple. He served a mission without the least physical impairment.

On February 1, 1839, Amanda and her four surviving children left the state of Missouri. They settled in Nauvoo, Illinois, where Amanda married another man, also named Warren Smith. She bore him three children before their divorce.

---

6  *Heroines of "Mormondom,"* 91.
7  Tullidge, *Women of Mormondom*, 124.
8  Tullidge, *Women of Mormondom*, 128.

Amanda was a member of the Female Relief Society of Nauvoo. In the summer of 1842, she accompanied Emma Smith and Eliza R. Snow on their journey to Quincy, Illinois, to see Governor Thomas Carlin. They presented to the governor a petition signed by the women of the Relief Society asking for protection of the Prophet Joseph Smith from illegal suits pending against him.

When religious persecution raged in Nauvoo, Amanda took her children to the Territory of Iowa. In 1850, they journeyed to the Salt Lake Valley. In the valley, Amanda became president of the Salt Lake 12th Ward Relief Society. A few months before her death, she moved to Richmond, Utah, to live with her daughter Alvira Hendricks. Amanda died of paralysis on June 30, 1886, in Richmond at age seventy-seven. Historian Andrew Jenson wrote of her, "Amanda Smith was beloved by all who knew her good works and sterling qualities. She was ever unflinching and firm in her faith in the gospel."[9]

**A Bridge to the Past**

Few can match the courage of Amanda when she cared for her son with militia looking on after the massacre at Hawn's Mill. Her courage is what legends are made of. She had the Lord on her side. We, too, have the Lord on our side when courage is needed most.

---

9   Andrew Jenson, *Latter-day Saint Biographical Encyclopedia: A Compilation of Biographical Sketches of Prominent Men and Women in the Church of Jesus Christ of Latter-day Saints* (Salt Lake City: Andrew Jenson History, 1914), 2:797.

*Bathsheba W. Smith*

(1822–1910)

---

WHEN THE FEMALE RELIEF SOCIETY of Nauvoo was organized on March 17, 1842, eighteen-year-old Bathsheba Smith was the youngest woman present. She wrote of Joseph Smith being at a Relief Society meeting: "He opened the meeting by prayer. His voice trembled very much, after which he addressed us. He said: 'According to my prayer I will not be with you long to teach and instruct you; and the world will not be troubled with me much longer.'"[1] She later wrote, "I stood face to face with a prophet of the living God, and I had no doubt in my mind about his authority."[2]

---

Bathsheba had a refined Southern childhood. She was reared on a three-hundred-acre homestead in Harrison County, Virginia. As she grew to maturity, Bathsheba had opportunities for schooling but found greater joy in spinning, weaving, and embroidery work. "I was somewhat religiously inclined," she said of her youth. "I attended to my secret prayers, studied to be cheerful, industrious, and happy, and was opposed to rudeness. I often attended the meetings of different sects, but did not see much difference in them. I liked to

---

1  "Recollections of the Prophet Joseph Smith," *Juvenile Instructor* 26 (1891), 345.
2  Bathsheba W. Smith, quoted in Lucy Woodruff Smith, "Past Three Score Years and Ten," *Young Woman's Journal* 12 (October 1901), 440; also quoted in *Daughters in My Kingdom: The History and Work of Relief Society* (Salt Lake City: The Church of Jesus Christ of Latter-day Saints, 2011), 34.

attend the Presbyterian meetings, because they had the handsomest church and the Reverend Mr. Bristol was so gentlemanly and pious; and could preach so eloquently."[3]

When Bathsheba was age sixteen, Latter-day Saint elders visited her neighborhood in Virginia. "I heard them preach and believed what they taught," she wrote. "I believed the Book of Mormon to be a divine record, and that Joseph Smith was a Prophet of God. I knew by the spirit of the Lord which [I] received in answer to prayer, that these things were true."[4] Bathsheba was baptized on August 21, 1837, as a member of The Church of Jesus Christ of Latter-day Saints by Elder Samuel James. Of her baptism, she wrote, "The Spirit of the Lord rested upon me, and I knew that He accepted of me as a member in His Kingdom."[5]

One of the missionaries who taught Bathsheba the gospel of Jesus Christ was Elder George A. Smith. They took a strong liking to each other and agreed that "with the blessings of the Almighty in preserving us, in three years from this time, we will be married."[6] In the meantime, George served a mission in England. As for Bathsheba,

> the spirit of gathering with the Saints in Missouri came upon me, and I became very anxious indeed to go there that fall with my sister Nancy and family. . . . I was told I could not go. This caused me to retire to bed one night feeling very sorrowful. While pondering upon what had been said to me about not going, a voice as it were said to me, "Weep not, you will go this fall." I was satisfied and comforted. The next morning I felt so contented and happy; on observing which my sister Sarah said, "You have got over feeling badly about not going to Zion this fall have you?" I quietly, but firmly replied, "I am going. You will see."[7]

In the fall of 1837, Bathsheba and her family moved from Virginia to Far West, Missouri. "On our journey the young folk of our party had much enjoyment," she wrote. "It seemed so novel and romantic to travel in wagons over

---

3   "Autobiography of Bathsheba W. Smith," 1822–1910, L. Tom Perry Special Collections, Harold B. Lee Library, Brigham Young University, Provo, Utah.
4   "Autobiography of Bathsheba W. Smith."
5   "Autobiography of Bathsheba W. Smith."
6   George Albert Smith, July 25, 1841, quoted in Janet Peterson and LaRene Gaunt, *Elect Ladies: Presidents of the Relief Society* (Salt Lake City: Deseret Book, 1990), 63.
7   "Autobiography of Bathsheba W. Smith."

hill and dale, through dense forests and over extensive prairies, and occasionally passing through towns and cities, sometimes traveling on Macadamized roads and camping in tents at night."[8] Their stay in Far West was cut short due to religious persecution and mobocracy. "In these distressing times," Bathsheba wrote, "the spirit of the Lord was with us to comfort and sustain us, and we had a sure testimony that we were being persecuted for the Gospel's sake, and that the Lord was not angry with none save those who acknowledged not his hand in all things."[9]

It was not until the spring of 1840 that Bathsheba and her family moved to Nauvoo. She recalled, "Here I continued my punctuality in attending meetings, had many opportunities of hearing Joseph Smith preach, and tried to profit by his instructions, and received many testimonies to the truth of the doctrines he taught. . . . I was present at the laying of the cornerstones of the foundation of the Nauvoo Temple, and had become acquainted with the Prophet Joseph and his family."[10] At the time, Bathsheba was "a tall, stately woman, with an abundance of beautiful brown hair, dark eyes, smooth fair complexion, . . . dignity of carriage, yet, with all that, she was easy to approach, lovable in manner. . . . She was artistic in temperament, loved the beautiful, appreciated refinement, and always dressed in good taste."[11]

Bathsheba married George Albert Smith, the elder she had met earlier in Virginia. They were married on July 25, 1841, fourteen days after he returned from his mission to England. They lived in a home given them by the Prophet Joseph Smith. Bathsheba confided in her journal, "I was ashamed to have any of my acquaintances see me in such a looking place. It had, however, the desirable qualities of neither smoking nor leaking."[12]

Her first son was born at 4:00 a.m. on July 7, 1842—George Albert Jr. Just two months later, her husband George left on another mission. During his absence, Bathesheba wrote to him often. In her letter of July 6, 1844, she wrote of the martyrdom of Joseph and Hyrum Smith:

> We have had strange times since you left. You will no doubt hear, before this reaches you, of the death of our beloved brethren Joseph and Hyrum Smith. They were killed at

---

8   "Autobiography of Bathsheba W. Smith."
9   "Autobiography of Bathsheba W. Smith."
10  "Autobiography of Bathsheba W. Smith."
11  Julia P. M. Farnsworth, "A Tribute to Bathsheba W. Smith," *Young Woman's Journal* 21 (November 1910), 608–9.
12  "Autobiography of Bathsheba W. Smith."

Carthage on the 27 of June and on the 28 they were brought home and such a day of mourning never was seen. It pains me to write such a painful tale, but the Lord has comforted our hearts in a measure.[13]

Bathsheba and her family left Nauvoo in the winter of 1846. "In company with many others, my husband took me and my two little children . . . and we crossed the Mississippi River to seek a home in the wilderness."[14] On their journey, Bathsheba was asked to remain in Winter Quarters as George journeyed back and forth to and from the Salt Lake Valley. Finally, by 1850, she and George went together to the valley.

From 1850 to 1910, Bathsheba and her family resided in the Salt Lake 13th Ward. Of her husband, George A. Smith, who was in the First Presidency of the Church, Bathsheba said, "I love my husband dearly. I believe but few in this wide world have been as happy as we have been. We have no differences, always agree on all points, our religion and our future hopes and expectations are the same."[15]

After George's death, Bathsheba turned to charitable work. She became the director of the Deseret Hospital and instigated the development of birthing hospitals throughout Utah. She presided over the women's department of the Salt Lake Temple. She served as a counselor in the presidency of the Central Board of the General Relief Society from 1888 to 1892 and in the presidency from 1892 to 1901. In 1901, she was called to be the president of the General Relief Society.

Bathsheba died on September 20, 1910, at age 88, the last of the original twenty members of the Female Relief Society of Nauvoo. Over 6,000 people attended her funeral. Anthon H. Lund of the First Presidency spoke:

> She lived the pure life of a saint. She never wavered or halted. She tasted the bitterness of adversity, passed through persecution and also enjoyed prosperous days, but whether in the days of adversity or the days of prosperity, we always found her the same. She was never depressed and there was always sunshine in her heart. Her faith was built on the rock of ages and was never shaken.[16]

---

13 Bathsheba W. Smith to George A. Smith, July 6, 1844, quoted in Peterson and Gaunt, *Elect Ladies*, 67.
14 "Autobiography of Bathsheba W. Smith."
15 "Autobiography of Bathsheba W. Bigler Smith," quoted in Diane Hill Zimmerman, *Mormon Pioneers of Harrison County (now West) Virginia in the 1830s* (n.p., 1997), 35.
16 "Glowing Tribute to Saintly Life," *Salt Lake Herald-Republican*, September 26, 1910.

## A Bridge to the Past

Bathsheba fell in love with missionary George A. Smith. Promises were made and years passed before their marriage. Of their marriage, Bathsheba said, "I love my husband dearly. I believe but few in this wide world have been as happy as we have been." In The Family: A Proclamation to the World, the First Presidency and Quorum of the Twelve Apostles said, "Successful marriages and families are established and maintained on principles of faith, prayer, repentance, forgiveness, respect, love, compassion, work, and wholesome recreational activities."[17]

---

17 "The Family: A Proclamation to the World," *Ensign* or *Liahona*, Nov. 2010, 29.

## Emma Hale Smith

(1804–1879)

---

EMMA SMITH TOLD HER SON Joseph Smith III:

> My belief is that the Book of Mormon is of divine authenticity—I have not the slightest doubt of it. I am satisfied that no man could have dictated the writing of the manuscripts unless he was inspired; for, when acting as his scribe, your father would dictate to me hour after hour; and when returning after meals, or after interruptions, he could at once begin where he had left off, without either seeing the manuscript or having any portion of it read to him. This was a usual thing for him to do. It would have been improbable that a learned man could do this; and, for one so ignorant and unlearned as he was, it was simply impossible.[1]

---

Emma is arguably the most famous Latter-day Saint woman of the nineteenth century. Much has been spoken and written of her life—both positive and negative. The topic of her life has left more than one writer frustrated because Emma did not keep a journal, write an autobiography, or pen vignettes of

---

1   Joseph Smith III, "Last Testimony of Sister Emma," *Saints' Herald* 26, no. 19 (October 1, 1879), 289.

key life events. Such omissions have left biographers looking to the collected works of those who knew her best.

Those who knew of her suffering at the hands of outraged mobs and of her anguish at the deaths of infants seldom wrote of her heartaches. Although they were recipients of her generosity and kindness and witnessed her loyalty to her husband Joseph, she in no way dominated their writings. The extant letters exchanged between Joseph and Emma and letters between Emma and her second husband, Lewis Bidamon, and those of her children are filled with short snippets of life's experiences but leave the inquisitive wanting more.

In turning to primary sources, Joseph Smith's journal entries provide factual information but precious little commentary. To the Prophet Joseph, she was "my beloved Emma—she that was my wife, even the wife of my youth, and the choice of my heart . . . undaunted, firm, and unwavering—unchangeable, affectionate Emma!"[2] Joseph's journal entries tell of his attentive care of her: "Emma began to be sick with fever; consequently I kept in the house with her all day. . . . Emma is no better. I was with her all day. . . . Emma was a little better."[3] His journal entries are replete with notations of their time together: "Spent the forenoon chiefly in conversation with Emma on various subjects, and in reading my history with her—both felt in good spirits and very cheerful."[4] His letters reveal abiding love for Emma: "I would gladly go from here to you barefoot, and bareheaded, and half naked, to see you and think it great pleasure."[5] It is not surprising that Joseph pled on behalf of Emma and their children: "Have mercy, O Lord, upon [my] wife and children, that they may be exalted in thy presence, and preserved by thy fostering hand."[6]

Emma was the first to know that Joseph received the gold plates from the angel Moroni. In her home in Harmony, Pennsylvania, the plates "often lay on the table without any attempt at concealment, wrapped in a small linen tablecloth, which I had given him to fold them in. I once felt of the plates, as they thus lay on the table, tracing their outline and shape."[7] She was the only woman to scribe the Book of Mormon translation. Joseph wrote, "[I] have commenced translating again, and Emma writes for me."[8] Emma recalled that

---

2   Smith, *History of the Church*, 5:107.
3   Smith, 5:165–66.
4   Smith, 5:92.
5   Joseph Smith, Letter to Emma Smith, April 4, 1839. Joseph Smith Papers.
6   D&C 109:69.
7   Smith, "Last Testimony of Sister Emma," 290.
8   Lucy Mack Smith, "Lucy Mack Smith, History, 1845," page 138, josephsmithpapers.org.

as Joseph was translating, "even the word *Sarah* he could not pronounce at first." He asked, "Emma, did Jerusalem have walls around it?" When she informed him that it had, Joseph replied, "Oh! I was afraid I had been deceived."[9]

Emma's testimony of the Book of Mormon and the prophetic calling of Joseph led to her baptism on June 28, 1830, by Oliver Cowdery. When asked years later about reasons behind her decision to be baptized, Emma said, "I know Mormonism to be the truth; and believe the Church to have been established by divine direction. I have complete faith in it."[10]

Days after Emma's baptism, in early July 1830, Joseph Smith received a revelation affirming her "sins [were] forgiven" and she was "an elect lady."[11] Emma was told in the revelation to "murmur not because of the things which thou hast not seen, for they are withheld from thee and from the world," an apparent reference to the gold plates.[12] Her "office" was to be "a comfort unto my servant, Joseph Smith, Jun., thy husband" and speak "consoling words, in the spirit of meekness" to him.[13] The revelation ended with a phrase of hope: "Lift up thy heart and rejoice, and cleave unto the covenants which thou has made. . . . A crown of righteousness thou shalt receive."[14]

On September 14, 1835, the Kirtland High Council and Presidency of the Church resolved that "Sister Emma Smith [should] proceed . . . to make a selection of sacred hymns, according to the Revelation, and that President W[illiam] W. Phelps be appointed to revise and arrange them for printing."[15] With the help of Phelps, Emma compiled the first hymnbook of the Church—*A Collection of Sacred Hymns, for the Church of the Latter Day Saints*. The total number of hymns in the hymnal was ninety, the first being "Know Then That Ev'ry Soul Is Free" and the last "The Spirit of God like a Fire is Burning." Several hymns in the original hymnal appeared in subsequent editions of the hymnal, giving Latter-day Saints an opportunity to sing the hymns of Zion selected by Emma Smith.

Emma became the mother of eleven children, raising five to adulthood. When Joseph Smith was confined in Liberty Jail, she and her children joined

---

9   Emma Smith to Edmund C. Briggs, "A Visit to Nauvoo in 1856," *Journal of History* 9 (January 1916), 454.
10  Smith, "Last Testimony of Sister Emma," 290.
11  D&C 25:3.
12  D&C 25:4.
13  D&C 25:5.
14  D&C 25:13, 15.
15  Joseph Smith History, Volume B-1, 1838–1856 [September 1, 1834–November 2, 1838], September 14, 1835, 612, The Joseph Smith Papers.

religious exiles traveling from Far West to the banks of the Mississippi River, a distance of nearly two hundred miles. On February 15, 1839, with two babies—Alexander and Frederick—in her arms and two children—Joseph and Julia—at her skirts, Emma walked across the frozen Mississippi to safety in Quincy, Illinois. In cotton bags under her dress, Emma carried Joseph's private papers and a manuscript of the inspired translation of the Bible.

On March 7, 1839, Emma wrote to Joseph,

> I shall not attempt to write my feelings altogether, for the situation in which you are, the walls, bars, and bolts, rolling rivers, running streams, rising hills, sinking valleys and spreading prairies that separate us, and the cruel injustice that first cast you into prison and still holds you there, with many other considerations, places my feelings far beyond description.
>
> Was it not for conscious innocence, and the direct interposition of divine mercy, I am very sure I never should have been able to have endured the scenes of suffering that I have passed through. . . .
>
> No one but God, knows the reflections of my mind and the feelings of my heart when I left our house and home, and almost all of every thing that we possessed excepting our little Children, and took my journey out of the State of Missouri, leaving you shut up in that lonesome prison. . . . But I hope there is better days to come to us yet.[16]

On March 21, 1839, from Liberty Jail, Joseph penned:

> Affectionate Wife . . .
>
> Dear Emma I very well know your toils and sympathize with you if God will spare my life once more to have the privilege of taking care of you I will ease your care and endeavor to comfort your heart. . . . I was in prison and ye visited me inasmuch as you have done it to the least [of] these you have done it to me these shall enter into life Eternal but no more
>
> > your Husband[17]

---

16  Letter from Emma Smith to Joseph Smith, March 7, 1839, 37, spelling standardized, The Joseph Smith Papers.

17  Letter from Joseph Smith to Emma Smith, March 21, 1839, [1, 3], spelling standardized, The Joseph Smith Papers.

## Glorious Truths about Women of the Restoration

Before many days had passed, Joseph escaped from his captors and joined Emma and their children in Quincy, Illinois. From Quincy, Joseph moved his family upriver to Commerce, where he found "the land was mostly covered with trees and bushes, and much of it so wet that it was with the utmost difficulty a foot man could get through, and totally impassible for teams." Yet with "no more eligible place, presenting itself," Joseph wrote, "I considered it wisdom to make an attempt to build up a City."[18]

In that city known as Nauvoo, Emma became the "First Lady." She graciously welcomed the poor and the acclaimed into her home. Joseph often assisted Emma with the task of feeding visitors. At a party held in their home, "twenty one [guests] sat down to the dinner table, and Emma and myself waited on them," Joseph wrote.[19] When Jesse Crosby observed Joseph doing "woman's work," he said to the prophet, "Brother Joseph, my wife does much more hard work than does your wife." Joseph replied, "If a man cannot learn in this life to appreciate a wife and do his duty by her, in properly taking care of her, he need not expect to be given one in the hereafter." Crosby wrote, "His words shut my mouth as tight as a clam. I took them as terrible reproof. After that I tried to do better by the good wife I had and tried to lighten her labors."[20]

On Thursday, March 17, 1842, Joseph organized the Female Relief Society of Nauvoo. Thirty-eight-year-old Emma Smith was elected president of the society. Joseph challenged the society to search out the needy and minister to their needs. Emma remarked, "We are going to do something *extraordinary*—when a boat is stuck on the rapids with a multitude of Mormons on board we shall consider *that* a loud call for *relief*—we expect extraordinary occasions and pressing calls."[21] Under Emma's able guidance, heavy burdens were lifted and necessities needed to sustain life freely proffered.

In a reflective mood, Joseph dictated his sentiments about Emma to his clerk William Clayton:

> With what unspeakable delight, and what transports of joy swelled my bosom, when I took by the hand on that night,

---

18   Joseph Smith History, 1838–1856, Volume C-1 [November 2, 1838–July 31, 1842], June 11, 1839, 954, The Joseph Smith Papers.
19   Joseph Smith History, 1838–1856, volume D-1 [August 1, 1842–July 1, 1843], January 18, 1843, 1455, The Joseph Smith Papers.
20   Hyrum L. Andrus and Helen Mae Andrus, comps., *They Knew the Prophet* (Salt Lake City: Bookcraft, 1999), 145.
21   Nauvoo Relief Society Minute Book, March 1842–March 1844, March 17, 1842, 12, The Joseph Smith Papers.

my beloved Emma, she that was my wife, even the wife of my youth; and the choice of my heart. Many were the re-vibrations of my mind when I contemplated for a moment the many scenes we had been called to pass through. The fatigues, and the toils, the sorrows, and sufferings, and the joys and consolations from time to time had strewed our paths and crowned our board. Oh! what a comingling of thought filled my mind for the moment, Again she [is] here, even in the seventh trouble, undaunted, firm and unwavering, unchangeable, affectionate Emma.[22]

On June 27, 1844, at about 8:00 a.m. in Carthage Jail, Joseph wrote:

> Dear Emma,
>
> I am very much resigned to my lot, knowing I am justified and have done the best that could be done. Give my love to the children and all my Friends. . . . God bless you all. Amen.
>
> Joseph Smith[23]

Around five in the afternoon on June 27, 1844, Joseph and his brother Hyrum were killed by a mob. Hyrum was the first to fall from an assassin's bullet. As Joseph moved toward the east bedroom window, two bullets hit him from the doorway, and two struck him from the outside. He fell from the second-story window to the ground below and was heard to exclaim, "O Lord my God!"[24]

Emma lived for many years without Joseph in Nauvoo. She remarried and lived to see her children mature and leave home. With the many changes that came her way, the constant was her testimony of Joseph Smith's prophetic calling. In her seventy-fourth year she said, "I believe he was everything he professed to be."[25]

As Emma's life began to ebb in the spring of 1879, family members were at her bedside for two weeks. In the evening hours on April 30, Emma's sons, Joseph III and Alexander, alternated turns sitting near her. Alexander heard his mother call out, "Joseph, Joseph, Joseph." He awakened his brother Joseph III,

---

22   Journal, December 1841–December 1842, 164, The Joseph Smith Papers.
23   Letter from Joseph Smith to Emma Smith, June 27, 1844, 1–[2], spelling standardized, The Joseph Smith Papers.
24   D&C 135:1.
25   Nels Madsen, in "Visit to Mrs. Emma Smith Bidamon," 1877, recorded by Historian's Office, November 27, 1931, Church History Library.

who hurried to his mother's bedside. Joseph saw his mother rise up and extend her left arm as she said, "Joseph! Yes, yes, I'm coming." "Mother, what is it?" Alexander asked, but his mother did not reply.[26] Emma died at 4:20 a.m. at age seventy-four.

**A Bridge to the Past**
When Emma eloped with Joseph Smith, she had no inkling that one day she would be the most famous woman in the history of The Church of Jesus Christ of Latter-day Saints. But as the years have passed, Emma, who wrote only a few letters and gave fewer speeches, is the one woman known among members of the Church throughout the world. Due to kind remembrances of loved ones, especially Joseph Smith, there is much known and much to celebrate about the life of Emma Smith. There is much to celebrate in your life too. Take a moment to reflect upon who you have become and all you have accomplished.

---

26  *Zion's Ensign*, December 31, 1903, quoted in Linda King Newell and Valeen Tippetts Avery, *Mormon Enigma: Emma Hale Smith* (Garden City, NY: Doubleday, 1984), 304.

# Julia Murdock Smith

(1831–1880)

---

"Until I was a child of five years old," wrote Julia, "I was happy, it was then I was first told I was not a Smith. . . . From that hour I was changed. I was bitter even as a child. O how it stung me when persons have inquired, 'Is that your *adopted* daughter?'"[1]

---

On April 30, 1831, Father John Murdock wrote in his journal, "[My wife Julia Clapp Murdock] brought forth two fine children, a son and a daughter . . . and she departed this life when the children were about six hours old."[2] When the twins were infants, Emma Smith recalled, "Brother Murdock came to me and asked me to take them, and I took the babes."[3] Joseph and Emma cared for the twins—Joseph Smith Murdock and Julia Murdock Smith—as if they were their birth parents. When Joseph Smith Murdock was eleven months old, he died from complications of measles in March 1832, a few days after Joseph Smith was tarred and feathered in Hiram, Ohio.

---

1 John Murdock, "A Synopsis of My History," typescript, 1864, Historical Department of the Church of Jesus Christ of Latter-day Saints, Salt Lake City, Utah, Sunny McClennan Morton, "On Being Adopted: Julia Murdock Smith," *Dialogue: A Journal of Mormon Thought* (Winter 2003): 168; see also S. Reed Murdock, *Joseph and Emma's Julia: The "Other" Twin* (Salt Lake City: Eborn Books, 2004), 25.
2 Murdock, *Joseph and Emma's Julia*, 9.
3 Joseph Smith III, "Last Testimony of Emma Smith," *Saints' Herald* 26, no. 19 (October 1, 1879): 289–90.

As a child and in her youth, Julia endured many trials that beset her family as they moved from Kirtland to Missouri and then on to Illinois. In Nauvoo, Julia attended school taught by Eliza R. Snow in her father's Red Brick Store on Water Street. After the martyrdom of Joseph Smith, at age thirteen, Julia attended a private school taught by James Monroe. Brother Monroe wrote of her, "Today I made Julia go out of the room for laughing and carrying on for which she is quite angry with me, I presume, but it will have a beneficial influence."[4]

In 1848, at age seventeen, Julia became acquainted with an unemployed magician named Elisha Dixon, who boarded at the Mansion House. At the time, Elisha was age thirty-six and suffering from ill health. According to one historian, Julia "took delight in taking the 'gypsy king' his meals and reading to him as he rested and recovered."[5] In spring of 1848, Elisha and Julia eloped and were married in St. Louis. In September 1849, John Bernhisel reported to Brigham Young about the marriage: "Julia, the adopted daughter of Emma, has been joined in the silken bonds of wedlock to a reformed gambler of the name of Dixon."[6]

By 1852, Julia and Elisha were living in an apartment near Galveston Bay, Texas. Elisha secured work on the steamboat *Magnolia*, which took excursion trips on the Trinity River out of Galveston. On the excursions, Elisha was gone from Julia for two weeks at a time. On one such trip, he was severely burned when the steamboat boiler exploded. Elisha suffered for three weeks before his death. Julia, distraught over his passing, packed her bags and returned to her mother Emma in Nauvoo. Although a widow, Julia was only twenty-two years old.

In Nauvoo, Julia captured the attention of John Middleton. Julia and John were married on November 19, 1856, by Reverend Waldenmeyer, a minister of the Presbyterian Church in town. A year after their marriage, on November 9, 1857, Julia joined her husband in the Catholic faith and was baptized at the Church of St. Francis Xavier in St. Louis.

By 1859, Julia and John had moved to St. Louis. They purchased a home, and John secured a job as a bookkeeper in a bank. Although it appeared to family and friends that they prospered, all was not well. John had become an alcoholic. His alcoholism negatively affected his employment and his marriage.

---

4   James Monroe Journal, quoted in Murdock, *Joseph and Emma's Julia*, 75.
5   Cecil McGavin, *The Family of Joseph Smith* (Salt Lake City: Bookcraft, 1963), 179, quoted in Murdock, *Joseph and Emma's Julia*, 83.
6   Letter of John Bernhisel to Brigham Young, Journal History of the Church, September 10, 1849, quoted in Murdock, *Joseph and Emma's Julia*, 84.

In 1871, Emma wrote to her son Joseph Smith III, "[John Middleton] is now clerk, and cashier in a pork house, but how long he will be remains to be seen, poor Julia has a trying life."[7]

Julia ended her relationship with John and returned to Nauvoo in 1876. As for John Middleton, he became a "vagabond." He lived somewhere in New Mexico after their separation.[8]

Four years after Julia returned to Nauvoo, her mother, Emma, died on Julia's birthday. (Julia lost both of her mothers on April 30—one in 1831 and the other in 1879.) Rather than live alone, Julia traveled with her brother Alexander and his family. Her traveling abruptly ended when it was discovered that she had breast cancer. Julia returned to Nauvoo and resided with friends James and Semantha Moffitt. She died on September 10, 1880, at the Moffitts' home. Her obituary appeared in the *Nauvoo Independent*:

> [Julia] was a woman of the most exemplary character—an advocate of all the graces and all the virtues and had a strong loving disposition for her friends which firmly endeared them to her. She was considerably above the medium of intelligence and of a[n] indomitable spirit which manifested itself in the trying ordeal of sickness through which she passed. . . . She leaves many friends who deeply regret her death.[9]

James and Semantha Moffitt made arrangements for Julia to be buried in their family plot in the St. Peter and Paul Cemetery in Nauvoo. The white tombstone that marks her grave was purchased by her brother John R. Murdock, the son of John and Julia Murdock. The inscription on the tombstone reads:

Julie M. Middleton
BORN
May 1, 1831
Died
September 10, 1880
Gone But Not Forgotten

---

7   Letter of Emma S. Bidamon to Joseph Smith III, December 5, 1871, quoted in Murdock, *Joseph and Emma's Julia*, 144.
8   Murdock, *Joseph and Emma's Julia*, 169.
9   *Nauvoo Independent*, September 10, 1880, quoted in Murdock, *Joseph and Emma's Julia*, 164.

**A Bridge to the Past**

Though Julia experienced bitterness in her life, it was later said of her that she "was a woman of the most exemplary character." You cannot be a passive participant in rising to the top, in life or in emotion. You discover the fury of a hurricane by walking against it, not by lying down on the ground. A woman who succumbs to disappointment simply does not know what it would have been like an hour, a week, or a lifetime later if she had risen above her sorrows. Just like the mythical phoenix crashes and burns, only to rise from its ashes, so, too, can we rise from our trials even stronger.

*Lucy Mack Smith*

(1775–1856)

---

"Mrs. Smith, we hear that you have a gold Bible, and we have come to see if you will be so kind as to show it to us." Lucy replied, "No, gentlemen, . . . we have no gold bible; but we have a translation of some gold plates which have been brought forth for the purpose of making know[n] to the world the plainness of the gospel, and of giving a history of the people which formerly inhabited this Continent." She then proceeded to inform the delegation from the Western Presbyterian Church of the contents of the Book of Mormon. "I wish, that, if you do believe those things that you will not say anything more upon the subject—I do wish you would not," advised Deacon George Beckwith. Lucy replied, "Deacon Beckwith, . . . if you should stick my flesh full of faggots, and even burn me at the stake, I would declare that Joseph has got the record, and that I know it to be true, as long as God [should] give me breath."[1]

---

Such boldness in defending the gospel of Christ was the hallmark of Lucy Mack Smith's life. Once, when she saw fellow Saints waiting to board a boat at Buffalo bound for the Fairport Harbor in Ohio, she asked "if they confessed to the people that they were Mormons." They replied, "No, indeed . . . neither mention a word about your religion; for, if you do, you will never be able to get a house or a boat either." Lucy told them that she "should tell the people

---

[1] Lucy Mack Smith, "Lucy Mack Smith, History, 1845," 162–63, josephsmithpapers.org.

precisely who I was" and what she professed. "If you are ashamed of Christ you must not expect to be prospered."² Within a few moments, a man asked Lucy, "Is the Book of Mormon true?" Without hesitation, she replied,

> That book . . . was brought forth by the power of God, and translated by the gift of the Holy Ghost; and, if I could make my voice [to] sound as loud as the trumpet of Micheal [*sic*] the Arch Angel, I would declare the truth of the same from land to land, and from sea to sea, and the echo should reach to every Isle, untill [*sic*] every member of the family of Adam should be left without excuse; for I do testify that, God has revealed himself to man again in these last days.³

When introduced to Reverend Ruggles, a Protestant minister in Pontiac, Michigan, the reverend said, "And you . . . are the mother of that poor foolish, silly, boy, Joe Smith; who pretended to translate the Book of Mormon." Lucy assured Reverend Ruggles, "I am sir, the Mother of Joseph Smith; but why do you apply to him such epithets as those?" Ruggles answered, "Because . . . he should imagine that he was going to break down all other churches with that simple Mormon book." Mother Smith asked the reverend if he had read the Book of Mormon. "No," he said. Lucy encouraged him to read the book for it "was writen [*sic*] for the salvation of your soul by the gift and power of the Holy Ghost." The reverend said, "Pooh, . . . nonsense—I'm not afraid of any member of my church being led astray by such stuff: they have too much intelligence." Lucy predicted, "Now Mr Ruggles, . . . mark my words—as true as God lives, before three years we will have more than one third of your Church; and sir, whether you believe it or not, we will take the very Deacon too."⁴ Within three years, one-third of the reverend's congregation joined with the Latter-day Saints, including the deacon.

Her assertiveness led Lucy in October 1838 to push her way through a crowd at Far West to the covered wagons where her sons Joseph and Hyrum were being held captive by the Missouri militia. "I am the mother of the prophet," she cried. "Is there not a gentleman here, who will assist me to that wagon, that I may take a last look at my children, and speak to them once more." Making her way through the crowd, she reached the wagon and pled, "Joseph do speak to your poor mother once more—I cannot bear to go till I hear your voice." Joseph cried aloud, "God bless you mother." Of his words, she said, "I found consolation, that surpassed all earthly comfort: I was filled with the spirit of God."⁵

---

2   Smith, 197–98.
3   Smith, 202.
4   Smith, 212–13.
5   Smith, 280–81.

Joseph said of his mother, "My mother... is one of the noblest, and the best of all women. May God grant to prolong her days."6 The Lord heard Joseph's plea and extended the life of his mother. She lived to see the slain bodies of her sons Joseph and Hyrum. She cried, "My God! My God! Why hast thou forsaken this family?"7 Although family sought to comfort her, she asked Elder Wilford Woodruff to give her a priesthood blessing. In the blessing, Lucy was told, "Let thy heart be comforted in the midst of thy sorrow for thou shalt be held forever in honorable remembrance in the congregations of the righteous."8

At the October 1845 conference in Nauvoo, at age seventy, Lucy was invited to speak. She spoke of being the mother of eleven children, seven of whom were boys. She also spoke of her sons being dead, all but one. She asked the assembled whether she should still be called "Mother Smith," an affectionate title given her by the Saints. Brigham Young, in response to her query, arose and asked the assembled, "All who consider Mother Smith as a Mother in Israel, signify it by saying yea! (loud shouts of Yes)."9 At that same conference in anticipation of going west, Lucy said, "If I go, I want to have my bones fetch[ed] back to be laid with my husband & children."10

For reasons of her own, Lucy did not join the Saints in following Brigham Young to the West. On April 4, 1847, the Quorum of the Twelve wrote to her,

> We felt we could not take our leave [for the Rocky Mountains] without addressing a line to mother Smith, to let her know that her children in the Gospel have not forgotten her....
>
> If our dear Mother Smith should at any time wish to come where the Saints are located, and she will make it manifest to us, there is no sacrifice we will count too great.11

---

6  Joseph Smith, Journal, December 1841–December 1842, 180, The Joseph Smith Papers.
7  Smith, 312–13.
8  Matthias F. Cowley, ed., *Wilford Woodruff, Fourth President of the Church of Jesus Christ of Latter-day Saints: History of His Life and Labors as Recorded in His Daily Journals* (Salt Lake City: Bookcraft, 1964), 228.
9  Ronald Walker, "Lucy Mack Smith Speaks to the Nauvoo Saints," *BYU Studies* 32, no. 1–2 (1991), 3.
10  Walker, "Lucy Mack Smith Speaks to the Nauvoo Saints," 6.
11  Quorum of Twelve to Lucy Mack Smith, April 4, 1847, quoted in Lavina Fielding Anderson, ed., *Lucy's Book: A Critical Edition of Lucy Mack Smith's Family Memoir* (Salt Lake City: Signature Books, 2001), 796.

In 1846, Church trustees purchased the Joseph Noble home near the southeast corner of Kimball and Hyde streets in Nauvoo for the comfort of Mother Smith. Her son William Smith wrote to the trustees saying, "[We are] perfectly satisfied with the dealings of said church with Mother Smith; and freely acknowledge that the said church is hereby released from all moral and legal obligation to us of either of us."[12]

Lucy and her eight-year-old granddaughter, Mary Bailey Smith, lived in the home for five months. During that interim, Lucy set up an Egyptian artifacts display. A correspondent from the *Albany Atlas* reported, "The old lady is the keeper of the Egyptian mummies, and various relics and curiosities, which she exhibits to the public at two bits per head." The correspondent concluded, "If she weeps as much with every one as she did while relating her stories to me, she would be invaluable in Broadway on a dusty day."[13] A traveler, identified only as Miss F. J., reported, "We found a pleasant looking old lady, of seventy, or thereabouts, and to our question, 'Are you the mother of the Prophet?' the mother of Washington could not have replied with greater dignity, or a prouder air. 'Yes! ladies, I am the mother of the Prophet.'"[14]

When the Battle of Nauvoo raged in September 1846, Lucy abandoned her home. For a time, she and her granddaughter Mary lived with the Arthur Millikin family in Webster, Illinois, and then in Fountain Green, Illinois. By the early 1850s, she had returned to Nauvoo and was living with the family of Emma Smith Bidamon. In the years that followed, Lucy spent much time in bed and in a wheelchair built by Lewis Bidamon. In 1855, she moved into the Smith farmhouse, located a few miles southeast of town, and resided with Joseph Smith III and his bride, Emeline Griswold. On July 2, 1855, John Lyman Smith reported, "Aunt Lucy has been confined to the bed for 10 months unable to walk with the Rheumatism."[15]

Lucy died on May 14, 1856, at age eighty-one. Joseph Smith III wrote to John Bernhisel, "Grandmother died the morning of the 14th of May last easily with her senses to the last moment. . . . I sat by her and held her hand in mine

---

12  William Smith, Arthur Millikin, and Lucy Millikin, "To the Public," Nauvoo Broadside, April 14, 1846.

13  Correspondence of the *Albany Atlas* reprinted in *Cleveland Herald* 11, September 13, 1845.

14  Miss F. J., "Visit to Nauvoo," *Ladies' Magazine and Casket of Literature* (Boston: A. H. Davis, 1848), 11, quoted in Ronald E. Romig, ed., *Lucy's Nauvoo* (Independence, MO: John Whitmer Books, 2009), 67.

15  John Lyman Smith, Journal, vol. 1, July 2, 1855, Church History Library.

till death relieved her—The first death scene I ever witnessed."[16] The next day, Lucy was buried near the Joseph Smith homestead in Nauvoo.

**A Bridge to the Past**
Lucy was a defender of the faith. People never had to guess where she stood on the topic of her son Joseph or the Book of Mormon. In her prime, Lucy would not be found retreating to a quiet corner in the house. But when she was older and had buried her husband and her sons, Lucy began to question whether she should still be referred to as "Mother." Brigham Young asked a gathering of Saints at a general conference, "All who consider Mother Smith as a Mother in Israel, signify it by saying yes!" Loud shouts of affirmation were heard. Even the greatest defenders of the faith need confirmation of their worth. An expression of gratitude and a thoughtful note is much appreciated.

---

16   Joseph Smith III to John Bernhisel, quoted in Anderson, *Lucy's Book*, 796.

# Lucy Meserve Smith

(1817–1892)

---

"I FIRST MET THE PROPHET Joseph Smith on a steamboat, when I landed at the ferry in Nauvoo," Lucy wrote.

The first words he said to our company were: "I guess you are all Latter-day Saints here, by the singing I heard when the boat landed." He then shook hands with each one in the company, and then took his sister, Lucy Millikan's seven months' old boy in his arms and sat down and wept for joy, as his sister was thought to be in a decline when she left home the year before with her husband. She was indeed the picture of health when she returned, which gave the Prophet double joy on meeting her with her son.

President Joseph Smith, the Prophet, looked the same to me when I met him as I saw him in a dream before I left home.[1]

---

Lucy's father, Josiah Smith, was the first in her family to join the Church of Jesus Christ, being baptized in 1835 by Daniel Bean. Before long, he was

---

1 "Lucy Meserve Smith," in Mark L. McConkie, comp., *Remembering Joseph: Personal Recollections of Those Who Knew the Prophet Joseph Smith* (Salt Lake City: Deseret Book, 2003), 107.

ordained the presiding elder of a small branch in Newry, Maine. Under his watchful care, Lucy was baptized on August 16, 1837, in "the lovely little stream called Bear River."[2] Lucy did not migrate to Nauvoo with her family in the early 1840s. Instead, she went to Lowell, Massachusetts, to work in a cotton factory. After earning enough money to travel, she journeyed to Nauvoo in hopes of seeing her family and meeting the Prophet Joseph Smith. Of the Prophet Joseph, she wrote, "The little children were very much attached to the Prophet, as he used to play with them as one of their equals. Indeed he was loved best by those who were the most acquainted with him."[3] Lucy heard the Prophet give his last sermon and recalled that he said, "Brethren and Sisters, Love one another, and be merciful to your enemies." According to Lucy, he repeated the phrase twice "in a very emphatic tone of voice with a loud 'Amen,' while the rain was pouring in torrents from the clouds, but the audience remained quiet. We didn't mind getting wet if we could hear the Prophet speak."[4]

Lucy was in Nauvoo when Joseph and his brother Hyrum Smith went to Carthage in late June 1844. Of June 27, she recalled,

> The evening the murder was committed at Carthage, such a barking and howling of dogs, and bellowing of cattle all over the city of Nauvoo I never heard before or since. News came in the morning of the awful tragedy! In the afternoon I repaired to the Mansion, and there witnessed the awful scene, the Prophet and Patriarch laying in their gore with kettles of bloody water, and cloths standing near, while every man, woman, and child were in tears.[5]

After the burial of Joseph and Hyrum Smith, Lucy was employed by Emma Smith. For a year and a half, she spun "rightly ten knotted skeins of fine marino wool yarn for which Emma paid me money." More important to Lucy, "Emma bore testimony of the truth of this latter-day work, as it came forth through His servant of the Lord (Joseph Smith), but she accused the Twelve of making bogus of Mormonism."[6]

---

2  "Lucy Meserve Smith Smith, daughter of Lucy Meserve Bean and Josiah Smith & second wife of Apostle George Albert Smith. Written by my own hand in the 72nd year of my age at Salt Lake City, Utah Territory. Apr. 19th 1888," FamilySearch; Lane R. Pendleton, "Lucy Meserve Smith," December 1999, FamilySearch.
3  "Lucy Meserve Smith," in McConkie, *Remembering Joseph*, 73.
4  "Lucy Meserve Smith Autobiography of her life dated August 14th, 1889," FamilySearch.
5  "Lucy Meserve Smith Autobiography."
6  "Lucy Meserve Smith Autobiography."

On November 23, 1844, Lucy became a plural wife of George A. Smith. On December 29, 1845, she was endowed in the Nauvoo Temple. And on February 9, 1846, she crossed the Mississippi River, seeking safety in Iowa. Of her leaving Nauvoo, Lucy wrote, "We were compelled to leave our comfortable homes and flee into the wilderness as a mob had control."[7] She traveled across Iowa with other wives and children of George A. Smith. She penned,

> We encountered some very severe cold weather with very strong high winds. I cannot forget how cold I was standing in the tent preparing food and washing dishes for our big family. When I would wash a dish and raise it out of the water there would be ice on it before I could get it wiped. I could not get warm from morning till night and from night until morning. In the morning the bed covers would be frozen stiff.[8]

Lucy wrote of days traveling "through rain, mud slush all day, when night came the mud was six inches deep and the men were completely drenched." She wrote of wind "[taking] off nearly every wagon cover, the dishes and brooms went whizzing through camp." She also wrote of giving birth to a son named Don Carlos Smith in Cutler's Park and of living in a log cabin "ten feet square with a sod roof, only the soft ground for a floor, and poor worn out cattle beef and corn cracked on a hand mill for our food." And she wrote of her feelings about the death of her only child: "I felt so overcome in my feelings, I was afraid I would lose my mind as I had not recovered from my sickness the previous winter."[9]

As her health returned, Lucy became a teacher at the Pawnee Mission School before leaving Kanesville, Iowa, on June 22, 1849, with the George A. Smith/Dan Jones Company. The pioneer company arrived tired and hungry in the Salt Lake Valley on October 27, 1849, at eleven o'clock at night.

Lucy slept in her wagon from October 1848 until January 1850. She then moved into a log cabin and later to an adobe house. She gave birth to a stillborn child. To support herself, Lucy taught school in the Salt Lake 17th Ward to fifty-six students.

From Salt Lake, Lucy moved to Provo, where she lived for seventeen years. She earned her living spinning and weaving. She wove hundreds of yards of cloth for bed coverlets, diapers, and carpets. In 1856, she headed the Provo

---

7 "Lucy Meserve Smith"; Pendleton, "Lucy Meserve Smith."
8 "Lucy Meserve Smith"; Pendleton, "Lucy Meserve Smith."
9 "Lucy Meserve Smith"; Pendleton, "Lucy Meserve Smith."

women's efforts to support survivors of the Willie and Martin Handcart Companies. Under Lucy's direction, women in Provo spun wool, created twenty-seven quilts, and made clothes.

Lucy was called to preside over the Relief Society in Provo. "Our society was short of funds then, we could not do much, but the four Bishops could hardly carry the bedding and other clothing we got together the first time we met," she wrote.[10] In her presidency, Relief Society sisters made a flag for the Provo Brass Band. Lucy was proud that the flag won the big prize at the Utah Territorial Fair.

In 1873, Lucy journeyed back to Maine and Massachusetts to visit her father, her brothers Freeborn and Jonathan, and her sister Catherine. George A. Smith spent the winter of 1874 in St. George with Brigham Young. On his return to Provo, he contracted a severe cold in his lungs. He never recovered, dying in September 1875.

Left a widow, Lucy rented a room for several years in Salt Lake City before leasing a cottage for an additional eight years. Her biographer wrote, "Being heavy and weak in her ankles, she was hindered in leading a public life in later years."[11] Lucy died on October 5, 1892, at age seventy-five.

**A Bridge to the Past**

Lucy had a particular fondness for children. Two of her written accounts about the Prophet Joseph Smith involved children. When it came to her own life and the bearing of children, her children died in infancy. At one point, she wrote, "I felt so overcome with my feelings." Rather than mourn her loss day after day, she spent her life in service. Have you ever watched the Christmas classic *It's a Wonderful Life*, starring Jimmy Stewart? In the movie, the angel Clarence shows George Bailey (Jimmy Stewart) what his kind deeds had done for others and the tragedy that would have befallen their lives if he had never been born. Likewise, the kind service of Lucy made all the difference in the lives of near neighbors and her loved ones.

---

10   "Lucy Meserve Smith"; Pendleton, "Lucy Meserve Smith."
11   "Lucy Meserve Smith"; Pendleton, "Lucy Meserve Smith."

# Mary Fielding Smith

(1801–1852)

---

MARY FIELDING, A CONVERT FROM Canada, attended a meeting held in the Kirtland Temple:

> [Hyrum Smith] spoke in a most pleasing manner . . . and exhorted us as we had received Christ Jesus the Lord so to walk in him. . . .
>
> . . . He asked us if we did not feel as humble as little children [and] he assured us that he for one did. . . . He was then affected to tears. . . . [He] had to sit down for a short time to give vent to his feelings, after which he again arose and begged the congregation to excuse his weakness. Before he concluded, he seemed to be filled with [the] Spirit and power of God. He reminded me of some of the Nephites' preachers of old when he assured us with great energy that from that hour the Church should begin to rise.[1]

---

In 1834, Mary migrated from England to Toronto to be with her brother Joseph and her sister Mercy, who had earlier migrated to Canada. Little did

---

1 Letter of Mary Fielding to Mercy Fielding, June 1837, quoted in Jeffrey S. O'Driscoll, *Hyrum Smith: A Life of Integrity* (Salt Lake City: Deseret Book, 2003), 154.

the Fielding siblings know that in two years they would be baptized, in May 1836, by Elder Parley P. Pratt, and within the year leave Upper Canada to be with the Saints in Kirtland, Ohio. In that small farming community, Mary was a schoolteacher and private tutor to young children. More importantly, at age thirty-six, she married thirty-seven-year-old widower Hyrum Smith on December 24, 1837.

On the day of her marriage, Mary became not only the wife of Hyrum Smith, but also a mother to five children born to Hyrum's first wife, Jerusha Barden Smith. Although Mary was capable and up to the task, there were external difficulties that beset her on all sides. For example, before the birth of Mary's first son, Hyrum and his brother Joseph and other Church leaders were imprisoned in Liberty Jail. "We endeavored to find out for what cause," Hyrum wrote, "but all we could learn was, that it was because we were 'Mormons.'"[2] Of Hyrum's imprisonment and the added responsibilities that befell her, Mary wrote to her brother Joseph Fielding:

> So great have been my afflictions, etc., that I know not where to begin; but I can say, hitherto has the Lord preserved me, and I am still among the living to praise him, as I do today. I have, to be sure, been called to drink of the bitter cup; but you know my beloved brother, this makes the sweet sweeter.
>
> . . . I suppose no one felt the painful effects of their confinement more than myself. I was left in a way that called for the exercise of all the courage and grace I possessed. My husband was taken from me by an armed force, at a time when I needed, in a particular manner, the kindest care and attention of such a friend, instead of which, the care of a large family was suddenly and unexpectedly left upon myself, and, in a few days after, my dear little Joseph F. was added to the number. . . .
>
> O, My dear brother, I must tell you, for your comfort, that my hope is full, and it is a glorious hope; and though I have been left for near six months in widowhood, in the time of great affliction, and was called to take joyfully or otherwise, the spoiling of almost all our goods, in the absence of my

---

[2] Smith, *History of the Church*, 3:419.

husband, and all unlawfully, just for the gospel's sake . . . yet I do not feel in the least discouraged. . . .

The more I see of the dealing of our Heavenly Father with us as a people, the more I am constrained to rejoice that I was ever made acquainted with the everlasting covenant.[3]

Hyrum escaped the confines of his imprisonment and wrote,

I had been abused and thrust into a dungeon, and confined for months on account of my faith, and the "testimony of Jesus Christ." However I thank God that I felt a determination to die, rather than deny the things which my eyes had seen, which my hands had handled, and which I hard [sic] borne testimony to, wherever my lot had been cast; and I can assure my beloved brethren that I was enabled to bear as strong a testimony, when nothing but death presented itself, as ever I did in my life.[4]

Hyrum joined Mary and his children in Quincy, Illinois. From Quincy, he moved his family to what would become Nauvoo. In Nauvoo, Mary gave birth to her daughter Martha Ann in 1841. Happy days followed but not for long. On June 27, 1844, Hyrum died a religious martyr in Carthage Jail when a ball struck him on the left side of the nose. He fell backward to the jail floor, exclaiming, "I am a dead man!"[5] As he fell to the floor, another bullet from outside the jail entered his left side. At the same instant, a bullet from the door grazed his breast and entered his head by the throat. A fourth ball entered his left leg. The next to fall from an assassin's bullet was the Prophet Joseph Smith. John Taylor, a witness to the barbaric scene, wrote:

Their names will be classed among the martyrs of religion; and the reader in every nation will be reminded that the Book of Mormon, and this book of Doctrine and Covenants of the church, cost the best blood of the nineteenth century to bring them forth for the salvation of a ruined world. . . . They lived for glory; they died for glory; and glory is their eternal reward.

---

3  Don Cecil Corbett, *Mary Fielding Smith, Daughter of Britain: Portrait of Courage* (Salt Lake City: Deseret Book, 1966), 99–100.

4  Hyrum Smith, "A History, of the Persecution, of The Church of Jesus Christ, of Latter Day Saints in Missouri," *Times and Seasons* 1, no. 2 (December 1839): 23.

5  D&C 135:1.

From age to age shall their names go down to posterity as gems for the sanctified.[6]

After the funeral and a period of mourning, Mary and some of the leading ladies of Nauvoo visited Robert Foster, a man suspected of being in the mob at Carthage. "[Mary] told him they would not bear his taunts and insults any longer. They ordered him to leave the city forthwith."[7] In fear, Robert Foster fled from Nauvoo.

Although Mary was encouraged by near relatives to remain in Nauvoo and not follow Brigham Young to the Rocky Mountains, she ignored the advice. After traversing the Territory of Iowa, she was ready to continue the journey west. When the captain of her pioneering company, Cornelius Lott, questioned her preparation for the journey ahead and suggested she wait behind, Mary told him that she would go ahead as planned and arrive at the destination before him. She did arrive in the Salt Lake Valley before Captain Lott but not before encountering difficulties.

While camped in the Missouri River bottoms for the night, her best yoke of oxen wandered off. In the morning, her son Joseph F. Smith and his uncle Joseph Fielding searched in the tall grass and nearby woods for the oxen. They returned to camp "fatigued, disheartened and almost exhausted." As Joseph F. approached camp, he saw his "mother kneeling down in prayer." He wrote, "I halted for a moment and then drew gently near enough to hear her pleading with the Lord not to suffer us to be left in this helpless condition, but to lead us to recover our lost team, that we might continue our travels in safety." She then walked toward the riverbank, where she found the cattle. She called to young Joseph and her brother to come quickly and see. "And like John, who outran the other disciple to the sepulchre, I outran my uncle and came first to the spot where my mother stood," wrote Joseph F. "There I saw our oxen fastened to a clump of willows growing in the bottom of a deep gulch . . . perfectly concealed from view." Joseph F. next wrote, "And we were soon on our way home rejoicing."[8]

Mary and her family arrived safely in the valley. They settled in a small home in Salt Lake City. Their circumstance was less than prosperous. Joseph F. wrote,

> One spring when we opened our potato pits [my mother] had her boys get a load of the best potatoes, and she took them

---

6  D&C 135:6.
7  Smith, *History of the Church*, 7:176.
8  Joseph Fielding Smith, comp., *Life of Joseph F. Smith* (Salt Lake City: Deseret News Press, 1938), 132–33.

to the tithing office; potatoes were scarce that season. I was a little boy at the time, and drove the team. When we drove up to the steps of the tithing office ready to unload the potatoes, one of the clerks came out and said to my mother: "Widow Smith, it's a shame that you should have to pay tithing." . . . My mother turned upon him and said: "William, you ought to be ashamed of yourself. Would you deny me a blessing?"

She insisted that he accept her tithing. "Though she was a widow, you may turn to the records of the Church from the beginning unto the day of her death, and you will find that she never received a farthing from the Church to help her support herself and her family."[9]

On September 21, 1852, Mary died of pneumonia in Salt Lake City at age fifty-one. Her death was greatly lamented by her family. Joseph F. Smith said of his mother, "Her name and deeds will be had in everlasting remembrance, associated as they are, with the persecutions of the Saints, and those tragic scenes that can never be forgotten. . . . She endured afflictions and overcame difficulties with a degree of patience and perseverance worthy of imitation."[10]

## A Bridge to the Past

Although others had lots of advice for her, Mary made up her own mind. Whether it was to take her family to the unchartered West or to pay tithing, she could not be swayed from her course. She was resolute—determined. Mary's determined faithfulness led M. Russell Ballard, her descendant and President of the Quorum of the Twelve, to say,

> Hyrum returned home from a mission after his beloved wife Jerusha died, leaving him with five living children, including a baby, and no mother for them. Shortly thereafter, heaven sent Mary Fielding to become Hyrum's wife to help him care for his family. Together they had two additional children, the oldest a boy they named Joseph Fielding, after the Prophet Joseph and Mary's brother Joseph Fielding. The little girl was named Martha Ann.
>
> Mary Fielding, with the background of a schoolteacher from England, certainly taught the children the basic skills of

---

9   Smith, *Life of Joseph F. Smith*, 158–59.
10  Smith, *Life of Joseph F. Smith*, 161, quoted in Leon R. Hartshorn, comp., *Remarkable Stories from the Lives of Latter-day Saint Women* (Provo, UT: Spring Creek, 1973), 141.

reading and writing, but more importantly, she instilled in them faith and trust in God.[11]

Honor awaits those who teach their children faith and trust in God.

---

11  M. Russell Ballard, "Joseph F. Smith and the Importance of Family," in *Joseph F. Smith: Reflections on the Man and His Times*, eds. Craig K. Manscill, Brian D. Reeves, Guy L. Dorius, and J. B. Haws (Provo, UT: Religious Studies Center, 2013), 5–6.

# Eliza Roxcy Snow

(1804–1887)

---

Through poetry, Eliza bore testimony of the Restoration of the gospel of Jesus Christ:

> This work is moving on apace,
> And great events are rolling forth;
> The kingdom of the latter days,
> The "little stone," must fill the earth.
> The "little stone," must fill the earth.
>
> Though Satan rage, 'tis all in vain;
> The words the ancient prophet spoke
> Sure as the throne of God remain;
> Nor men nor devils can revoke.
> Nor men nor devils can revoke.
>
> All glory to his holy name
> Who sends his faithful servants forth
> To prove the nations, to proclaim
> Salvation's tidings through the earth.
> Salvation's tidings through the earth.[1]

---

Eliza grew to womanhood in Mantua in northeastern Ohio. Her father was a farmer, justice of the peace, and a devout Baptist. Her mother was a Baptist

---

1   "Though Deepening Trials," *Hymns*, no. 122.

too but willingly opened her home to preachers of any Christian denomination. Of her parents, Eliza penned, "[They] carefully imprest on the minds of their children, that useful labor is honorable—idleness and waste of time disgraceful and sinful." Fortunately for Eliza, her parents did not view reading as a waste of time. "I was partial to poetical works, and when very young frequently made attempts at imitation of the different styles of favorite authors," recalled Eliza. "In school I often bothered my teachers by writing my lessons in rhyme."[2] By age ten, she had won prizes for her literary skills.

In 1825, Eliza published her first poem. Within four years, eleven of her poems were printed in the *Western Courier* and twenty in the *Ohio Star*. "Being shy and perhaps lacking confidence, she signed her poetry with 'assumed signatures,' or, as she penned, 'wishing to be useful as a writer, and unknown as an author.'"[3] Along the way, she had suitors and "very flattering proposals" of marriage, but none she was willing to accept.[4]

Timidity still marked her ways in autumn of 1829 when at age twenty-five, she first learned of Joseph Smith and his sacred record. "A Prophet of God—the voice of God revealing to man as in former dispensations, was what my soul had hungered for," she wrote, "but could it possibly be true—I considered it a hoax—too good to be true."[5] But upon meeting Joseph Smith in the winter of 1831, all doubts fled. On April 5, 1835, Eliza entered baptismal waters. By December 1835, she "bade a final adieu to the home of my youth, to share the fortunes of the people of God" in Kirtland.[6]

In that agrarian community, she resided with the Joseph Smith family and supported herself as a seamstress and a schoolteacher. Her stay in Kirtland was cut short, however, as violent persecution forced Latter-day Saints from the area. Eliza and her loved ones migrated to Missouri, settling in a "double log house" at Adam-ondi-Ahman.[7] When persecution reared in Missouri, Eliza moved on, penning,

---

2  *Eliza R. Snow, an Immortal: Selected Writings of Eliza R. Snow* (Salt Lake City: Nicholas G. Morgan Sr. Foundation, 1957), 2.

3  Eliza R. Snow quote in Susan Easton Black and Mary Jane Woodger, *Women of Character: Profiles of 100 Prominent LDS Women* (American Fork, UT: Covenant Communications, Inc., 2011), 304.

4  Eliza R. Snow, "Sketch of My Life," in Maureen Ursenbach Beecher, *The Personal Writings of Eliza Roxcy Snow* (Salt Lake City: University of Utah Press, 1995; repr., Logan: Utah State University Press, 2000), 16.

5  *Eliza R. Snow, an Immortal*, 5–6.

6  *Eliza R. Snow, an Immortal*, 7.

7  Eliza R. Snow Smith, *Biography and Family Record of Lorenzo Snow* (Salt Lake City: Deseret News, 1884), 28.

It was December [1838] and very cold when we left our home, and, after assisting in the morning arrangements for the journey, in order to warm my aching feet, I started on foot and walked until the teams came up. When about two miles out I met one of the so-called Militia, who accosted me with "Well, I think this will cure you of your faith." Looking him squarely in the eye, I replied, "No, Sir, it will take more than this to cure me of my faith." His countenance dropped and he responded, "I must confess you are a better soldier than I am." I passed on, thinking that, unless he was above the average of his fellows in that section, I was not complimented by his confession.[8]

Unfortunately, years of religious persecution and upheaval had their way with Eliza—especially her poetic urges. It appeared to some that her ability to express herself through poetry had ended. Joseph Smith, who married Eliza under the law of plural marriage, did not agree. He designated Eliza "Zion's Poetess" and encouraged her to write again. With renewed determination, she took up the pen and wrote of the debauchery of government officials and the suffering of the Saints. She submitted twenty poems about religious prejudice and persecution to the *Quincy Whig* under the pen of a "Mormon girl."[9]

In Nauvoo, at age thirty-five, Eliza filled Latter-day Saint newspapers—*Times and Seasons*, the *Wasp*, and the *Nauvoo Neighbor*—with her inspired poetry. "While time shall last," wrote Emmeline B. Wells, "Sister Eliza's songs will be sung in Zion, and her memory live in the hearts of the people, and her name be immortalized as Zion's Poetess."[10] Generations of Latter-day Saints have been stirred by the lyrics of "Though Deepening Trials," "Behold the Great Redeemer Die," "How Great the Wisdom and the Love," "O My Father," and "Awake, Ye Saints of God, Awake!"[11] These familiar poems are only a few of nearly four hundred poems written by Eliza R. Snow.

In March 1842, Eliza was elected secretary of the Female Relief Society of Nauvoo. She scribed sermons of Joseph Smith given to the Relief Society sisters. Of his words, Eliza penned, "His expansive mind grasped the great plan of salvation and solved the mystic problem of man's destiny."[12]

---

8   *Eliza R. Snow, an Immortal*, 9–10.
9   *Eliza R. Snow, an Immortal*, 11.
10  E. B. W, "Pen Sketch of an Illustrious Woman," *Woman's Exponent* 10, no. 11 (November 1, 1881), 82.
11  *Hymns*, nos. 122, 191, 195, 292, 17.
12  Snow, "Sketch of My Life," in Beecher, *Personal Writings of Eliza Roxcy Snow*, 11.

After the martyrdom of Joseph and Hyrum Smith, Eliza's poetic leanings were unpredictable. Recognizing the problem, she wrote, "I have a pen that freely moves / Or does not move at all."[13]

Eliza joined the Latter-day Saint exodus from Nauvoo to Iowa and then to the Salt Lake Valley. In the valley, she resided in a row of log dwellings until 1856, when she moved into the Lion House. When the Endowment House was dedicated, she was given oversight of women who participated in sacred temple ordinances. She was later asked to head the Relief Society (1868) and introduce organizations for young women (1870) and children (1878). Of her responsibilities, Eliza penned, "I have traveled from one end of Utah Ter[ritory] to the other—into Nevada & Idaho, in the interests of these organizations."[14] On each visit, she tried to elevate and inspire women to speak up: "Were we the stupid, degraded, heartbroken beings that we have been represented, silence might better become us; but, as women of God . . . we not only speak because we have the right, but justice and humanity demand that we should."[15]

By age eighty, Eliza had been closely associated with Church leaders for half a century. She died on December 5, 1887. The Assembly Hall was draped in white for her funeral. A choir sang, "Bury Me Quietly When I Die":

> On the "iron rod" I have laid my hold;
> If I keep the faith, and like Paul of old
> Shall have "fought the good fight," and Christ the Lord
> Has a crown in store with a full reward
> Of the holy Priesthood in fullness rife,
> With the gifts and the powers of an endless life,
> And a glorious mansion for me on high;
> Bury me quietly when I die.[16]

## A Bridge to the Past

At age twenty-one, Eliza had her first poem published. By age twenty-five, thirty-one of her poems had been printed in newspapers, but all under

---

13 "To—," in Eliza R. Snow, 1842–1882 Journal, quoted in Jill Mulvay Derr and Karen Lynn Davidson, comps. and eds., *Eliza R. Snow: The Complete Poetry* (Provo, UT: Brigham Young University Press; Salt Lake City: University of Utah Press, 2015).
14 Snow, "Sketch of My Life," 37.
15 "Great Indignation Meeting," *Deseret Evening News* (January 19, 1870), 2.
16 *The Life and Labors of Eliza R. Snow Smith* (Salt Lake City: Juvenile Instructor Office, 1888), 35.

"assumed signatures." She submitted twenty poems to the *Quincy Whig* under the pen name of "Mormon girl." Despite the fact that her talents in poetry were remarkable, it took Eliza time to gain confidence. It wasn't until she was age thirty-five that she attached her own name to her poetry. Confidence is hard to come by, especially when there isn't a referee holding your hand high and announcing your victory. But with confidence in the Lord, we can all accomplish great things.

(1830–1914)

As Eunice recalled her days in Nauvoo, she said,

> Some of the most impressive moments of my life were when I saw the "Nauvoo Legion" on parade with the prophet, then General Joseph Smith, with his wife, Emma Hale Smith, on horseback at the head of the troops. . . . He was so fair and she so dark in their beautiful riding habits. He was in full military suit and she wore her habit trimmed with gold buttons, and neat cap on her head, and a black plume in it, while the prophet wore a red plume in his, and a red sash across his breast. His coat was black and his white pants had red stripes on the outside seams. He also wore a sword at his side.[1]

Eunice was about a year old when her parents joined the Church of Jesus Christ. She was about four years old when they were driven from Jackson County, Missouri, because of their religious beliefs. She was age eight when she first remembered seeing the Prophet Joseph Smith and singing for him. "The first time I ever sang for the prophet, Father and Mother were called upon to sing 'Redeemer of Israel.' I sang a part alone. Joseph watched me all the time we were singing."[2]

---

1  "Eunice Billings Warner Snow Tells Her Own Story," ed. Marba Peck Hale, September 1910, November 1911, August 1914 with other dates unknown, FamilySearch.
2  "Eunice Billings Warner Snow Tells Her Own Story."

Her most vivid youthful memories were of the Prophet Joseph's family. Eunice was a childhood friend of Julia Murdock Smith, Joseph's adopted daughter. She often played with Julia in the Mansion House. Eunice said, "The prophet took me on his lap every time I went to his home and had me sing for him. He thought it was so nice because I could sing alto while so young. . . . He said to me at one time when my father, mother, and myself had been singing for him, 'My little sister, you shall be able to sing songs of Zion for as long as you desire.'"3

Joseph requested that Eunice sing in the Nauvoo Choir even though she was younger than other singers. She sang in the choir at the Nauvoo Temple dedication, recalling that the first hymn sung was "Oh, Oh, For the Temple's Completed, The Lord Hath a Place for His Head." Following the dedication, she received her temple endowment on her sixteenth birthday. She recalled that "the Temple was partitioned off in rooms, with canvas" and that on the last night the temple was open, they took down the canvas and danced. "There was room enough for one hundred people to dance at one time," Eunice wrote. "We surely had a fine time."4

Eunice also recalled events leading up to the martyrdom of Joseph Smith and his brother Hyrum:

> I remember when the "Nauvoo Expositor" was destroyed [June 10, 1844]. This was a paper established by the apostates and it was creating considerable trouble—so much that our brethren felt that it should not exist. It was destroyed after a short time and many of the people were very much enraged at the time, and it pointed to the beginning of mobocracy. . . .
> 
> After the destruction of the "Expositor" many of the apostates became wild and revengeful, thirsting for the prophet's blood. . . .
> 
> On the last day which he spent in Nauvoo, he [the Prophet Joseph Smith] passed our house with his brother Hyrum, both riding [June 24, 1844]. My mother and I were standing in the door yard and as he passed he bowed with uplifted hat to my mother. Hyrum seemed like one in a dream, sad and despondent, taking no notice of anyone. They were on their way to the Carthage jail, and it was the last time I saw the prophet alive. 5

---

3 "Eunice Billings Warner Snow Tells Her Own Story."
4 "Eunice Billings Warner Snow Tells Her Own Story."
5 "Eunice Billings Warner Snow Tells Her Own Story."

Eunice described the confusion in Nauvoo following the martyrdom of the Prophet Joseph Smith:

> The condition of the church was a pitiable sight with confusion on every hand. . . .
>
> There were so many opinions as who would be the leader of the Saints at that time. Sidney Rigdon was sure he was the man. He stood up and declared that he was the one, but he was called down and Brigham Young stood up and spoke with the power and voice of Joseph. He surely had the Prophet Joseph's mantle on.[6]

Eunice and her family followed Brigham Young and other Latter-day Saints in their exodus from Nauvoo. They trekked across Iowa to reach Council Bluffs, nestled on the bank of the Missouri River. They then journeyed across the plains to the Rockies, arriving in the Salt Lake Valley in 1848. They settled in Bountiful, eight miles north of Salt Lake City. In that small settlement, Eunice married John E. Warner, a musically talented young man. To their union were born eight children. Eunice claimed that she and John ate only one meal in their log home in Bountiful before Brigham Young called them to settle in Manti, Utah. "We prepared for our journey and started in the latter part of October [1849]," Eunice recalled. They reached Manti on November 21, 1849. Eunice's first impression of Manti was that "everything was bleak and dreary. There was . . . no house in sight, only the brush covering the ground." For six weeks, she and John lived in a wagon "with only a brush covering to protect us from the storms."[7]

John helped build a log meetinghouse where Church services were held. He was asked to lead the Manti choir and serve as the clerk of the Manti ward and as a clerk to Judge Peacock during sessions of the district court. As for Eunice, she sang in the Manti choir, played in the first theater organized in town, and was a member of the Thespian Society.

"We lived in Manti fourteen years and I shall always cherish fond recollections of the place," said Eunice. "We came to it when it was bare and desolate and we saw it grow into a beautiful settlement."[8] Yet in Manti, Eunice faced her

---

6 "Eunice Billings Warner Snow Tells Her Own Story."
7 "A Sketch of the Life of Eunice Billings Snow," *Woman's Exponent* 39, no. 3 (September 1910), 22.
8 "Sketch of the Life of Eunice Billings Snow," 23.

greatest trial. "The Indians were very troublesome from the first of our settling, as they said, on their land. They were mad. They would drive off our cattle and kill them to eat, as they said it was as much their right to take our cattle without our consent, as it was for us to live on their land and not get their consent."9

Tensions between settlers in Manti and Indians led to the Walker War. On August 4, 1853, Eunice's husband, John, was killed by Indians in the Manti Canyon. After his death, an Indian wearing John's necktie and carrying his gun, and another Indian with John's pocketknife, came to her parents' home. Eunice said,

> There happened to be a butcher knife on the table. I grabbed the knife and started for them. My Father saw me rise from the table. He caught me in his arms and carried me out of the room. (This happened only a short time before my son was born. He was born six months after his father was killed.) . . .
>
> . . . I prayed as earnestly as ever I did for the Lord to take that terrible feeling from me. It was taken to some degree, but it has never entirely left me.10

Eunice was supported in her trials by her parents and friends. She wrote, "I lived a widow three years, then I was married to Brother George W. Snow. . . . I had four children belonging to him."11

On June 15, 1905, at age seventy-five, Eunice received her patriarchal blessing in the Manti Temple by John B. Maben. In her blessing, she was told,

> Thou hast passed through many ordeals of trial, of difficulty, and of question, nevertheless the Lord has wonderfully preserved thee for a good and wise purpose. . . . You shall not seek the Lord in vain. His blessings and mercies shall be continued unto you and shall be vouchsafed by the goodness of God, and His grace shall be sufficient for you to fulfull [sic] and complete your mission on the earth with honor and great success, that shall entitle you hereafter to recognition with your loved ones that have gone before, especially him to whom you have been sealed by the keys and authority and powers of the Holy Priesthood.12

---

9   "Eunice Billings Warner Snow Tells Her Own Story."
10  "Eunice Billings Warner Snow Tells Her Own Story."
11  "Eunice Billings Warner Snow Tells Her Own Story."
12  "Eunice Billings Warner Snow Tells Her Own Story."

Eunice lived another nineteen years and enjoyed "fairly good health."[13] She died on November 28, 1914, at age ninety-four.

## A Bridge to the Past

As a child, Eunice received a promise from the Prophet Joseph Smith: "My little sister, you shall be able to sing songs of Zion for as long as you desire." Eunice sang for the Prophet, in the Nauvoo choir, at the Nauvoo Temple dedication, and later in the Manti Choir. But when her husband was killed by Indians in the Manti Canyon, Eunice stopped singing. It took years for her to again sing the songs of Zion. Life has a way of knocking each of us down. What is important is to get up as quickly as you can and reach for talents that have always brought joy.

---

13 "Eunice Billings Warner Snow Tells Her Own Story."

# Priscilla Mogridge Haines
(1823–1899)

As Priscilla recalled her baptism as a member of The Church of Jesus Christ of Latter-day Saints by Elder Orson Hyde, she reflected on the courage of the converts and elders in England:

> It is proper to here state that baptism was a trial to the converts in England in those days. They had to steal away, even unknown to their friends oftentimes, and scarcely daring to tell the saints themselves that they were about to take up the cross; and not until the ordinance had been administered, and the Holy Ghost gave them boldness, could they bring themselves to proclaim openly that they had cast in their lot with the despised Mormons. Nor was this all, for generally the elders had to administer baptism when the village was wrapt in sleep, lest persecutors should gather a mob to disturb the solemn scene with gibes and curses, accompanied with stones or clods of earth torn from the river bank and hurled at the disciple and minister during the performance of the ceremony.[1]

---

1  Edward W. Tullidge, *The Women of Mormondom* (New York: Tullidge and Crandall, 1877), 286–87.

Priscilla grew to womanhood in Wiltshire, England. She was brought up in the Episcopal faith and believed as her parents until she matured and "thought more about religion." Priscilla wrote, "I became dissatisfied with the doctrines taught by that Church, and I prayed to God my Heavenly Father to direct me aright, that I might know the true religion."[2]

On the heels of her prayer came missionaries from The Church of Jesus Christ of Latter-day Saints preaching about Joseph Smith and the Book of Mormon. Priscilla wrote, "[I] believed it. God had sent the true gospel to me in answer to my prayer."[3] She determined to be baptized although it was midwinter and the weather was bitter cold. Priscilla walked four miles to a local elder's house on the evening of her baptism. She recorded,

> Arriving at his house, we waited until midnight, in order that the neighbors might not disturb us, and then repaired to a stream of water a quarter of a mile away. Here we found the water, as we anticipated, frozen over, and the elder had to chop a hole in the ice large enough for the purpose of baptism. It was a scene and an occasion I shall never forget. Memory to-day brings back the emotions and sweet awe of that moment. None but God and his angels, and the few witnesses who stood on the bank with us, heard my covenant; but in the solemnity of that midnight hour it seemed as though all nature were listening, and the recording angel writing our words in the book of the Lord. Is it strange that such a scene, occurring in the life of a latter-day saint, should make an everlasting impression, as this did on mine?[4]

At this point, Priscilla had never contemplated leaving her home in England or voyaging to America. But "no sooner had I emerged from the water, on that night of baptism, and received my confirmation at the water's edge, than I became filled with an irresistible desire to join the saints who were gathering to America." On December 27, 1843, at age nineteen, Priscilla prayed and then headed to the port city of Liverpool alone. When she "saw the ocean that would soon roll between me and all I loved, my heart almost failed me. But . . . there was no turning back."[5]

With about 250 other Latter-day Saints, most of them converts like herself, Priscilla boarded the sailing vessel *Fanny* and voyaged to America. When the

---

2  Tullidge, 285–86.
3  Tullidge, 286.
4  Tullidge, 287.
5  Tullidge, 288.

vessel docked in New Orleans, Priscilla had planned to board the steamer *Maid of Iowa* and continue up the Mississippi River to Nauvoo, Illinois. But the *Maid of Iowa* was embargoed and lashed to the wharf. Priscilla wrote, "A lady of fortune was in the company—a Mrs. Bennett—and out of her private purse she not only lifted the embargo, but also fitted out the steamer with all necessary provisions, fuel, etc., and soon the company were again on their way."6

Their journey upriver was under the command of Captain Dan Jones. "At nearly every stopping place the emigrants were shamefully insulted and persecuted by the citizens," wrote Priscilla. "At Memphis some villain placed a half consumed cigar under a straw mattress and other bedding that had been laid out, aft of the ladies' cabin, to air. When we steamed out into the river the draft, created by the motion of the boat, soon fanned the fire into a quick flame. Fortunately I myself discovered the fire and gave the alarm in time to have it extinguished."7

At another landing, a mob gathered with plans to harm Latter-day Saints aboard the steamer. Captain Jones maneuvered the boat upriver past the mob. At yet another landing, Priscilla wrote, "A mob collected and began throwing stones through the cabin windows, smashing the glass and sash, and jeopardizing the lives of the passengers." According to Priscilla, Captain Jones "informed the mob that if they did not instantly desist, he would shoot them down like so many dogs; and like so many dogs they slunk away."8

When the steamer was nearing Nauvoo, Priscilla recalled,

> I had never before seen any of those assembled, yet I felt certain, as the boat drew near, that I should be able to pick out the prophet Joseph at first sight. This belief I communicated to Mrs. Bennett, whose acquaintance I had made on the voyage. She wondered at it; but I felt impressed by the spirit that I should know him. As we neared the pier the prophet was standing among the crowd. At the moment, however, I recognized him according to the impression, and pointed him out to Mrs. Bennett, with whom I was standing alone on the hurricane deck.
>
> Scarcely had the boat touched the pier when, singularly enough, Joseph sprang on board, and, without speaking with

---

6  Tullidge, 289.
7  Tullidge, 289.
8  Tullidge, 290–91.

any one, made his way direct to where we were standing, and addressing Mrs. Bennett by name, thanked her kindly for lifting the embargo from his boat, and blessed her for so materially aiding the saints.[9]

Priscilla resided in Nauvoo and enjoyed a brief season of peace. She married Samuel Lowry and gave birth to a daughter who died a few years later. It is assumed that her marriage to Lowry ended in divorce. With other Latter-day Saints, Priscilla fled from religious persecution in Nauvoo to Iowa and from there to the Rocky Mountains. It was not until 1854 that she married again, becoming a plural wife of Thomas Stephen Williams on December 23, 1854. Their marriage was solemnized in the Endowment House on Temple Square in Salt Lake City. The marriage ended in divorce.

Eleven years later, Priscilla married William C. Staines, a native of England. William had joined the Church in September 1841 after listening to the Restoration message preached by George J. Adams. He had arrived in Nauvoo on April 12, 1843. The next day, he heard the Prophet Joseph preach: "When I saw him that day he had on the same hat and coat that I saw him in when at sea. I heard him preach a number of times and saw him in and around the city, giving counsel, and I always believed in him from my first seeing him until his death, that he was the leader of this dispensation and God Almighty's prophet."[10]

William worked as a plasterer on the Nauvoo Temple before becoming one of the first Latter-day Saints to leave Nauvoo in the exodus to the West, arriving in the Salt Lake Valley on September 15, 1847. William was in charge of the endowment rooms in the Council House in Salt Lake City until being called on a mission to England in December 1860. It was in England that William received his testimony of the Book of Mormon: "I was speaking to a large congregation, bearing my testimony to the truth of the gospel, when I lifted up the Book of Mormon, saying, 'I know that this book I hold in my hand—the Book of Mormon—was translated by the power of God through Joseph Smith, and will go to every nation, kindred, tongue and people, as a testimony of the truth of the gospel.' This was the first testimony I had ever had of its truth."[11]

---

9   Tullidge, 291.
10  "Reminiscences of William C. Staines," *Contributor* 12 (1890–1891): 121–23, FamilySearch.
11  "Reminiscences of William C. Staines."

William and Priscilla were married on October 2, 1865. No children were born to their union. However, theirs was a happy marriage. Priscilla and William resided in Salt Lake City. Priscilla died on January 4, 1899, at age seventy-five.

**A Bridge to the Past**
Priscilla knew the answer to "Why pray?" The answer is simple—prayer expresses the soul's sincere desire. For Priscilla, she was dissatisfied with the doctrines of the Episcopal Church and asked the Lord in prayer to direct her to a "true religion." In answer to her "soul's sincere desire" expressed in prayer, missionaries taught her about the Restoration of the gospel. Consider the words of James Montgomery:

> Prayer is the soul's sincere desire,
> Uttered or unexpressed,
> The motion of a hidden fire
> That trembles in the breast.
>
> Prayer is the burden of a sigh,
> The falling of a tear,
> The upward glancing of an eye
> When none but God is near.[12]

---

12  "Prayer Is the Soul's Sincere Desire," *Hymns*, no. 145.

## Leonora Cannon Taylor

(1796–1868)

---

IN THE DAYS PRECEDING THE martyrdom of Joseph and Hyrum Smith, Leonora recalled, "Joseph Smith urged Emma to go to Carthage with him. She refused on account of having chills and [a] fever. He replied, if they did not hang me I do not know how they [will] kill me."[1]

---

When Leonora was thirteen years old, her father died at sea. As he had been the sole support of the family, his death plunged his widow and children into poverty. As a young teenager, Leonora was forced to seek gainful employment. She left the Isle of Man to work for a lady of status and rank in London.[2] In the bustling city, she found opulence in the upper crust of society. She also found her Savior. Leonora committed herself to a Christian life, allowing the Lord to direct all her movements. Concluding that her curly hair was sinful, she made a covenant with God to never show her curls in public. Although her actions appear extreme in our day, it evidences Leonora's commitment to live a self-effacing Christian life.

In her twenties, Leonora returned to her family on the Isle of Man. Her stay was brief but long enough for her to befriend the daughter of the private

---

1 "Leonora C. Taylor," in Mark L. McConkie, *Remembering Joseph: Personal Recollections of Those Who Knew the Prophet Joseph Smith* (Salt Lake City: Deseret Book, 2003), 401.
2 See B. H. Roberts, *The Life of John Taylor* (Salt Lake City: Bookcraft, 1963), 471.

secretary to Lord Aylmer, the newly appointed governor of Canada. The daughter insisted that Leonora become her companion on their voyage to the New World. Leonora declined the opportunity until reading in Genesis 12:1, "Get thee out of thy country, and from thy kindred, and from thy father's house, unto a land that I will shew thee." Believing the scripture to be a heavenly answer, in 1832, Leonora took passage aboard a steamer in Liverpool and voyaged to America. On the voyage she wrote, "I have thought for some days I should never live to see land, if it is my Father's will may I be resigned to it if He is with me all shall be well, it matters little what becomes of the Body. But the Lord is good unto me an unworthy Worm I find is not in vain to call upon Him praised be his name for ever. . . . Lord help me to be thankful that I am what I am and whom I am."[3]

When the steamer docked in the New York Harbor, Leonora went with her friend and her family across Lake Ontario to Toronto. On July 29, 1832, Leonora wrote, "I thank God for the kindness I meet with from the Family he hath placed me in I want to beg of the Lord that he would shine upon their Hearts bless them in there [sic] Souls. and Bodys."[4]

In Toronto, Leonora attended a bible class taught by John Taylor. His story of joining the Methodist Church and coming to America intrigued her. As a boy in England, John saw "in vision, an angel in the heavens, holding a trumpet to his mouth, sounding a message to the nations." The importance "of this vision he did not understand until later in life," but it led him to seek for greater truth.[5] Perceiving spiritual light in the Methodist dogma, at age sixteen, John abandoned his affiliation with the Church of England. A year or so later, he was recognized as a Methodist exhorter, a distinction that followed him to Canada. His unusual perception of the Methodist faith, however, led to his dismissal as an exhorter. Wanting to continue preaching, John organized Bible study classes.

When John first proposed marriage to Leonora, she declined. John was age twenty-five and Leonora was thirty-seven. A dream caused Leonora to change her mind and accept his proposal. In the dream, she saw "'herself associated with him [John Taylor]' in his life-work . . . [and] she was convinced that

---

3   B. H. Roberts, *The Life of John Taylor* (Salt Lake City: Bookcraft, 1963), 471–72.
4   Biographical Sketch of Leonora Cannon Taylor, FamilySearch.
5   Roberts, 28.

he would be her husband."⁶ John and Leonora were married on January 28, 1833, in Canada.

Three years later, they hosted in their home Parley P. Pratt, an Apostle of the Lord Jesus Christ. Elder Pratt overheard Leonora tell a neighbor, "[Elder Pratt] may be a man of God."⁷ Leonora and John attended Elder Pratt's study lessons and concluded that he spoke the truth. They entered baptismal waters on May 9, 1836.

Following their baptisms, the Taylors packed up their possessions and moved to Kirtland, Ohio. Unfortunately, in the agrarian community of Kirtland, they were confronted with religious persecution. Rather than stay in the unfriendly environment, in fall of 1838, the Taylors moved to Far West, Missouri. The extermination order issued by Governor Lilburn W. Boggs of Missouri against Latter-day Saints forced the Taylors to move once again. They sought refuge in log barracks in Montrose, Iowa.

John did not remain long with his family in the barracks. He had been ordained an Apostle and called to be a missionary in the British Isles. As his departure for England drew near, Leonora suffered greatly from sickness and a fever. Before departing,

> He [John] dedicated his wife and family to the care of the Lord, and blessed them in His name. At the thought of the hardships they had endured, of the uncertainty of their continuing in the house they then occupied, and that only a solitary room, the prevalence of diseases, the poverty of the brethren, their insecurity from mobs, together with the uncertainty of what might take place during his absence, produced feelings of no easy character. These solicitations, paternal and conjugal, were enhanced also by the time and distance that was to separate us. The thought of going forth at the command of the God of Israel to revisit my native land, to unfold the principles of eternal truth and make known the things God had revealed for the salvation of the world overcame every other feeling.⁸

---

6   Mary Jane Woodger, "The Lord Often Led Me," in *Women of Faith in the Latter Days, Volume One, 1775-1820*, eds. Richard E. Turley Jr. and Brittany A. Chapman (Salt Lake City: Deseret Book, 2011), 412.
7   Richard L. Jensen, "The John Taylor Family," *Ensign*, Feb. 1980, 51.
8   Mary Alice Cannon Lambert, "Leonora Cannon Taylor," *Young Woman's Journal* 20, no. 8 (August 8, 1908), 247.

Leonora recovered from her illness and was able to care for herself and her children in John's absence. John's mission to the British Isles proved a great blessing to himself and Leonora. Numbered among his first converts were Leonora's brother George Cannon and George's wife, Ann Quayle Cannon.[9]

After John returned to Nauvoo, he became prominent in civic affairs. He was elected to the Nauvoo City Council and named a regent of the Nauvoo University. He became the associate editor of the *Times and Seasons* and the proprietor of the *Nauvoo Neighbor*.

John was with the Prophet Joseph Smith and his brother Hyrum in Carthage Jail on June 27, 1844. In the afternoon, John sang, "A Poor Wayfaring Man of Grief." At 5:15 p.m., Joseph Smith and his brother Hyrum were murdered. John was severely wounded with four bullets penetrating his body.

Leonora wrote to Governor Thomas Ford of Illinois on July 22, 1844, about the tragedy:

> *Sir,*— The peculiarity of my situation will, I hope, plead my excuse for troubling your Excellency on the present occasion.
>
> Mr. [John] Taylor, who was severely wounded in the jail at Carthage, is still ill, and obliged to be lifted in and out of bed; his wounds are slowly healing, and we hope he will finally get well, if suffered to do so. But, sir, I am sorry to say the murderers and mobbers are still at large in our neighborhood; as there has been no steps taken to bring them to justice, they have taken fresh courage and held meetings to carry out their work of destruction. I have been told they have sent messengers to Missouri to collect all the force they can, to come and exterminate the Mormons after harvest....
>
> ... Nothing but the urgency of the case could have induced me to remind your Excellency of your promise to bring the *murderers* to *justice*. If a step of that kind is not taken soon, I much fear that it cannot benefit us as a people.
>
> We are without arms, in a great measure, having delivered them up at your Excellency's request.[10]

In spite of her letter, Governor Ford failed to provide Latter-day Saints with protection. As religious persecution raged, Leonora and John and their

---

9  See Jensen, "John Taylor Family," 52.
10 "Leonora Taylor's Womanly Letter to Governor Ford," July 22, 1844, in Smith, *History of the Church*, 7:201.

children fled from Nauvoo to safety in Iowa, leaving behind property worth ten thousand dollars with little hope of recompense. They had not traveled far when John received another mission assignment to England. His acceptance meant leaving Leonora and his children in difficult circumstances. Leonora recorded on the back page of her diary how she survived the separation from John and the ordeals of life:

> The Lord often led me by a way that I knew not and in a path that I naturally did not wish to go, every sweet has had its bitter, the way seemed to me narrower every day without his almighty power to help me I cannot walk in it to whom shall I go or look for succor but unto thee my Father and only Friend.[11]

Leonora and her children eventually journeyed to the Salt Lake Valley. In the valley, she continued to be very supportive of her husband but knew much of loneliness as he was often called to serve away from home. Leonora died on December 9, 1868, at age seventy-two.

## A Bridge to the Past

Leonora made and kept sacred covenants. She was blessed with strength to endure religious persecution, care for her wounded husband, and cross the plains to reach the westward Zion. President Russell M. Nelson recently said, "The Lord is gathering those who are willing to let God prevail in their lives."[12] Leonora epitomized his statement, for she was willing to be led by the Lord in "a way that I knew not and in a path that I naturally did not wish to go."

---

11  Roberts, *Life of John Taylor*, 474.
12  President Russell M. Nelson, "Let God Prevail," *Ensign*, Oct. 2020.

## Mercy Rachel Fielding Thompson

(1807–1893)

---

AFTER THE DEATH OF HER husband, Robert Thompson, Mercy wrote, "This indeed was a time of sorrow, but I can never forget the tender sympathy and brotherly kindness he [the Prophet Joseph Smith] ever showed toward me and my fatherless child. When riding with him and his wife Emma in their carriage I have known him to alight and gather prairie flowers for my little girl."[1]

---

In 1832, Mercy Fielding migrated to Upper Canada with her brother Joseph and sister Mary. In 1836, the Fielding siblings, who had become disenchanted with Methodism, were introduced to The Church of Jesus Christ of Latter-day Saints by John Taylor. They were baptized on May 21, 1836, by Elder Parley P. Pratt. Following their baptisms, the siblings journeyed to Kirtland to be with the Saints of God.

In Kirtland, Mercy was reacquainted with Robert Thompson. Robert had joined the Methodist Church at an early age. He migrated to Canada from England in 1834, where he also was baptized by Elder Parley P. Pratt. Robert moved to Kirtland in May 1837. One month later, he was married to Mercy on June 4, 1837, by the Prophet Joseph Smith.[2]

---

1 "Recollections of the Prophet Joseph Smith," *Juvenile Instructor* 27, no. 13 (July 1, 1892), 399.
2 See Dan T. Holmes, "Brief Life Story of Mercy Fielding Thompson," FamilySearch.

Before the Thompsons moved from Kirtland to Far West, Missouri, Mercy received a patriarchal blessing in the Kirtland Temple from Joseph Smith Sr. The Thompsons arrived in Far West in May 1838. Their only child, Mary Jane Thompson, was born on June 14, 1838. Five months later, on October 25, 1838, Robert stood next to Elder David W. Patten when he was mortally wounded in the Battle of Crooked River. Within days of Elder Patten's death, Robert was threatened with mob violence and fled from Far West to Quincy, Illinois. Mercy wrote, "To describe the sufferings and privations we endured while there would be past my skill. . . . Some few things however I will relate. My husband with many of the men being chased by a mob fled into the wilderness in November leaving me with an infant not five months old through months of distressing worry before I could get a message from him."[3]

During this distressing period, Mercy stayed with her sister, Mary Fielding Smith. Mercy wrote,

> It was during this time that I stayed with my sister who gave birth to a son November 13, 1838 while her husband [Hyrum Smith] was in prison. She took a severe cold and was unable to attend to her domestic duties for four months. This caused much of the care of the family which was very large to rest upon me. Mobs were continually threatening to massacre the inhabitants of the city. At times I feared to lay my baby down lest they should slay me and leave it to suffer worse than death.
>
> About the first of February 1839, by the request of her husband, my sister was placed in a bed in a wagon and taken a journey of about 40 miles to visit him in the prison. Her infant son Joseph Fielding Smith being then eleven weeks old. I had to accompany her with my own baby being eight months old. The weather being extremely cold, we suffered much on the journey.

Mercy wrote an anecdotal account of their experience in Liberty Jail:

> It would be beyond my power to describe my feelings when we were admitted into the jail by the keeper and the door was locked behind us. We could not help feeling a sense of horror on realizing that we were locked up in that dark and dismal den, fit only for criminals of the deepest dye; but there we beheld Joseph, the Prophet, the man chosen of God, in

---

3   "My Story by Mercy Rachel Thompson," December 20, 1880, FamilySearch.

the dispensation of the fullness of time to hold the keys of His kingdom on the earth, with power to bind and loose as God should direct, confined in a loathsome prison for no other cause or reason than that he claimed to be inspired of God to establish His church among men. There we also found his noble brother, Hyrum, who, I believe was not charged with any other crime than that of being a friend to his brother Joseph. . . . The night was spent in fearful forebodings, owing to a false rumor having gone out that the prisoners contemplated making an attempt to escape, which greatly enraged the jailor and the guards.[4]

After leaving Liberty Jail, Mercy and her sister, Mary, returned to Far West. In mid-February in extreme cold weather, the sisters began their journey out of the state of Missouri. Mercy wrote, "My husband had engaged a room for our accommodation [in Quincy, Illinois], but my sister being obliged to be with me on account of her baby the whole of Bro. Hyrum's family of ten remained with us until April."[5] When Hyrum escaped from imprisonment in Missouri, he arrived in Quincy and made other housing arrangements for his family.

It was not long before the Thompsons and the Smiths had moved upriver to Commerce. Robert became a private secretary to the Prophet Joseph Smith. At the general conference in October 1840, he was sustained as the Church historian. In addition, Robert was asked to give the funeral sermon for Joseph Smith Sr. He also wrote the hymn, "See, the Mighty Angel Flying."[6] Due to Robert's being the private secretary of Joseph Smith and having a personal relationship with the Smith family, Mercy had many occasions to be with the Prophet Joseph. She wrote, "I saw him by the bed-side of Emma, his wife, in sickness, exhibiting all the solicitude and sympathy possible for the tenderest of hearts and the most affectionate of natures to feel." More important to Mercy, she saw the Prophet "by the death-bed of my beloved companion, I saw him stand in sorrow, reluctantly submitting to the decree of Providence, while the tears of love and sympathy freely flowed." Robert died on August 27, 1841. The Prophet Joseph "took charge of the funeral ceremonies, strictly adhering to my husband's wish that there should be no military or other display at his burial."[7]

4   "Recollections of the Prophet Joseph Smith," *Juvenile Instructor*, July 1, 1892, 398.
5   "Recollections of the Prophet Joseph Smith," 398.
6   "See, the Mighty Angel Flying," *Hymns*, no. 330.
7   "Recollections of the Prophet Joseph Smith," 399.

As to being a widow with a young daughter, Mercy wrote,

> With diligence and economy and the helping of the Lord, our wants were supplied, but to me it was a lonesome life to be deprived of my husband, whose like could rarely be found. I believe all who knew him would agree with me in saying that his meekness and humility and integrity he could not be easily excelled, if equaled. . . .
>
> Being deprived of my husband[']s society caused me to mourn so deeply that my health was impaired very much.[8]

After two years of living in very trying, lonely circumstances, on August 11, 1843, Mercy recorded,

> I was called by direct revelation from Heaven through Brother Joseph Smith the prophet to enter into a state of plural marriage with Hyrum Smith the patriarch. This subject when first communicated to me, tried me to the very core. All my former traditions and every natural feeling of my heart rose in opposition to this principle, but I was convinced that it was appointed by him who is too wise to err. And too good to be unkind. Soon after my marriage I became a partner with my sister in the house of Hyrum Smith, where I remained until his death. Sharing with my sister the care of his numerous family. I had from the time I moved to his house been a scribe recording patriarchal blessings.[9]

At one point Mercy was "seeking diligently to know from the Lord if there was any thing I could do for the building up of the Kingdom of God." She experienced "a most pleasant sensation" and heard the words, "Try to get the sisters to subscribe one cent per week for the purpose of buying nails and glass for the temple." When she told the Prophet Joseph of the whisperings of the still small voice, he encouraged her to move forward with the subscription. Mercy wrote, "Not with standing the poverty of the community we had collected from the sisters by the time the committee was ready for the glass and nails in the treasury $500.00."[10]

In late 1845, when the Nauvoo Temple was ready for use, Brigham Young called Mercy to "take up [her] abode there" and assist with the female ordinances.

---

8   "My Story by Mercy Rachel Thompson."
9   "My Story by Mercy Rachel Thompson."
10  "My Story by Mercy Rachel Thompson."

Mercy described herself as "laboring night and day keeping my child with me" in the temple.[11]

She remained in Nauvoo until September 1846, crossing the Mississippi River a day or two before the mob commenced firing on the city. She recalled,

> I traveled to winter quarters where I remained until the following June. Then I started with a company of Saints led by Parley P. Pratt for the west. We arrived in the valley of the Great Salt Lake in 16 weeks.
>
> I shared with [the] saints the privations eating thistle roots, fighting crickets and grasshoppers, but I do not remember of having uttered one mummer of complaint. The blessings of the Lord have attended me and crowned my labors with success so that I have been able to assist in emigrating the poor saints as well as contributing for the poor here in the building of the temples and so forth. I would not give up my religion for all the gold in America.[12]

Mercy closed her autobiographical sketch by saying,

> I know too that if I had not embraced the gospel as revealed by Joseph Smith the Prophet in these the last days and endeavored to live up to the requirements of the law of God, I could never be permitted to dwell in the presence of God in his celestial kingdom. I am now in my 74th year and have written this sketch without spectacles mostly by lamp light.[13]

Mercy died on September 15, 1893, in Salt Lake City, at age eighty-six.

**A Bridge to the Past**

Mercy passed through horrific scenes in Missouri and saw the destruction of Latter-day Saint property. She witnessed the Prophet Joseph Smith being confined in Liberty Jail and cared for Hyrum Smith's family when her sister, Mary Fielding Smith, was too weak from childbirth to do so. Mercy cared for the poor and administered to their wants in the Salt Lake Valley without any thought of compensation. Intermixed with her charity were enough joys to cause Mercy to say, "I would not give up my religion for all the gold in

---

11   "My Story by Mercy Rachel Thompson."
12   "My Story by Mercy Rachel Thompson."
13   "My Story by Mercy Rachel Thompson."

America." Mercy had learned a great secret—don't dwell on past sorrows. She replaced such thinking with notations of the tender mercies of the Lord on her behalf, such as the Prophet Joseph alighting from his carriage to pick prairie flowers for her little girl and Brigham Young inviting her to serve in the Nauvoo Temple day and night. By focusing on the here and now, Mercy was able to write, "[The] blessings of the Lord have attended me and crowned my labors with success." I hope you could write a similar statement.

(1816–1902)

---

OUT OF HER BEDROOM WINDOW, Nancy could see "the masons at work [on the Nauvoo Temple] and could hear the click of their hammers and hear their sailor songs as they pulled the rock in place with pulleys."[1] One day as she looked toward the temple, she saw a crowd gathered and decided to investigate:

> I thought I would go over. I put on my bonnet and shawl and made my way over. Brother Joseph [Smith] was there and seemed busily engaged over something. Finally, he looked up and saw us women. He said for the brothers to stand back and let the sisters come up. So they gave way, and we went up. In the huge chief corner stone was cut out a square about a foot around and about as deep lined with zinc, and in it Brother Joseph had placed a Bible, a Book of Mormon, a hymn book, and other church works along with silver money that had been coined in that year. Then a lid was cemented down, and the temple was reared on the top of

---

1  Nancy Naomi Alexander Tracy wrote her life history three times. In 1880 at age sixty-four she wrote thirty-six pages. The original of it is in the Bancroft Library in Berkeley, California. In 1885 at age sixty-nine she wrote eighty-one pages in longhand. A typed copy is housed in the Utah Historical Society in Salt Lake City. In 1896 at age eighty she wrote again. The typed copy is seventy-six pages long in possession of her family. The following notes are from these sources and appear as "Life History of Nancy Naomi Alexander Tracy Written by Herself," FamilySearch.

this. It made me think of the prophets in ancient days hiding up their records to come forth in some future generation.[2]

---

"My parents were church-going people, my Mother a Baptist, my Father . . . was a Universalist," wrote Nancy. Her father died when she was four years old. He had left her mother "a nice little farm and comfortable home, but misfortunes overtook her and she lost all."[3] Unable to support all of her children, Nancy's mother sent her to be raised by her grandparents. She wrote,

> I had a good home and good care. As soon as I was old enough, they sent me to school. I was taught in all the common branches. As I grew older, I had acquired a fair education. When I was 15, I could spin and weave, knit and sew, and I always felt thankful to grandmother for teaching me.[4]

While living with her grandparents, Nancy attended the Methodist Church and "read the Bible and went and prayed with all the sincerity in the world, for I wanted to be a Christian and be happy." As a teenager, she attended camp revival meetings and was put on an "anxious seat, as they called it, but I failed to get that change of heart."[5]

After ten years of living with her grandparents, at age sixteen, Nancy moved back home with her mother. "Mother got me a place to board and sent me to school again," Nancy wrote. To support herself, she became a housekeeper for Abram Tracy. While working in his home, she met Moses Tracy. "He became my escort when I went out," wrote Nancy. "I found him to be a young man of good habits and a working man. I accepted his offer of marriage." Nancy and Moses were married on July 15, 1832. "Everything was bright before us," Nancy penned. "As yet we had not tasted the bitter. Those were happy days."[6]

In 1833, Nancy heard "rumbles about a gold bible that a gold-digger had dug up. . . . Newspapers were full of the vilest slander about Joseph Smith, the finder of these golden records." When Latter-day Saint missionaries came to her neighborhood, Nancy "determined to go and see and hear what those

---

2 "Life History of Nancy Naomi Alexander Tracy."
3 "Life History of Nancy Naomi Alexander Tracy."
4 "Life History of Nancy Naomi Alexander Tracy."
5 "Life History of Nancy Naomi Alexander Tracy."
6 "Life History of Nancy Naomi Alexander Tracy."

horrid creatures looked like and had to say, for I hardly expected they were human from what I had heard." She listened to the preaching of Elder David W. Patten, an Apostle of the Lord Jesus Christ. "It seemed as though his influence put all prejudice under his feet," Nancy recalled. "I believed with my whole soul . . . and told the folks that for the first time I had heard the true Gospel preached."[7]

On May 10, 1834, Nancy and Moses were baptized. After their baptisms, they desired to gather with other Latter-day Saints in Kirtland, Ohio. They bid farewell to family and friends and traveled about four hundred miles to reach Kirtland. On the Sabbath following their arrival, they attended a meeting. "For the first time we saw [the] Prophet Joseph and heard him preach," Nancy said.[8]

After securing a room for themselves, the Prophet Joseph and Oliver Cowdery stopped by to see them. Nancy wrote,

> He [Joseph] wanted some money, for he was encumbered. My husband readily gave him the desired amount of fifty dollars, and he sat down to write a note. My husband told him he did not want a note and that his word was sufficient. Joseph made the reply, "Brother Tracy, business is business and we want to do it correctly." He gave the note payable one day after date. He said, "When you think you need the money, let me know in time, so I can get it for you." Brother Tracy told him he should not need it until the next spring.[9]

Nancy was able to attend both days of the Kirtland Temple dedication. She wrote, "They were two of the happiest days of my life. . . . I felt that it was heaven on earth. . . . Solemn Assemblies were called. Endowments were given. The Elders went from house to house, blessing the Saints and administering the Sacrament."[10] Following the temple dedication, many of the elders were sent on missions, including Moses Tracy. When he returned from the mission, Moses asked the Prophet Joseph whether he should take his family to Missouri. According to Nancy,

> Brother Joseph bowed his head for a moment, and then said, "It is the will of the Lord for you to go to that land, and you

---

7 "Life History of Nancy Naomi Alexander Tracy."
8 "Life History of Nancy Naomi Alexander Tracy."
9 "Life History of Nancy Naomi Alexander Tracy."
10 "Life History of Nancy Naomi Alexander Tracy."

will need the money I owe you, and you shall have it although I do not know how I am going to get it. Get ready and let me know a day or two before you start."

... Brother Joseph sold half an acre of land and came and paid the money, saying, "I told you you should have it."[11]

After the Tracys moved to Far West, Missouri, they found "the Saints were in destitute conditions and circumstances in consequence of persecution and being driven from their homes." Nancy penned, "It was the same with us. Our clothes and shoes were giving out." Moses found work at a mill and soon acquired forty acres of land three miles from Far West. Nancy took in sewing. But before long, Missourians started to "plunder . . . and insult women and children and abuse them, and to take the brethren prisoners into their camps, until, at last, the brethren could stand it no longer." The Battle of Crooked River followed in the wake of atrocities. "News of this battle spread like wildfire," wrote Nancy, "and soon the whole state was in arms against" the Latter-day Saints.[12]

Nancy was in her home when the Missouri militia marched into Far West. She wrote,

> They stationed one company near my house and there camped. I was alone except for my little children. My husband had to leave, for all those who were in the Crooked River battle were being hunted for by the soldiers. So I was at their mercy. Still they assured me that I would not be molested. However, they searched the premises and put a double guard around my house. So I was a prisoner in my own home with no one to care for me but my little boy.[13]

When it was relatively safe to do so, Nancy and her family fled from Far West. "Imagine our feelings in leaving our homes and starting out not knowing where we were going and leaving our Prophet and leaders in prison at the mercy of those bold fiends of human shape," she penned before adding, "Notwithstanding our afflictions, the hand of the Lord was over His people."[14]

Nancy and her children made it safely across the Mississippi River to Quincy and then on to Commerce, Illinois. Of Commerce, Nancy wrote, "It was a very sickly place, but the only one we had to go to. . . . Here we were again

---

11   "Life History of Nancy Naomi Alexander Tracy."
12   "Life History of Nancy Naomi Alexander Tracy."
13   "Life History of Nancy Naomi Alexander Tracy."
14   "Life History of Nancy Naomi Alexander Tracy."

to start anew to make another home. . . . We were not conquered in spirit but determined to live our religion and stand by the principles of the Gospel and help to build up the kingdom of God on the earth."[15]

Nancy and Moses and their four children enjoyed a season of peace in what became the city of Nauvoo. Moses was employed in a mercantile store, and Nancy taught school. She also joined the Female Relief Society of Nauvoo. Of that society, she penned,

> Sometimes Emma would bring the Prophet in to give instructions. One in particular, I remember. He opened the meeting by prayer. He was so full of the Spirit of the Holy Ghost that his frame shook and his face shone and looked almost transparent. This was about the time that the order of Celestial marriage was given by revelation to him. He had taught it to a few who would hear it, but I heard him say at one time when he was preaching (turning to those that sat behind him[)], "If I should reveal to these, my Brethren, who now seem to be my bosom friends, what God has revealed to me, they would be the first to seek my life." And it was so. Even when this law of Celestial marriage was taught, these very men, William Marks, the Laws, and others, turned vipers against him.[16]

When Nancy and Moses learned of the deaths of Joseph Smith and his brother Hyrum, Nancy penned, "We were horror-stricken. My husband sobbed aloud, 'Is it true? Can it be true?'" She wrote that the killing of Joseph Smith cast a "dark gloomy shadow over Nauvoo," for "all the Saints near and far . . . loved the Prophet of God."[17]

Nancy attended an August 8, 1844, meeting in which "Sidney Rigdon and his followers were on hand to contest their right to be the leaders of the Saints." She wrote, "I can testify that the mantle of Joseph fell upon Brigham that day as that of Elijah did fall upon Elisha, for it seemed that his voice, his gestures, and all were Joseph. It seemed that we had him again with us."[18]

In 1846, Nancy and her family joined the Latter-day Saint exodus from Nauvoo. They crossed the mighty Mississippi and camped along the way before reaching the bluffs near the Missouri River. They stayed for three years at the

---

15 "Life History of Nancy Naomi Alexander Tracy."
16 "Life History of Nancy Naomi Alexander Tracy."
17 "Life History of Nancy Naomi Alexander Tracy."
18 "Life History of Nancy Naomi Alexander Tracy."

bluffs before continuing their journey to the Salt Lake Valley. Gazing upon the valley, Nancy wrote, "Oh how beautiful and grand the valley, dotted with dwellings and with the Great Salt Lake sparkling in the sunlight, appeared. We feasted our eyes upon the scene. It looked like paradise."[19]

The Tracys resided first in the Session Settlement, next Provo, and then in Marriottsville. At each location, Moses was ill. He suffered from paralytic strokes before his death in August 1858. "In all our married life or ever since we had joined the Church of Latter-day Saints," wrote Nancy, "it had been one continual scene of persecution, traveling from one place to another to find a resting place from our enemies."[20]

Left alone in very destitute circumstances, she penned, "There was nothing grown upon which to subsist, the children were practically naked, and I was worn out myself. I felt to cry unto the Lord for help." In recalling these difficult days and those that followed, Nancy wrote, "I marvel, for I was never a strong woman. I feel to acknowledge the hand of the Lord in it all and that I am alive today to tell the tale."[21]

On April 8, 1860, she married the brother of Moses Tracy—Horace Tracy. "I had been married 15 months when I had a daughter born, my last child," Nancy wrote. "This made eleven children of whom three were dead and another gone and perhaps dead also. I know not what has become of him."[22]

On her eighty-third birthday on May 14, 1899, Nancy penned—

> Eighty-three summers are past and gone
> Since I first beheld the light of morn.
> And in my heart I know full well
> I have not long on earth to dwell.
>
> But e'er I pass behind the veil,
> A message I bear, truth will prevail,
> Though Satan's powers may it assail;
> God is at the helm and will steer the ship,
> And anchor it safe in the harbor of bliss;
>
> . . . . . . . . . . . . . . . . . . . . . . . . . . . . . .
>
> Now to my friends and kindred dear
> I bid you all adieu, my work on earth is done;

---

19 "Life History of Nancy Naomi Alexander Tracy."
20 "Life History of Nancy Naomi Alexander Tracy."
21 "Life History of Nancy Naomi Alexander Tracy."
22 "Life History of Nancy Naomi Alexander Tracy."

> Though you may shed the bitter tear,
> Tis well with me, so never fear;
>
> . . . . . . . . . . . . . . . . . . . . . . . . . . . . .
>
> The angels will meet you at the gate,
> If you have been true and kept the faith;
> Your reward is sure, so be firm and endure,
> In the haven of rest to dwell with the blessed.[23]

Nancy died three years after writing the poem, in 1902, at age eighty-six.

## A Bridge to the Past

From the time of her baptism until her death, Nancy epitomized the pioneer song "Faith in Every Footstep" and in so doing had the "happiest of days." Sure, there was a mix of disappointments and sorrows thrown along Nancy's path as there are in yours. It appears that Nancy viewed her sorrows as stepping-stones, not stumbling blocks. Her hope for a bright future did not dim with age. Hers was a hope that the Lord would prevail and blessings would follow—now and in the future.

---

23 "Life History of Nancy Naomi Alexander Tracy."

# Emmeline B. Wells

(1828–1921)

---

Although Emmeline B. Wells had met Joseph Smith only months before his death, the Prophet still made a lasting impression on Emmeline and her faith. She recounted:

> As we neared our destination in sailing up the Mississippi . . . a crowd of people were coming toward the bank of the river. As we stepped ashore the crowd advanced, and I could see one person who towered away and above all the others around him. . . . His [Joseph Smith's] majestic bearing, so entirely different from any one I had ever seen (and I had seen many superior men) was more than a surprise. It was as if I beheld a vision; I seemed to be lifted off my feet, to be as it were walking in the air, and paying no heed whatever to those around me. I made my way through the crowd, ther. I saw this man whom I had noticed, because of his lofty appearance, shaking hands with all the people, men, women and children. Before I was aware of it he came to me, and when he took my hand, I was simply electrified,—thrilled through and through to the tips of my fingers, and every part of my body, as if some magic elixir had given me new life and vitality. I am sure that for a few minutes I was not conscious of motion. . . .

> I heard him preach all his last sermons, and frequently met him and shook hands with him, and always felt in my inmost soul, he is indeen [sic] a man unlike all others.[1]

---

While away from home earning a teaching certificate at the New Salem Academy in Massachusetts, Emmeline's mother and three of her sisters joined The Church of Jesus Christ of Latter-day Saints. When fourteen years old, Emmeline returned home and entered baptismal waters, even though town authorities, ministers, and others at the water's edge threatened harm.[2]

On July 29, 1843, at age fifteen Emmeline married sixteen-year-old James Harvey Harris, the son of her branch president. With James and his family, Emmeline journeyed to Nauvoo in March 1844. There she met the Prophet Joseph Smith. Two months later, Joseph and his brother Hyrum were killed in Carthage.

The death of Joseph led even the faithful to reevaluate their religious commitment. Among those who withdrew from the faith was Emmeline's husband, James. Emmeline refused to relinquish her faith. In spite of their religious differences, James bid her an affectionate farewell and boarded a steamer heading to St. Louis with the promise he would return in about two weeks. Although James wrote letters to Emmeline, she never saw him again.

Grieving over the loss of her husband, the death of an infant son, and her loneliness in Nauvoo, there was little comfort for Emmeline until she attended a meeting held on August 8, 1844. She wrote,

> I could see very well, and every one of them thought it [Brigham Young] was really the Prophet Joseph risen from the dead. But after Brigham Young had spoken a few words, the tumult subsided, and the people really knew that it was not the Prophet Joseph, but the President of the quorum of the Twelve Apostles. It was the most wonderful manifestation, I think, that I have ever known or seen.[3]

---

1 Emmeline Blanche Wells, in "Joseph Smith, the Prophet," *Young Woman's Journal* 16, no. 12 (December 1905), 555–56.
2 See Orson F. Whitney, *History of Utah* (Salt Lake City: George Q. Cannon & Sons, 1904), 4:587.
3 Preston Nibley, comp., *Faith Promoting Stories* (Salt Lake City: Deseret Book, 1943), 138.

In 1845, Emmeline became a plural wife of Bishop Newel K. Whitney. To their union were born two children. At the time of the exodus from Nauvoo, Emmeline journeyed with the Whitney family to the Territory of Iowa. When the family reached Winter Quarters, Emmeline taught school. In 1848, she journeyed to the Salt Lake Valley. In 1850, Newel K. Whitney died.

In October 1852, Emmeline married Daniel H. Wells, by whom she bore three daughters. While her children were young, Emmeline devoted herself to motherhood. After they reached maturity, she turned to writing. On May 1, 1875, she became the assistant editor of the *Exponent*. In July 1877, she was appointed senior editor. Of this appointment, Brigham Young said, "I give you a mission to write brief sketches of the lives of the leading women of Zion, and publish them."[4] Emmeline was pleased and said, "Although the historians of the past have been neglectful of woman, and it is the exception if she be mentioned at all; yet the future will deal more generously with womankind and the historian of the present age will find it very embarrassing to ignore woman in the records of the nineteenth century."[5]

Along with writing and editing the *Exponent* for more than a quarter of a century (1877–1914), Emmeline published a book of poetry—*Musings and Memories* (1915). Her best-known poem is "Our Mountain Home So Dear."[6] She later wrote "Aunt Em's Stories." Of her intellect, it was said, "Her marvelous memory is an encyclopedia of facts upon any subject in which she is interested."[7]

Emmeline played a key role in the organization of the Relief Society, Young Ladies, and Primary Associations. For nearly thirty years, she represented Utah women in the National Woman's Suffrage Association. When Utah women were franchised in February 1870, Emmeline was among the "first to wield the ballot."[8] She chaired the Utah Women's Republican League and for twenty-two years was general secretary of the Relief Society. When asked how she accomplished so much, she answered, "Work is [my] most congenial atmosphere, [my] very breath of life."[9]

4   "The Jubilee Celebration, The Need of Press Representation," *Woman's Exponent* 20, no. 17 (March 15, 1892), 132.
5   "Self-Made Women," *Woman's Exponent* 9, no. 19 (March 1, 1881), 148.
6   "Our Mountain Home So Dear," *Hymns*, no. 33.
7   Whitney, *History of Utah*, 4:590.
8   Whitney, *History of Utah*, 4:588.
9   Whitney, *History of Utah*, 4:590.

On October 3, 1910, President Joseph F. Smith called eighty-two-year-old Emmeline B. Wells to be the fifth General President of the Relief Society, the oldest woman ever called to the position.[10] At that time, Emmeline "stood barely five feet tall and weighed only a hundred pounds. She refused to wear black dresses or a veil over her face, preferring instead pastel colors and soft, flowing scarves at her neck. Delicate earrings dangled from her pierced ears, layers of slender chains hung around her neck, and rings adorned her fingers."[11] Emmeline accepted the call and penned, "I feel deeply the great responsibility resting upon me in being called to fill this public office; [sic] but hope to be guided and sustained by the Holy Spirit in this calling and duty that I may keep humble and be qualified to do all things that are required of me."[12] Under her leadership, the motto "charity never faileth" was given to Relief Society.

In 1918, at age eighty-nine, Emmeline fell into the elevator shaft at the bishop's building and would have fallen fifteen feet if she hadn't grabbed the lifting cable and hung on until rescued. She suffered a stroke in April 1921 and lay in a comatose state for three weeks before her death on April 25, 1921. Flags were flown at half-mast at prominent Church structures throughout Salt Lake City in honor of a woman for the first time. Her funeral was held in the Salt Lake Tabernacle with President Heber J. Grant presiding and speaking. A tribute to her life stated, "She is about as near the personification of true charity as it is possible for a mortal to be; and in her there is neither selfishness nor guile. She has a heart as broad as humanity, a sympathy that knows no bounds."[13]

In 1928, on the hundredth anniversary of her birth, women of Utah placed a marble bust of Emmeline B. Wells in the state capitol building in Salt Lake City. The inscription on the memorial reads, "A Fine Soul Who Served Us."

## A Bridge to the Past

Brigham Young invited Emmeline to write and publish brief life sketches of leading Latter-day Saint women. By accepting Brigham's invitation, Emmeline

10   See Annie Wells Cannon, "Mothers in Israel," *Relief Society Magazine* 3, no. 2 (February 1916), 63, 66.
11   Janet Peterson and LaRene Gaunt, *Elect Ladies* (Salt Lake City: Deseret Book, 1990), 79.
12   "Diary of Emmeline B. Wells," April 1, 1875; available at churchhistorianspress.org/emmeline-b-wells.
13   "A Mother in Israel. A tribute to Emmeline B. Wells: Aunt Em," *Juvenile Instructor*, May 1913, 1.

was the first to write of the sacrifice, faith, and devotion of sisters in Zion. With pen in hand and the press of the *Woman's Exponent* at her disposal, for twenty-five years, Emmeline faithfully preserved in print stories of women that have blessed readers for generations.

Have you written the story of your life, your faith, and your successes? Have you shared the inspiring stories of those around you? They are stories worth preserving.

## Mary Musselman Whitmer

(1778–1856)

Lucy Mack Smith wrote in the summer of 1829, when Joseph Smith, Oliver Cowdery, and David Whitner returned to the Whitmer log house,

> It was between 3 & 4 o'clock Mrs. [Mary Musselman] Whitmer & Mr. Smith [Joseph Smith Sr.] and myself were sitting in a bedroom I sat on the bedside when Joseph came in he threw himself [down] beside me Father!— Mother!— said he you do not know how happy I am The Lord has caused the plates to be shown to 3 more besides me who have also seen an angel and will have to testify to the [truth] of what I have said for they know for themselves . . . and it does rejoice my soul that I am not any longer to be entirely alone in the world. Martin Harris then came in he seemed almost overcome with excess of Joy He then testified to what he had seen and heard as did also the others Oliver and David [and] their testimony was the same in substance as that contained in the book of Mormon.[1]

Mary and her husband, Peter Whitmer, reared seven children to adulthood—Christian, Jacob, John, David, Catherine, Peter Jr., and Elizabeth Ann. The

---

1  Lucy Mack Smith, "Lucy Mack Smith History, 1844–1845," book 8, page 11, josephsmithpapers.org.

Whitmer family resided in Pennsylvania before moving to Waterloo, New York, in 1809 and settling on a hundred-acre farm in Fayette Township. In Fayette, Peter Whitmer was known as "a hard-working, God-fearing man, a strict Presbyterian [who] brought his children up with rigid sectarian discipline."[2] He attended the German Reformed Church and held morning devotionals in his home with prayers, hymns, and reading of the scriptures.

His pastor, Diedrich Willers Sr., said that Father Whitmer was "a quiet unpretending, and apparently honest, candid, and simple-minded man." In 1829, Reverend Willers warned Peter of "errors and delusions" being perpetuated by Joseph Smith.[3] Peter ignored the warning and encouraged his son David to bring Joseph and his scribe to their home, a distance of 135 miles from Harmony, Pennsylvania. Peter was convinced that "there must be an overruling hand in this."[4]

Joseph and Emma Smith and Oliver Cowdery were guests in the Whitmer home in 1829. During their stay, Mary Whitmer claimed to see the gold plates. Church Historian Andrew Jenson wrote, "If her statement is reliable, she is the only woman on earth who has ever enjoyed the privilege of seeing the holy treasure."[5]

Years later, David Whitmer repeated her claim to Orson Pratt and Joseph F. Smith. When Edward Stevenson and Andrew Jenson visited Richmond, Missouri, in 1888, her grandson John C. Whitmer testified,

> I have heard my grandmother (Mary M. Whitmer) say on several occasions that she was shown the plates of the Book of Mormon by a holy angel, whom she always called Brother Nephi. (She undoubtedly refers to Moroni, the angel who had the plates in charge.) It was at the time, she said, when the translation was going on at the house of the elder Peter Whitmer, her husband.... My grandmother in having so many extra persons to care for, besides her own large household, was

---

2 *Chicago Tribune*, December 17, 1885, quoted in Richard Lloyd Anderson, "The Whitmers: A Family That Nourished the Church," *Ensign*, Aug. 1979, 35.
3 Diedrich Willers to Ellen E. Dickinson, January 19, 1882, quoted in Ellen E. Dickinson, *New Light on Mormonism* (New York: Funk & Wagnalls, 1885), 249–52, quoted in Anderson, "Whitmers," 36.
4 Lucy Smith, *Biographical Sketches of Joseph Smith the Prophet, and His Progenitors for Many Generations* (Liverpool: S. W. Richards, 1853), 136.
5 Andrew Jenson, "The Eight Witnesses," *Historical Record* 7, nos. 8–10 (October 1888), 621.

often overloaded with work to such an extent that she felt it to be quite a burden. One evening, when (after having done her usual day's work in the house) she went to the barn to milk the cows, she met a stranger carrying something on his back that looked like a knapsack. At first she was a little afraid of him, but when he spoke to her in a kind, friendly tone, and began to explain to her the nature of the work which was going on in her house, she was filled with unexpressible joy and satisfaction. He then untied his knapsack and showed her a bundle of plates, which in size and appearance corresponded with the description subsequently given by the witnesses to the Book of Mormon. This strange person turned the leaves of the book of plates over, leaf after leaf, and also showed her the engravings upon them; after which he told her to be patient and faithful in bearing her burden a little longer, promising that if she would do so, she should be blessed; and her reward would be sure, if she proved faithful to the end. The personage then suddenly vanished with the plates, and where he went, she could not tell.[6]

Her grandson concluded his remarks by saying, "I knew my grandmother to be a good, noble and truthful woman, and I have not the least doubt of her statement in regard to seeing the plates being strictly true. She was a strong believer in the Book of Mormon until the day of her death."[7] If John C. Whitmer's remembrance was correct, Mary's experience preceded the account of the Eleven Witnesses of the Book of Mormon.

Of the Eleven Witnesses, Mary was the mother of five—David, Christian, Jacob, Peter Jr., and John. She was the mother-in-law of Oliver Cowdery and Hiram Page, two additional witnesses of the Book of Mormon. In other words, whether by blood or marriage, Mary Whitmer was related to seven of the Eleven Witnesses of the Book of Mormon.

In addition, it was in her home that the Church was organized on April 6, 1830. Church conferences were held in the home in 1830 and 1831, and about half of the revelations contained in the Doctrine and Covenants in the New York period were received in the Whitmer home.

As to her receptivity to the gospel, Mary Whitmer was known among the faithful as "Mother Whitmer." She was baptized on April 18, 1830, in Seneca

---

6 Jenson, "Eight Witnesses," 621.
7 Jenson, "Eight Witnesses," 621.

Lake by Oliver Cowdery. She helped make clothing for missionaries sent to the Lamanites to preach the gospel of Jesus Christ. She and her family gathered with the Saints in Kirtland, Ohio, in 1831. By the next year, they were in Jackson County, Missouri, helping establish a Latter-day Saint settlement in Independence. They fled from religious persecution in Jackson County in 1833. The Whitmers were with the Saints in Clay and Caldwell counties from 1833 to 1838. But then the family broke away from the leadership of Joseph Smith.

Mary never affiliated with the Church after 1838. She died in Richmond, Missouri, in January 1856.

**A Bridge to the Past**
The translation of the Book of Mormon was completed in her home, and it was said of her that she saw an angel and the plates. Seven of the Witnesses to the Book of Mormon were sons or sons-in-law, and the Church was organized in her home. Mary enabled those around her to reach their full potential and build up the kingdom of God. No other woman could claim the blessings that Mary had in the early days of the Church. Which people in our lives could we help to bless if we encouraged them along the covenant path?

*Elizabeth Ann Whitney*

(1800–1882)

---

THE PROPHET JOSEPH SMITH WROTE of Elizabeth's husband, Newel K. Whitney, "Thou art a faithful friend in whom the afflicted sons of men can confide, with the most perfect safety. Let the blessings of the Eternal also be crowned upon his head. How warm that heart! how anxious that soul! for the welfare of one who has been cast out, and hated of almost all men. Brother Whitney, thou knowest not how strong those ties are that bind my soul and heart to thee."[1]

---

When Elizabeth was eighteen years old, she was sent to live with a maiden aunt, Sarah Smith, in northeastern Ohio. There she met Newel K. Whitney, a young merchant who was buying and selling furs. "Shortly after entering my twenty-first year I became acquainted with a young man from Vermont, Newel K. Whitney, who, like myself, had left home and relatives and was determined to carve out a fortune for himself," Elizabeth wrote. "We met and became acquainted; and being thoroughly convinced that we were suited to each other, we were married."[2]

---

1 Smith, *History of the Church*, 5:108.
2 Edward W. Tullidge, *The Women of Mormondom* (New York: Tullidge and Crandall, 1877), 34.

Elizabeth and Newel were married on October 20, 1822, in Kirtland, Ohio, by Reverend J. Badger, a Presbyterian minister. The newlyweds believed that "ours was strictly a marriage of affection. Our tastes, our feelings were congenial, and we were really a happy couple, with bright prospects in store."[3] Elizabeth and Newel became the parents of eleven children—seven sons and four daughters.

In their first years of marriage, Elizabeth recalled, "We prospered in all our efforts to accumulate wealth, so much so, that among our friends it came to be remarked that nothing of Whitney's ever got lost on the lake [Erie], and no product of his exportation was ever low in the market; always ready sales and fair prices."[4]

During this prosperous time, Newel and Elizabeth examined religious thought. Neither had ever formally professed a specific religious creed, though Elizabeth claimed, "I was naturally religious." After examining various creeds, the Whitneys united with a restorationist movement—the Campbellites—believing the movement "seemed most in accordance with scriptures."[5]

One evening in prayer, Newel and Elizabeth expressed their earnest desire to know how they could receive the Holy Ghost. Elizabeth wrote that while in prayer,

> The spirit rested upon us and a cloud overshadowed the house.
> It was as though we were out of doors. The house passed away from our vision. . . .
> . . . A solemn awe pervaded us. We saw the cloud and we felt the spirit of the Lord.
> Then we heard a voice out of the cloud saying:
> "Prepare to receive the word of the Lord, for it is coming!"[6]

The word of the Lord was brought to the Whitneys by missionaries from the newly organized Church of Jesus Christ. In November 1830, Newel and Elizabeth were baptized—Elizabeth first and Newel a few days later.

The Whitneys were anxious to meet the Prophet Joseph Smith. Joseph, in turn, was anxious to meet them. He had seen Newel in vision praying

---

3   Elizabeth Ann Whitney, "A Leaf from an Autobiography," *Woman's Exponent* 7, no. 6 (August 15, 1878), 41.
4   Tullidge, *Women of Mormondom*, 34.
5   Tullidge, *Women of Mormondom*, 34–35.
6   Tullidge, *Women of Mormondom*, 42.

upon his knees and pleading with the Lord that the Prophet would come to Kirtland. Of the arrival of Joseph Smith in Kirtland on or about February 1, 1831, Elizabeth wrote, "I remarked to my husband that this was the fulfilment of the vision we had seen of a cloud, as of glory, resting upon our house."[7]

When the Prophet Joseph proposed calling Newel K. Whitney to be a bishop, Newel staggered and said to Joseph, "I cannot see a Bishop in myself." The Prophet answered, "Go and ask Father for yourself." The Lord spoke to Newel in a voice from heaven saying, "Thy strength is in me."[8] Newel served as a bishop for eighteen years.

The Prophet Joseph and his wife were welcomed guests in the Whitney home. Joseph wrote of receiving "every kindness and attention which could be expected, and especially from Sister Whitney."[9] He referred to Elizabeth as "The Sweet Songstress of Zion," for she had the gift of tongues in song.[10] The Prophet promised Elizabeth "that if she kept the faith, the gift would never leave her."[11] Elizabeth sang in tongues in the Kirtland Temple. Elder Parley P. Pratt interpreted her lyrics by saying that her hymn was "descriptive of the different dispensations from Adam to the present age."[12]

Elizabeth had other talents too, none more pronounced than her generous spirit. After attending a three-day feast in January 1836, in which the Whitneys fed the poor, the Prophet Joseph wrote, "Attended a sumptuous feast at Bishop Newel K. Whitney's. This feast was after the order of the Son of God—the lame, the halt, and the blind were invited, according to the instructions of the Savior. . . . We . . . received a bountiful refreshment, furnished by the liberality of the Bishop. The company was large."[13]

When religious persecution raged in Kirtland, the Whitneys moved on to Missouri and then Illinois, always seeking a safe place to worship God. On March 17, 1842, Elizabeth was one of twenty women privileged to

---

7   Andrew Jenson, *Latter-day Saint Biographical Encyclopedia: A Compilation of Biographical Sketches of Prominent Men and Women in the Church of Jesus Christ of Latter-day Saints* (Salt Lake City: Andrew Jenson History, 1901), 1:224.
8   Jenson, *Latter-day Saint Biographical Encyclopedia*, 1:224.
9   Smith, *History of the Church*, 1:146.
10  "Mother Whitney Dead," *Salt Lake Herald-Republican* (February 16, 1882).
11  Newel Kimball Whitney Papers, 1825–1906, L. Tom Perry Special Collections, Harold B. Lee Library, Brigham Young University, Provo, Utah.
12  Jenson, *Latter-day Saint Biographical Encyclopedia*, 3:564.
13  Smith, *History of the Church*, 2:362.

attend the foundational meeting of the Female Relief Society of Nauvoo. At that meeting, Elizabeth put forth the name of Emma Smith to be president of the society. After being elected to that office, Emma chose forty-one-year-old Elizabeth Whitney to be one of her counselors. As Elizabeth recalled that first meeting, she said, "The Relief Society then was small compared to its numbers now, but the Prophet foretold great things concerning the future of this organization, many of which I have lived to see fulfilled."[14] Elizabeth encouraged sisters of the society to assist the poor and "cast in our mites to assist the brethren in building the Lord's House."[15]

In 1846, Elizabeth and her family fled from religious persecution in Nauvoo to the Territory of Iowa. As Elizabeth trekked across Iowa, she suffered greatly from inclement weather. Yet she continued her journey to Winter Quarters and on to the Salt Lake Valley, arriving in the valley with the Heber C. Kimball Company in fall of 1848.

Two years after her arrival, Newel died in September 1850. Although distraught and left with children to rear, Elizabeth pressed forward. She raised her children to adulthood and strengthened her friends by sharing her "most implicit faith in a divine power, in infinite truth emanating from God the Father."[16] In spite of her age and service as a temple ordinance worker, Eliza R. Snow selected Elizabeth as her counselor in the Relief Society General Presidency.

In celebration of her lifetime of commitment, Emmeline B. Wells hosted a party to celebrate Elizabeth's eighty-first birthday. At the party, Elizabeth sang in tongues.[17] She died of general debility in February 1882 in Salt Lake City.

**A Bridge to the Past**
Elizabeth was a generous hostess. She welcomed the Prophet Joseph and his wife as guests in her home. Joseph wrote of receiving "every kindness and attention which could be expected, and especially from Sister Whitney." Elizabeth and her husband hosted a three-day feast in January 1836 for the poor in the Kirtland

---

14   Elizabeth Ann Whitney, "A Leaf from an Autobiography," *Woman's Exponent* 7, no. 12 (November 15, 1878), 91.
15   Nauvoo Relief Society Minute Book, June 16, 1843, [90]. Joseph Smith Papers.
16   Elizabeth Ann Whitney, "A Leaf from an Autobiography," *Woman's Exponent* 7, no. 5 (August 1, 1878), 33.
17   See Jenson, *Latter-day Saint Biographical Encyclopedia*, 3:564.

vicinity and rejoiced in the opportunity. Being a generous hostess will bring more friends to your home as well.

# *Mary Ann Stearns Winters*

(1833–1912)

---

IN JULY 1843, MARY ACCOMPANIED her stepfather, Parley P. Pratt, on a boat excursion down the Mississippi River from Nauvoo to Quincy, Illinois. Of their return trip, Mary recalled,

> Our progress was slow, the little boat being too small to stem the rapids successfully, and it was nearly morning before we landed at Nauvoo. Early in the evening, being tired and sleepy, my Pa took me on his lap to rest. He was sitting on the deck opposite Brother Joseph [Smith], so near that their knees almost touched. Brother Joseph was preaching, and numbers crowded around, listening. He stopped and gently raised my feet upon his knees, and when I would have drawn them away, he said, "No, let me hold them; you will rest better." I was soon sound asleep, and the next I knew, it was morning, and we had landed at Nauvoo.[1]

---

In August 1836, Elder Brigham Young and others of the Quorum of the Twelve Apostles held a conference in Vermont. "Many were baptized at that time," wrote Mary. Her mother, the widow Mary Ann Frost, was baptized by Elder David W. Patten. After baptism, "the spirit of gathering rested upon the

---

[1] Mary Ann Stearns Winters, "An Autobiographical Sketch of the Life of the Late Mary Ann Stearns Winters," FamilySearch.

converts, and agreeable to the counsel given, all who could do so, gathered to the body of the Church" at Kirtland, Ohio. As young Mary and her mother were journeying to Kirtland from Vermont, they stopped in Boston. In that bustling seaport, Mary saw for the first time the Prophet Joseph Smith, who had been preaching in the vicinity. "To me he seemed larger and nobler than any other man," she wrote. "I watched him closely and realized that what he was saying was good and true."[2]

After arriving in Kirtland, Mary received a blessing from Joseph Smith Sr. Of that blessing, she wrote, "I felt a new light. A new intelligence had entered my soul from that time, and right here I want to bear testimony that the power and influence of that blessing has followed me through all the days of my life."[3]

Mary's mother took her inside the Kirtland Temple and showed her "the place on the pulpit where the Savior had stood when He appeared to the Prophet, and where afterwards Moses and Elias came and delivered the keys for the gathering of the Saints (Israel), and the redemption of the dead." Her mother also took her "to see the Egyptian mummies that were in the upper corridor of the temple. . . . They frightened me very much—they had such an unearthly look to me. They were dark in color, and hard as metal, and the cloth they were wrapped in was petrified like the bodies."[4]

In 1837, Mary's widowed mother wed Elder Parley P. Pratt. "I was grafted into that family and was called by that name for a number of years," wrote Mary.[5] When persecution raged in Kirtland, she and her new family moved on to Far West, Missouri, and from there across the Mississippi River to Illinois. They were not in Illinois long, however, as Mary and her mother accompanied Parley P. Pratt on his mission to England.

It was not until 1842 that the Pratt family settled in Nauvoo. In that city, Mary recalled,

> peace and prosperity had wrought great changes, many good buildings had been erected, the temple walls were up to the arch of the basement windows, the font was in place with a temporary covering, and the hearts of the Saints rejoiced exceedingly in the presence of their Prophet and Patriarch to cheer them on in the work of salvation.[6]

---

2  Winters, "Autobiographical Sketch."
3  Winters, "Autobiographical Sketch."
4  Winters, "Autobiographical Sketch."
5  Winters, "Autobiographical Sketch."
6  Winters, "Autobiographical Sketch."

Mary attended a school taught by Miss Alvira Wheeler in the Orson Spencer home. She wrote of her school friends,

> We enjoyed our schools, our meetings, and our play times, little dreaming what the future had in store for . . . us. One of our most enjoyable pastimes was to visit the temple and run around on its walls, until it grew so high that it was considered dangerous, and we were prohibited from that pleasure.[7]

Mary was present when Joseph Smith preached his last Sunday sermon around ten o'clock on June 16, 1844, eleven days before the martyrdom. Hundreds, and perhaps thousands, gathered in a grove located a quarter mile east of the Nauvoo Temple to hear his message. Of that event, Mary Ann wrote,

> One Sunday morning early in June, 1844, I was at a meeting in the grove east on Mulholland Street, when Brother Joseph arose and said he wanted all the children that could to bring their testaments and hymn books and meet there the next Sabbath and have a Sunday School. He said, "I don't know as I will be here, I will if I can, but Brother Stephen Goddard will be here and take charge of you, won't you, Brother Goddard?" Brother Goddard assented and then Brother Joseph called for teachers and a number volunteered. He spoke at some length on the importance of this move, and as far as I know this was the first Sunday School in the history of the Church.[8]

Mary ended her entry about Sunday School by penning, "I attended the next Sabbath and my teacher was Sister Clara [Clarissa] Chase. I cannot remember of meeting but twice in the Sunday School when those awful days came that terminated in the martyrdom of Brother Joseph and Hyrum Smith."[9]

Mary was also present

> at the great meeting when the mantle of Brother Joseph rested upon Brigham Young until his whole being seemed changed and his voice was like that of the Prophet. The people around me, rising to their feet to get a better chance to hear and see, I and my little companion of the day, Julia Felshaw, being small of stature, stood upon the benches that we, too

---

7 Winters, "Autobiographical Sketch."
8 Winters, "Autobiographical Sketch."
9 Winters, "Autobiographical Sketch."

might behold the wonderful transformation, and I know that from that time on the power of that change remained with Brother Brigham Young as long as he lived on earth.[10]

The meeting was followed by a time in Nauvoo when "every soul was nerved to greater effort and the memory of our martyred Prophets was a constant incentive to greater faithfulness," Mary wrote.[11] Brick houses were built, the temple walls rose, and the Saints worshipped the Lord as never before. Yet religious persecution went unchecked, and the faithful were at the mercy of the mob-like element.

In February 1846, many of the Latter-day Saints fled from Nauvoo. On February 14, 1846, Mary and her family crossed the Mississippi. Mary wrote,

> After crossing the river on the ferry boat, it commenced snowing, and as we traveled along we passed camp after camp of the Saints just by the roadside, sitting around the campfire with the snow coming down in great flakes and melting under their feet, women and children with damp and drabbled clothing, men wading around caring for the cattle that were to be their propellers to a place of safety, mothers trying to prepare food for their families over the blazing log heaps, a sight fit to daunt the stoutest heart, but no, everyone of our acquaintances that we greeted in passing had a cheering word and a smiling countenance.[12]

In 1852, the Pratt family joined a pioneer company to cross the plains to the Rockies. In the company, Mary met Oscar Winters. They courted on the westward trek and, on August 6, 1852, were married by Elder Lorenzo Snow. After entering the Salt Lake Valley, Brigham Young called Mary and Oscar Winters to settle in Pleasant Grove. They remained in Pleasant Grove the rest of their days. Mary died in 1912 at age seventy-nine.[13]

## A Bridge to the Past

Mary Ann wrote an autobiography. In that thoughtful remembrance for her posterity, she wrote of Joseph Smith directing the organization of Sunday

---

10  Winters, "Autobiographical Sketch."
11  Winters, "Autobiographical Sketch."
12  Winters, "Autobiographical Sketch."
13  Mary Ann Sterns Winters obituary, "Prominent Pioneer Lady Passes Away," newspaper clipping, 1912, FamilySearch.

School on June 16, 1844. Her recollection of Sunday School in Nauvoo gives Church historians a reason to reconsider the much-repeated notion that Sunday School was organized in December 1849 in the Salt Lake Valley:

> On Sunday morning, December 9, 1849, at eight o'clock, about 30 children between the ages of 8 and 13 arrived in a small classroom that had been built in a home. They stamped their feet on the threshold, shook the snow off their coats and hats, then took their places on simple benches. They waited expectantly for the class to begin. It was a cold, snowy day outside, but the fireplace radiated a warm and friendly glow. Richard Ballantyne's eyes shone brightly as he called the Sunday School to order. He led the boys and girls in a song, and then he gave a quiet but fervent prayer dedicating this room in his home for teaching children the gospel of Jesus Christ.[14]

Have you written your autobiography? Intermixed with family and other events in your life, write of important events in the Church.

---

14  L. Tom Perry, "Teach Them the Word of God with All Diligence," *Ensign*, May 1999.

### (1821–1901)

"On the 10 [November 1836]," Zina wrote, "I saw the Prophet's face for the first time. He was 6 feet, light auburn hair and a heavy nose, blue eyes.... When he was filled with the spirit of revelation or inspiration to talk to the saints his countenance would look clear & bright.... When warning the saints of approaching danger if we forsook the path of truth & right ... it was truly affecting and any one that ever heard, I should think, could never forget."[1]

Zina described her childhood as uneventful. Yet her father, who was a prosperous New York farmer, had declared that "none of the churches were right according to the way he read the Bible, for none of them had the organization peculiar to the primitive church."[2] As he searched for the true church, he saw to it that Bible reading, prayers, and hymnal singing were a daily practice in his home.

When Zina was in her mid-teens, she earnestly prayed to find greater religious truths. She was taught great truths by missionaries Hyrum Smith and David Whitmer. She said of her conversion,

---

1 Zina Diantha Huntington, "Autobiographical sketch" [holography], 4, as cited in Janet Peterson and LaRene Gaunt, *Elect Ladies* (Salt Lake City: Deseret Book, 1990), 47.
2 Zina D. H. Young, "How I Gained my Testimony of the Truth," *Young Woman's Journal* 4, no. 7 (April 1893), 317.

> One day on my return from school I saw the Book of Mormon, that strange, new book, lying on the window sill of our sitting-room. I went up to the window, picked it up, and the sweet influence of the Holy Spirit accompanied it to such an extent that I pressed it to my bosom in a rapture of delight, murmuring as I did so, "This is the truth, truth, truth!"[3]

Zina later said, "From the day I received the sweet testimony of the Spirit, when grasping the precious Book of Mormon in my hands to my breast, I have never doubted nor faltered in my faith."[4] On August 1, 1835, at age fourteen, Zina was baptized by Hyrum Smith.

In October 1836, Zina and her family gathered with the Saints in Kirtland, Ohio. There her mother often took "Zina in her buggy and hunt[ed] out the distressed and needy in and about that place" and provided comfort.[5] Religious persecution forced Zina and her family to pack up their belongings in Kirtland and head to Far West, Missouri, hoping to find a peaceful place to live. Unfortunately, they arrived in Far West at the height of mob persecution. Zina and her family pressed on to Illinois, hoping to escape religious intolerance.

At age twenty, Zina married Henry Bailey Jacobs on March 7, 1841. She became the mother of two sons and one daughter. (Zina was later sealed to Joseph Smith and married for time to Brigham Young.) She joined the Latter-day Saint exodus from Nauvoo to the Territory of Iowa on February 9, 1846, and wrote, "Clear and cold. We left our house, all we possessed, in a wagon. . . . Shall I ever forget . . . leaving our homes for the wilderness trusting God like Abriham [sic]."[6]

As she crossed the plains to the Salt Lake Valley, Zina provided comfort to women on the trek. Emmeline B. Wells wrote, "She so distinguished herself among the sick and the sorrowing, that she . . . gained with many the appellation of 'Zina, the comforter.'"[7] At Brigham Young's suggestion, Zina attended classes on herbal medicine, home nursing, and midwifery. In 1872, she helped

---

3   Young, "How I Gained My Testimony of the Truth," 318.
4   Young, "How I Gained My Testimony of the Truth," 319.
5   Orson F. Whitney, *History of Utah* (Salt Lake City: George Q. Cannon & Sons, 1904), 4:577.
6   Diary of Zina D. H. Young, 13, quoted in Mary Brown Firmage, "Great-Grandmother Zina: A More Personal Portrait," *Ensign*, Mar. 1984.
7   "Zina D. H. Young, A Distinguished Woman," *Woman's Exponent* 10, no. 12 (November 15, 1881), 91.

establish the Deseret Hospital in Salt Lake City, serving as vice president of the hospital board.

Zina is best remembered for her work with the Relief Society. She served as the first counselor to Eliza R. Snow in the Relief Society General Presidency. "Some spoke of the two as the head and the heart of the women's work in Utah," wrote Susa Young Gates. "Sister Snow was keenly intellectual, and she led by force of that intelligence. Sister Zina was all love and sympathy, and drew people after her by reason of that tenderness."[8] She later added, "There have been many noble women, some great women and a multitude of good women associated, past and present, with the Latter-Day work. But of them all none was so lovely, so lovable, and so passionately beloved as was 'Aunt Zina.'"[9]

At age sixty-seven, Zina was called to be the General President of the Relief Society. She was set apart for the assignment by Wilford Woodruff. President Woodruff blessed Zina that she would have a heart "'drawn out towards . . . [the] sisters' and that she would 'do much good and relieve the suffering of those who are sick and afflicted.'"[10] During her years as General President, she often bore her testimony—"I know this is the Church and Kingdom of God, and I rejoice in putting my testimony before the daughters of Zion, that their faith may be strengthened, and that the good work may roll on. . . . If you will dig in the depths of your own hearts you will find, with the aid of the Spirit of the Lord, the pearl of great price, the testimony of the truth of this work."[11]

During Zina's final years, she expressed the hope that her influence and that of other Latter-day Saint women would continue so "the future may have reason to praise God for the noble Women of this generation."[12] Zina died on August 28, 1901.

---

8   Susa Young Gates, *History of the Young Ladies' Mutual Improvement Association of the Church of Jesus Christ of Latter-day Saints, From November 1869 to June 1910* (Salt Lake City: Deseret News, 1911), 21.
9   Gates, *History of the Young Ladies' Mutual Improvement Association*, 21.
10  Wilford Woodruff, "Blessing of Zina D. H. Young," October 11, 1888, Salt Lake City, quoted in Peterson and Gaunt, *Elect Ladies*, 56–57.
11  Young, "How I Gained my Testimony of the Truth," 319.
12  Zina Card Brown Family Collection, quoted in Mary Firmage Woodward, "Zina D. H. Young," *Encyclopedia of Mormonism*, ed. Daniel H. Ludlow (New York: Macmillan, 1992), 4:1613.

**A Bridge to the Past**
Zina wrote of herself, "I have never doubted or faltered in my faith." That alone is a reason to follow such a leader. Adding to it, in her early youth, Zina went with her mother to comfort the sick and the needy and learned much of charity and compassion. As she left Nauvoo for an unchartered wilderness, she put her trust in God that all would be well. When she reached the Salt Lake Valley, her tenderness toward those who suffered was spoken of throughout the valley. She rejoiced in testifying of the truthfulness of the gospel of Jesus Christ. Because of whom she had become, Zina was so loved in her leadership role that women throughout the Latter-day Saint settlements in the Rockies referred to her affectionately as "Aunt Zina." Consider this question: How have you been prepared to be a leader among women?

# Epilogue

---

President Russell M. Nelson said, "Jesus Christ invites us to take the covenant path back home to our Heavenly Parents and be with those we love."[1] The covenant path begins in baptismal waters. *Glorious Truths about Women of the Restoration* has presented the stories of fifty women who knew the Prophet Joseph Smith and entered the covenant path by being baptized and becoming members of The Church of Jesus Christ of Latter-day Saints.

Each woman in this book faced the choice of whether to stay or leave the covenant path—a path that included sacred temple ordinances. For some, it was the death of a loved one that caused them to step away from the path. For others, it was the pull of family members to apostatize. And for still others, it was religious persecution, ridicule, and threats of physical violence.

The women who moved with the faithful from New York to Ohio and then to Missouri and Illinois were extraordinary. Their repeated choice of faith, no matter the locale or circumstance, created a pattern of righteousness. The thread that held the pattern together was their belief that Joseph Smith was a prophet of God and that the gospel of Jesus Christ was restored. With uncompromising belief and a determination to stay on the covenant path, these women pressed forward against great odds, creating a legacy of faith that has endured for generations. Ask any Latter-day Saint whose ancestors knew Joseph Smith about these women and discover how they are spoken of with great applause as courageous, noble, faithful, and illustrious.

---

1  Russell M. Nelson, "Come, Follow Me," *Ensign*, May 2019.

By writing the stories of these women, I have strengthened my own commitment to follow the prophet and in so doing have discovered unexpected blessings. One blessing is the knowledge that faith is not just a choice—it is *the* choice. Another blessing is learning that sacrifice coupled with faith is what sincere prayer is all about. Perhaps more important, I have learned much from the women who wandered off the covenant path and had the courage to turn back and follow the prophet—not just for a day but for the rest of their lives. They were embraced and welcomed back. What are we waiting for? The Lord loves us. Blessings await.

## About the Author

Dr. Susan Easton Black joined the faculty of Brigham Young University in 1978 and taught Church history and doctrine until she retired to serve multiple missions with her husband, George Durrant. She is also past associate dean of general education and honors and director of Church history in the Religious Studies Center.

The recipient of numerous academic awards, she received the Karl G. Maeser Distinguished Faculty Lecturer Award in 2000, the highest award given a professor on the BYU Provo campus. Susan has authored, edited, and compiled more than 100 books and more than 250 articles.